Teachers College Studies in Education

Other Titles in this Series

Forum and Focus for the Junior College Movement

The American Association of Junior Colleges

MICHAEL BRICK

TEACHERS COLLEGE PRESS
Teachers College, Columbia University
New York

Manufactured in the United States of America

Preface

MARCH 2, 3, and 4, 1960, were cold days in Louisville, Kentucky. A snowstorm had hit the city just as hundreds of delegates were gathering to attend the 40th anniversary convention of the American Association of Junior Colleges. Three hundred and fifty-three delegates registered and came together as they had done for the past forty years to exchange ideas and to discuss developments in the junior college movement.

This was a far cry from June 30 and July 1, 1920, when thirty-four delegates representing twenty-two junior colleges met in St. Louis, Missouri, to organize the AAJC. Not only were the numbers different but so was the weather. They were oppressively hot days and many of the delegates wondered if all this sweat were worthwhile as Dr. George Zook, specialist in higher education for the United States Bureau of Education, came to the platform to call the assemblage to order.

Forty years elapsed between the torrid days in St. Louis and the freezing days in Louisville; and much had happened in these forty years. Much had happened not only to the AAJC but also to the junior college movement.

It is the purpose of this study to examine these years and to trace the development of the AAJC from its inception in 1920 through its forty-second annual meeting in 1962. In one sense this is an institutional history; in another, it is a study of an educational movement, for the Association and the junior college movement are closely interwoven. The literature of higher education pays scant attention to the history of the junior college movement. This study discloses the movement from its birth to its present status.

One of the characteristics of American higher education is the absence of centralized control. Leadership in every branch of American higher learning is provided by voluntary membership and participation in special organizations. Voluntary national organizations have arisen to promote standards and professionalism of institutions as well as to act as spokesmen for educational movements. The AAJC is such a voluntary, national organization. As have similar groups, the AAJC has served as a forum for the junior colleges of the country. At the annual meetings junior college educators debate educational concepts. The Association has provided leadership and direction for the junior colleges. This study will provide narrative, descriptive, and interpretive material on the role and meaning of a national organization that coordinated the efforts of individual two-year colleges which were developing throughout the country during the twentieth century. The AAJC acted as a cohesive force, giving the two-year colleges the strength and prestige needed to make an impact on higher education in the United States. The AAJC was the only national organization through which the two-year college could speak, and this study will show how the national organization acted as spokesman for a rapidly growing movement.

There is no doubt that two-year colleges would have developed without the Association. To ascribe specific influences on the junior college movement to this one educational association would leave one wide open to criticism. Few would deny, however, that the history of the junior college movement in America would have been very different if the AAJC had not existed.

The term junior college will be used to cover all institutions offering primarily the thirteenth and fourteenth years of education. Although junior colleges vary greatly in their purposes, organization, and programs, it is possible to identify certain functions that are characteristic of the majority of these institutions. They offer programs duplicating the freshman and sophomore years of the traditional college to students who plan to transfer and obtain the baccalaureate degree. They provide terminal programs to students not going on to a four-year college. In addition, the junior college attempts to ascertain and respond to the educational demands of its constituency and offers continuing education to adults. In the main, admission policy for the junior college is not restrictive. Tuition is low and the emphasis on counseling and guidance services and good teaching is high.

In a study of this nature it is impossible to overlook the many persons who have influenced, guided, and inspired the venture.

Special gratitude is due to the individuals connected with the AAJC who gave me insights into the Association's history. These include Leland Medsker, C. C. Colvert, Henry Littlefield, Roscoe Ingalls, Curtis Bishop, and Lawrence Bethel, all past presidents of the Association; and James Reynolds, for many years editor of the *Junior College Journal.* The late Walter Crosby Eells and Doak Campbell, former executive secretaries of the AAJC, were very helpful in filling in the early history of the Association. Dr. Eells made available his private papers, which explained many of the events that took place during his years as executive secretary. These papers are now in the possession of the author.

I am indebted to Edmund J. Gleazer, Jr., executive director of the AAJC, who made available the facilities of the Washington headquarters and without whose cooperation I could never have written this history. Dr. Gleazer and his staff, including William Shannon, Thomas Merson, Jesse Barnet, William Harper, Martha Trainor, and Isabel Coll-Pardo, gave me free access to the materials they had on file and gave of their time—at times under difficult conditions.

I owe special thanks to Dr. Maurice Seay, director, Division of Education, W. K. Kellogg Foundation, for making available the Kellogg files concerning contacts with the AAJC. He gave encouragement when needed and took the time to read parts of the manuscript.

I wish to thank Professor Frederick Kershner of the Teachers College, Columbia University, history department, who offered skillful advice and welcome encouragement. Professor Earl McGrath made valuable suggestions from his firsthand knowledge of higher education.

There are two men whom I must single out for special thanks because of their guidance, patience, helpful suggestions and perhaps most of all, their friendship, throughout the development of this report. They are Professor Erling Hunt and Professor Walter Sindlinger of Teachers College, Columbia University.

The endless chore of typing the several versions of this manuscript was handled by Mr. Emory Rarig with his usual effortless efficiency.

Finally, the writer wishes to thank his wife Barbara and son Barrett, whose understanding and encouragement have made it all worthwhile.

M. B.

Contents

1

The Junior College Idea

THERE WAS AN AIR of excitement in Louisville, Kentucky, in March, 1960, as delegates gathered for the annual meeting of the American Association of Junior Colleges. The excitement was engendered by the fact that this was the fortieth-anniversary convention of an Association which many had thought would not last out its first year. Also, many of the delegates knew that a momentous announcement was going to be made concerning a financial commitment by the W. K. Kellogg Foundation to the AAJC.

The junior college movement had come a long way from the days of the late nineteenth and early twentieth centuries when the junior colleges had little status generally, and even less recognition from other educational institutions. By 1960 the junior college movement was one of the fastest growing and most talked about developments in the field of higher education. The Association representing these junior colleges was taking its place as a powerful spokesman dedicated to the promotion of the junior college idea. How and why did all this growth take place?

One of the distinguishing features of American higher education is its diversity. A variety of forms of educational institutions has unfolded since the founding of Harvard in 1636: liberal arts college, technical institute, state university, land-grant college, professional school, normal school, teachers college, state college, municipal college, and, most recently, the junior college. Each arose as a response to the failure of existing institutions to meet the demands for a new or additional type of educational experience.

The development of the junior college as a response to the educational demands of society was in the same vein as the develop-

1

ment of state universities and land-grant colleges which arose to meet changing educational demands. The difficulties overcome and the successes achieved by educational institutions in the nineteenth century paved the way for the acceptance of the junior college idea by the public and by local and state legislatures.

American higher education today represents the end product of interaction between the Western European university heritage and the native American environment. From these processes of transplantation and continuous adaptation have emerged the aspects of academic culture which we have come to recognize as characteristically American.

SOCIO-ECONOMIC FORCES AND THE DEVELOPMENT OF THE JUNIOR COLLEGE IDEA

Four basic social and economic forces led to the junior college idea: (1) equality of opportunity, (2) use of education to achieve social mobility, (3) technological progress, and (4) acceptance of the concept that education is the producer of social capital.

Equality of Opportunity

Equality of opportunity has long been an ideal and a principle of the American people. Although the principle does not go back to the beginning of the English settlement, it did gain support at an early stage along the northern Atlantic seaboard.

As early as 1642, the Massachusetts Bay Colony made it obligatory upon all parents and masters to teach their children and apprentices to read and understand the principles of religion and the capital laws of the country, and to give them training "in some honest lawful calling, labour or employment, that may be profitable for themselves, or the Country." [1] Five years later, the General Court of the Colony passed a law requiring all communities of the Colony to erect and maintain schools for the children who would not otherwise be educated. This "Deluder Satan Act" of 1647 was a precedent for universal education, state enforced and financed by imposition of taxes.

[1] William Brigham (ed.), *The Compact with the Charter and Laws of the Colony of New Plymouth* (Boston: Dutton and Wentworth, 1836), pp. 270–71.

The purpose of such laws, of course, was not to train people for democratic dissent. However, literacy itself is a demonstrable danger to tyranny.

The leaders of the early national period fostered the concept of equality of opportunity. George Washington felt keenly the need for expansion of the colonial educational efforts.[2] Thomas Jefferson firmly believed in the paramount importance of careers freely open to all the talented. He was devoted to the principle of universal schooling and stated that "the ultimate result of the whole scheme of education would be the teaching of all the children of the State reading, writing and common arithmetic. . . ."[3] Jefferson's views are taken for granted today, but when they were written they expressed a revolutionary doctrine—a belief that every potential citizen should receive at least a minimum of formal instruction.

This unique character of the American way of life has been repeatedly emphasized. Lincoln in his first message to Congress declared that "the leading object of the Government for whose existence we contend is to elevate the conditions of men; to lift artificial weights from all shoulders; to clear the paths of laudable pursuit for all; to afford all an unfettered start and a fair chance in the race of life."[4] Frederick Jackson Turner, the historian of the West, summed up the case as follows: "Western democracy through the whole of its earlier period tended to the production of a society of which the most distinctive fact was freedom of the individual to rise under conditions of social mobility. . . ."[5]

It may be that the West has been more a myth than a reality in its influence on American thought. The romantic West, the demo-

[2] Letter to John Armstrong, April 25, 1788, in John C. Fitzpatrick (ed.), *The Writings of George Washington* (Washington, D.C.: U. S. Government Printing Office, 1939), XXIX, 467; letter to Roger Brooke, governor of Virginia, March 16, 1795, in Worthington Chauncey Ford (ed.), *The Writings of George Washington* (New York: G. P. Putnam & Sons, 1892), XIII, 53.

[3] John Dewey, *The Living Thoughts of Thomas Jefferson* (London: Cassell & Co., 1941), pp. 115–16.

[4] Special session message to Congress by Abraham Lincoln, July 4, 1861, in James D. Richardson, *A Compilation of the Messages and Papers of the Presidents, 1789–1897* (Washington, D.C.: United States Government Printing Office, 1898), VI, 30.

[5] Frederick Jackson Turner, *The Frontier in American History* (New York: Henry Holt & Co., 1920), p. 266.

cratic West lose both romance and democracy on closer scrutiny. Even if there were no strange elixir of freedom in the air—and indeed, there were often more agues and miasmas—established patterns of status and prestige were less fixed, and social fluidity somewhat more real in the early West. In the Midwest the principle that every child must be given educational opportunity was firmly established by the middle of the nineteenth century.

In the twentieth century, the ideal of equality of opportunity culminated in the report of the President's Commission on Higher Education which proposed the immediate abolition of all barriers to educational opportunity.

American colleges and universities must envision a much larger role for higher education in the national life. They can no longer consider themselves merely the instrument for producing an intellectual elite; they must become the means by which every citizen, youth, and adult is enabled and encouraged to carry his education, formal and informal, as far as his native capacities permit.[6]

Social Mobility

Closely associated with this ideal of equal opportunity is the concept of using education to achieve social mobility. The first campaign for free public elementary schools, waged under the generalship of leaders such as Horace Mann in Massachusetts, Henry Barnard in Connecticut, and Thaddeus Stevens in Pennsylvania, was won by the middle of the nineteenth century. But this was only the first phase of the struggle. Before it was over came the attempt to extend the system upward by providing free secondary education, and finally many states and municipalities established universities and colleges where higher education was virtually free to their citizens.

A survey conducted for *Fortune* by Elmo Roper in 1949 showed that "eighty-three per cent of all the people would want a son of theirs (if they had one) to go to college, sixty-nine per cent want college for their daughters." Of those who wanted their son or daughter to go to college, sixty-six per cent gave as their chief

[6] President's Commission on Higher Education, *Higher Education for American Democracy* (New York: Harper & Brothers, 1947), I, 101.

reason for sending a son to college, "preparation for a better job, a trade, or profession, greater earning power." The corresponding figure for daughters was forty-eight per cent.[7]

A group of sociologists stated the basic fact this way:

Still believing that their children should rise and seeing in the secondary school and college the principal avenues of mobility, the people sent their children to secondary school and college. The American people learned what the people of older cultures have learned, that the schools are the social elevators in a hardening social structure.[8]

Jesse P. Bogue, a leader in the junior college movement, indicated that a democratic society needed well-educated people, and he was convinced that the majority of the American citizenry were determined to have it so. "To write this belief into public policy," said Bogue, "has been one of the longest and hardest fought battles for social welfare." [9]

Education through the twelfth year is almost universal. The next logical step was to provide for the junior college years. Robert M. Hutchins, president of the University of Chicago, in 1934 stated that it would become the usual thing for high school graduates to attend a junior college near home. William H. Kilpatrick, in a valedictory address upon retirement from the faculty of Teachers College, Columbia University, prophesied that "the Junior College bids fair to become well nigh universal." [10] In 1947, junior college leaders predicted that by 1970 at least 50 per cent of our youth of college age would be enrolled in the junior college.[11]

Thus the public junior college represents a natural extension of the public school system, and a partial realization of the democratic ideal that secondary school and college education should be available to everyone.

[7] "Higher Education," *Fortune*, XL (September, 1949), Supplement, 1–16.

[8] W. Lloyd Warner, Robert J. Havighurst, and Martin B. Loeb, *Who Shall Be Educated?* (New York: Harper & Brothers, 1944), pp. 48–49.

[9] Jesse P. Bogue, *The Community College* (New York: McGraw-Hill Book Co., 1950), p. 4.

[10] *Junior College Journal*, V (December, 1934), 134; VIII (April, 1938), 341.

[11] C. C. Colvert, "A Half-Century of Junior Colleges," *Junior College Journal*, XVII (February, 1947), 247.

Technological Progress

Given impetus by the Civil War, business expansion and industrialism gained a dominant role by the beginning of the twentieth century. The virtual completion of the national railway network, tremendous increases in productive capacity, and a great outpouring of material goods marked the physical aspect of the conquest. Concomitant factors included an increase in urbanization with its attendant social problems, a shift in the locus of political and economic power, and an increasing awareness from a diverse camp of critics of a growing challenge to democracy.

Between 1865 and the present, a major element in American social thought defined itself. This element was "the business way" which held as principal ideas: (1) material success comes as the reward of superior virtue, (2) there is an insignificant amount of social injustice in the existing society, (3) the fittest and best survive the tests of our society, and (4) wealth tends to be socially benevolent. The business way, which had conquered the economic sphere almost completely and which influenced politics, sought also to win the mind of America. A varied and considerable group of men and institutions helped to define the business pattern of thought: Andrew Carnegie, William Graham Sumner, James McCosh, William McGuffey, Horatio Alger, Elbert Hubbard, Herbert Hoover, the Chamber of Commerce, and the National Association of Manufacturers. Buttressing their arguments by appeals to religion, science, political economy, psychology, anthropology, sociology, and the patience of the common man, they created an atmosphere from which President Calvin Coolidge could draw inspiration for his dictum: "The business of America is business."

Educators as well as businessmen led the way in reshaping educational patterns in America. Charles W. Eliot at Harvard was an example of the new educational leader. Business influence on boards of trustees of academic institutions began to increase.[12]

Discussions of educational objectives reflected the needs of an expanding industrial civilization. The issue of practical versus classical offerings in the college curriculum was argued. There

---

[12] Richard Hofstadter and C. DeWitt Hardy, *The Development and Scope of Higher Education in the United States* (New York: Columbia University Press, 1952), pp. 32–33.

were new demands for training at both professional and technical levels. Demands that education become more practical increased.

The developers of educational programs kept in mind the expansion and direction of industry and business. Industry demanded better-trained personnel. A developing technology was not only producing goods that called for highly skilled labor but was also changing the nature of the economic scene. Important for the junior college movement was the fact that the fields of endeavor which were expanding required for initial entry an educational background comparable to that provided by the junior college. New occupations developed: laboratory technician, medical secretary, dental secretary, aviation mechanic, junior accountant, engineer's assistant, and scores of other mid-level or semiprofessional occupations. Every advance in technology reduced the need for unskilled labor, including that of children and youth of school and junior college age. At the same time technology opened employment opportunity for those who had training beyond the high school.

The increasing diversity in the educational requirements of jobs in the work force is well presented in the "Rockefeller Report" published in 1958. The report states that

One of the striking features of contemporary life is the growing range and complexity of the tasks on which our social organization depends. The reasons for this lie in the explosive route of technological change and the increasing complexity of our social organizations.[13]

The report reveals that certain selected skills and occupations with high educational requirements that in 1910 accounted for 32.8 per cent of the labor force, in 1957 accounted for 47.6 per cent. The trend will accelerate in the years ahead, aided by automation and the discoveries of research.[14]

Coincident, then, with the expansion of our industrial system, the college for the few became the college for the many. The former was largely the privilege of the elect, the latter the assumption of a birthright secured by the extension of the notion of natural equality from a political to an educational sense. Society demanded

[13] Rockefeller Brothers Fund, *The Pursuit of Excellence: Education and the Future of America* (Garden City, N.Y.: Doubleday & Co., 1958), pp. 6–7.

[14] *Ibid.*, pp. 7–8.

from the colleges and universities curricula nearly inclusive enough to invite every type.

Education As Social Capital

After 1940 a profound change took place in the public attitude toward higher education. Social interest in higher education equalled or transcended the interest of the individual and his family. Higher education is now looked upon as a producer of social capital, with awareness that the national well-being is linked to the development of the nation's human resources.

Every thoughtful American is aware of the growing importance of higher education in American life and culture. The reasons are easy to find. In addition to the technological advances already discussed, great attention is being given to the conquest of space, the exploitation of the vast resources of the seas, and the search for breakthroughs in the field of medicine. The emergence of the United States as a world power and the concomitant assumption of the mantle of world leadership have added grave responsibilities of government.

American scientific advances and growing world responsibilities have created an unprecedented demand for college-trained men and women. The American people have come to understand that their national security and welfare depend fully as much on their human resources as upon existing productive capacity and natural resources. They have come to understand that men and women increase in value both to themselves and to society when they are educated. Thus in the public mind higher education has ceased to be an individual matter. It is now the producer of social capital.

EDUCATIONAL FORCES AND THE JUNIOR COLLEGE IDEA

The junior college is intimately related to the entire American educational enterprise. Studies of the junior college's origin and history demonstrate that this institution is descended from the secondary school on the one hand and from the college and university on the other. The secondary school founders of the junior college hoped to extend the educational opportunity of youth through two additional years. The colleges conceived the new institution as chiefly a selective agency to restrain all but the strongest of the rapidly increasing numbers who sought admission to the college and university, thereby providing partial relief to the over-burdened parent.

The Public High School Movement

The public high school was neither an accident nor a diabolic scheme of professional educators. It emerged in response to the economic and social demands of a society. The American high school rose from lowly origins in the 1820's to dazzling heights by the twentieth century. What accounted for this growth? Some of the answers to this question also explain the later development of the junior college.

The high school was to be many things to many people. As Wesley points out in his history of the National Education Association, for the colleges the high school was a preparatory school; for the state it was a training ground for democracy and citizenship; for parents it was a prolongation of education within reach of the parental roof; and for the proclaimers of equality it was the people's college.[15]

An important factor in explaining the rise of high schools was the presence of growing numbers of colleges which enlarged the distance between themselves and the elementary schools. This gap had to be filled. While the colleges would have preferred traditional academies to untried high schools, they saw no chance of getting them in the West and exerted some help in the establishment of high schools, giving up their preparatory departments as high schools arose to fill the void.

As the high school developed, arguments arose as to the nature of this institution which were closely related to the arguments that raged over the functions of the junior college when that institution emerged. At the St. Louis meeting of the National Education Association in 1871, Newton Bateman, state superintendent of public instruction of Illinois, examined the question of the state's

---

[15] Edgar B. Wesley, *NEA: The First Hundred Years* (New York: Harper & Brothers, 1957), p. 60. The paragraphs that follow in regard to high school developments are based on Wesley, *NEA*, pp. 61, 63, 70.

obligation to support high schools. The state, according to Bateman, should provide common schools for all and high schools and universities for all that want them. The university lifts up and challenges the high school, and the high school provides perpetual incentive toward high standards in elementary schools. To deny a high school and college education to the poor would perpetuate the barriers between the indigent and the affluent; it would create an aristocracy of learning to aggravate that of wealth. Such a restriction seems to say to the children of the poor: "Thus far, but no farther."

Even though the evolving high school grew rapidly in enrollment, broadened its program, adjusted itself to community conditions, and gave less attention to college requirements, the theory of its function did not develop correspondingly. The evolving high school encountered some opposition because next to endowed academies it seemed raw and crude. The high schools had no traditions and were feared by denominational academies and private schools as a threat to their existence. The colleges feared that their control over courses and programs would be impaired and college faculties looked upon high schools as a threat to scholastic standards.

A long educational war was waged by the colleges and the high schools in the definition of function for the emerging public high school. The alternatives for the high schools were either educational independence or subservience to colleges. High schools generally tried to avoid domination by the colleges because they felt they had a different mission. They were to educate citizens, train workers, disseminate culture; they were to serve society and not the colleges; they were the people's college and not the college's preparatory school. Most colleges, in contrast, held that high schools should be preparatory schools, for they sincerely believed that a high school that served a college was better than one that developed its program for other purposes. Definition of purpose for the high school is still an oft-debated issue today at the meetings of the NEA.

The public high school, then, became established as the pattern of secondary education in this country. What the public high school had done was to democratize secondary education. As more students attended and graduated from high school, there was a corresponding increase in the number who sought a college education. In some high schools "postgraduate" courses were established for those students who because of location or cost lacked the opportunity for college work.

The process of high school elongation had begun.

High School Stretching

One of the first states to start the stretching process was Colorado. The high school of Greeley, Colorado, for example, added an extra year of work, the thirteenth grade, in the 1880's.[16] A few years later, in the 1890's, the University of Michigan accepted one year of college work by students from the stronger high schools. By 1895, the East Side High School of Saginaw gave freshman college work in Latin, algebra, trigonometry, English and history.[17] By 1897, eight students had graduated from the University of Michigan in three years, "after doing a year's work beyond the four-year high school course of study in the East Side High School." [18]

Another early high school venture into the area of postgraduate work was the plan at Goshen, Indiana, where two years' work was added to the curriculum. In August, 1904, the local paper carried a notice announcing that beginning in September, the Goshen High School would offer a postgraduate course "that shall be equivalent to and accredited as one year's work in the best colleges and universities. . . . If sufficient numbers shall enroll for the first year's work the course will be extended to cover two years." Arrangements were finally made with the University of Chicago to accept the work for advanced standing.[19]

Nearly all such experiments were eventually abandoned. But in a few cases, as at Joliet, Illinois, the plan to extend the work

[16] Tyrus Hillway, *The American Two-Year College* (New York: Harper & Brothers, 1958), p. 36.

[17] Walter Crosby Eells, *The Junior College* (Boston: Houghton Mifflin Co., 1931), p. 53.

[18] A. A. Gray, "The Junior College in California," *School Review*, XXIII (September, 1915), 465–73.

[19] Waldo L. Adams, "The Junior College at Goshen, Indiana," *Junior College Journal*, IV (November, 1933), 74; Victor W. B. Hedgepeth, "The Six-Year High School Plan at Goshen, Indiana," *School Review*, XIII (January, 1905), 19–23.

of the secondary school resulted in the establishment of a separate junior college. Joliet not only claims to be the first public junior college but also illustrates the informal beginnings of the junior college movement.[20]

Junior colleges developed similarly in other parts of the country. J. Stanley Brown, superintendent at Joliet, reported in 1904 at the Conference of the Academies and High Schools affiliated with the University of Chicago that Philadelphia, Muskegon, Saginaw, St. Joseph, Goshen, Joliet, and eighteen semi-public institutions in different sections of the country were working out the six-year plan, giving collegiate work in connection with the high school.[21] As early as 1907 at the University of Missouri, the annual conference of teachers in accredited schools recommended giving college credit for one or two years of college level work done in high schools of larger cities. Eells, professor of education at Stanford University, blamed the matter of expense for preventing the high schools from taking advantage of the plan until 1915, when Hannibal, Kansas City, and St. Joseph, Missouri, organized junior colleges in connection with their high schools. Other institutions that began such work early included both Crane and Lane High Schools in Chicago.

Public institutions were not the only ones to become enamored of the stretching process. The earliest instance of postgraduate work being added to the high school is to be found at Newton, Maryland, where the first Catholic college in what is now the United States was founded in 1677. According to Eells, it might be called the earliest junior college, since in addition to secondary work it carried its students into the freshman year in college. Its students who wished further education were then sent to St. Omer's in Belgium to complete their studies. By the 1930's many academies, seminaries, and finishing schools added two years of junior college work to their courses of study.

California accepted the additional two years of high school most rapidly. The passage by the state legislature in 1907 of a measure authorizing high schools to offer higher educational serv-

[20] See Elbert K. Fretwell, Jr., *Founding Public Junior Colleges* (New York: Bureau of Publications, Teachers College, Columbia University, 1954), pp. 9–21.

[21] Information relative to the early development of junior colleges is based on Eells, *The Junior College*, pp. 55–58.

ices, which some were already offering, was the first such major development. The law provided that the board of trustees of any city, district, union, joint union, or county high school could prescribe postgraduate courses of study for the graduates of its high school or other high schools. This legislation was merely permissive and did not provide support to districts undertaking such service.

The California state legislature took the next important step in 1917 when it passed a bill providing for state and county financial support for junior college students on the same basis as for high school students. This legislative action was secured by the determined efforts of interested secondary school people, guided and directed by firm leadership from the state department of education.[22]

In 1921 California took another step forward with legislation providing for the organization of an independent junior college district with its own board, budget, and operating procedures. The junior college flourished in the favorable climate of California.

Thus very strong motivation for the junior college idea came from the high schools themselves.

The State University

From its inception the junior college idea received encouragement and direction from the colleges and universities. The new institution was christened "junior" and in its early infancy bore unmistakable evidence of the relationship which its name implied. The junior college inherited a number of characteristics from the four-year colleges and became practically a replica of the first two years of the regular college.

Not only have the ideas of university leaders contributed to a definition of the primary purpose of the first two years of college, but the development of the state university idea helped redefine education in America. The American liberal arts college as it existed in the mid-nineteenth century was not adequate to the needs of a rapidly changing society. The liberal arts college had done its job well but in terms of the few rather than the many. Growing

[22] Will C. Wood, "The Junior College," *Second Biennial Report of the State Board of Education of California* (Sacramento: 1916), pp. 163–64.

secularism, the subsequent development of industry, and the emergence of science called for changes in the educational pattern.

While the state university idea found literary expression in the seventeenth and eighteenth centuries, it was not until the nineteenth century that the university itself was fully developed. The rising state universities were characterized by the conviction that the recipients of higher education should not be an intellectual elite, but should be "all citizens capable of benefitting from such training." [23] As it was taking shape in the mid-nineteenth century, the state university idea assumed that a democratic social order required education on every level and that all had an equal right to higher education.

Closely related to the belief that all citizens should have an opportunity for higher education was the idea that the curriculum of a state-supported institution should reflect the professional and practical needs of the citizens. Economic and technological developments were transforming American society and economy and demanded specialized skills. Faced with these social demands for a more functional type of higher education than that being offered by the traditional liberal arts institutions, a few college presidents in the 1820's and 1830's spoke out against the educational *status quo.*

James Marsh of the University of Vermont, Eliphalet Nott of Union College, Philip Lindsley of the University of Nashville, and others attempted to introduce into the classical curriculum applied courses in the arts and sciences. The publication in 1842 of *Thoughts on the Present Collegiate System of the United States,* by President Francis Wayland of Brown University, reflected the ideas of those dissatisfied with the classical curriculum. Wayland denounced the program of the old-time college as ill-suited for equipping young men with the skills most needed in the everyday life of banking, milling, canal-making, bridge-building, and farming. The classical curriculum, Wayland contended, did not provide society with the techniques indispensable to its further material and moral progress.

[23] Merle Curti and Vernon Carstensen, *The University of Wisconsin* (Madison: University of Wisconsin Press, 1949), I, 22. The following paragraphs on curriculum change follow Curti and Carstensen, I, 26, 29.

In the main, the western state universities did not immediately adopt these much needed practical programs, partly because the faculties were liberal-arts oriented. It was only when the Federal Government in 1862 made land grants for the support of agricultural and mechanical education that the movement gained momentum. "Even thereafter," says Curti, "the battle, whether against the wily politicians, the indifferent farmers, or the champions of classical education, was won only after countless skirmishes." [24]

The Land-Grant College

Into the pre-Civil War period the American nation was still clinging to the Old World for its thinking and precepts. However, forces already at work in the first half of the nineteenth century would, when channeled, eventually lead to the establishment of a new type of collegiate education. Charles and Mary Beard, describing these pre-Civil War forces, found that "all in all the epoch of 'Jacksonian democracy,' the 'era of the common man,' the 'fabulous forties,' and the 'fermenting fifties,' was a time of dramatic mental activity and creative thinking in respect of everything human." [25]

Into this booming new civilization came the land-grant college movement. The changes it brought about in American higher education undoubtedly prepared the way for the eventual acceptance of the junior college idea. The questions raised by the establishment of the land-grant colleges in the nineteenth century were the same that junior college leaders debated in the twentieth century. Can the "liberal" and "practical" in higher education be successfully combined? Should post-high school education be limited to an educational elite or include all those who can profit from advanced study?

As the land-grant college curriculum developed, subjects were introduced and taught on the basis of their practical value. The concept of training for citizenship in a democratic society was also part of the program. By giving some measure of dignity to the vo-

---

[24] Curti and Carstensen, *The University of Wisconsin*, p. 29.
[25] Charles A. and Mary R. Beard, *A Basic History of the United States* (New York: The New Home Library, 1944), p. 245.

cations pursued by many Americans, the land-grant colleges helped pave the way for the acceptance of vocational training by higher educational institutions. The "new education" was partly responsible for breaking the concept of the fixed and prescribed classical curriculum.

Criticism of the land-grant colleges was both favorable and disparaging. Noah Porter, on assuming his duties as president of Yale in 1871, spoke of the "breeze of public interest and public criticism which is now blowing so freshly through the halls of ancient learning," [26] and Andrew D. White, president of Cornell University, speaking of the land-grant colleges, was to claim "in all the annals of republics, there is no more significant utterance of confidence in national destiny out from the midst of national calamity." [27]

Unfavorable criticism, however, came from many quarters. Isaac Roberts, a professor at Cornell, reported:

When the Press announced one fall that a large number . . . had entered the Freshman class, a leading denominational journal declared that 300 "fresh recruits for Satan" had entered this "Godless college." Another journal called it "a school where hayseeds and greasy mechanics were taught to hoe potatoes, pitch manure and be dry nurses to steam engines." [28]

To sum up, a unique system of higher education evolved through the years in response to societal demands. This kind of evolution marks the development not only of the American state university system and the land-grant colleges, but also of the junior college movement. By disrupting the traditional classical liberal arts curriculum, by being committed to the concept that the state and the nation prosper in proportion to the development of the individual, by democratization of higher education through their belief that intellectual capacity and achievements are not confined to the wealthy and privileged, by their insistence on the equality of studies; by all these, the land-grant colleges broke the monopoly

[26] W. Carson Ryan, *Studies in Early Graduate Education* (New York: The Carnegie Foundation for the Advancement of Teaching, 1939), p. 5.
[27] Cornell University, *Account of the Proceedings at the Inauguration*, October 7, 1868, p. 6.
[28] Quoted in Edward Danforth Eddy, Jr., *Colleges for Our Land and Time* (New York: Harper & Brothers, 1956), p. 73.

of the classical colleges and the stranglehold of the fixed and pre-scribed curriculum. They contributed a program and philosophy to American higher education from which the junior colleges bor-rowed heavily.

The Community Concept

The attempt to implement the concept of equal opportunity for all has led to growing enrollments in the colleges and universi-ties of the country. Such growth, together with the demands of so-ciety for a greater variety of trained personnel because of changing technology, has led to a new dimension in higher education. This new dimension is a growing concern about the quality of com-munity life, shown by the growing attempts to meet the needs of the community through higher education.

The idea of a college dedicated to meeting people's needs is not new to Americans. The American state university has had a good deal to do with fostering and furthering the ideal of service to the needs of the community. In the early twentieth century, the Uni-versity of Wisconsin realized the ideal of service to all the needs of the community. Wisconsin's President Charles R. Van Hise, in his inaugural address of 1904, indicated that Wisconsin was to be an institution for all the people of the state. The university would be a "watchtower," taking an active part in improving society and serving as an essential instrument of public service.[29]

The rise of state universities was paralleled by a movement for democratic higher education in the urban areas of America. The municipal university was created to provide higher education for the people of the cities at public expense. As early as 1847 the Free Academy of the City of New York, later to become the City College of New York, was established, and its course of studies had "especial reference to the active duties of operative life . . . the laboring class of our fellow citizens may have the opportunity of giving to their children an education that will more effectually fit them for the various departments of labor and toil, by which they will earn their bread." [30] Other municipal universities devel-

---

[29] John S. Brubacher and Willis Rudy, *Higher Education in Transition* (New York: Harper & Brothers, 1958), p. 163.

[30] John S. Diekhoff, *Democracy's College* (New York: Harper & Brothers, 1950), p. 9.

oped, the net result of which was to accelerate and broaden the movement for democratic higher learning.

An added impetus to the developing concept of the community and education working together came with the growing number of adults who sought learning of all kinds. Education was conceived as a continuing process in which the junior college was seen to be especially qualified to render service.

"In addition to preparatory and terminal curricula," said Earl J. McGrath,

the junior colleges can offer a third type of instruction which will be in great demand in the near future. Such instruction may be described as casual or service courses. . . . The junior colleges, enmeshed in the warp and woof of the community which sustains them, and untrammeled by tradition, are admirably equipped to offer this casual or service type of adult education.[31]

The acceptance by the junior colleges of a community function led to the emergence of the junior college as a community-serving educational institution. This concept went much deeper than the earlier one which thought of the junior college as a local institution designed to provide the community's youth with transfer and terminal curricula.

Community service is a rather recent development. There is little in the literature prior to 1930 which reveals this new conception of the junior college. A series of catastrophic events during the Depression, World War II, and more recently in America's assumption of world leadership, changed the characteristics of the junior college that had emerged in the early 1900's.

The very nature of the young and flexible junior college made possible a closer integration of campus and community without violating hallowed traditions. The opportunity of junior colleges during World War II to work closely with industry, business, and the military in the development of tailor-made programs to meet war training needs helped establish a new pattern. The development was accelerated by the report of the President's Commission

---

[31] Earl J. McGrath, "The Junior College of the Future," *Junior College Journal,* XV (February, 1945), 266–67. McGrath was then dean of administration and professor of education at the University of Buffalo.

on Higher Education. Using the term community college for the first time, the report indicated new potentialities:

Whatever form the community college takes its purpose is educational service to the entire community, and this purpose requires of it a variety of functions and programs. It will provide college education for the youth of the community certainly, so as to remove geographic and economic barriers to educational opportunities and discover and develop individual talents at low cost and easy access. But, in addition, the community college will serve as an active center of adult education. It will attempt to meet the total post high school needs of its community! [32]

THE MEN AND THE IDEA

Purification rites are of great significance in the tribal ceremonies of cultures. Many "big chiefs" in American higher education desired such purification rites as they surveyed the American university in the nineteenth century. One of these "chiefs" was Henry P. Tappan, president of the University of Michigan from 1852 to 1863. Earlier, Tappan had begun to form what were then considered advanced views on the subject of education, especially higher education in the United States. These views took final form during an extended visit to Europe; they were published in 1851 in a book entitled *University Education,* an exposition of the German system.[33] As early as 1852 he suggested that universities transfer the work of secondary departments to the high schools.[34] Others, enamored of the European approach to university education, advocated that the first two years of college work be completed before entrance to the university. The university should deal only in specialized or professional preparation. William Watts Folwell of the University of Minnesota, in his inaugural address as president of the university in 1869, indicated the great desirability of transferring the "body of work for the first two years in our ordinary American colleges to the secondary schools." [35]

[32] President's Commission, *Higher Education for American Democracy* I, 67–68.

[33] Henry P. Tappan, *University Education* (New York: George P. Putnam, 1851).

[34] B. A. Hinsdale, *History of the University of Michigan* (Ann Arbor: The University of Michigan, 1906), p. 43.

[35] William W. Folwell, *University Addresses* (Minneapolis: The H. W. Wilson Co., 1909), pp. 37–38.

Edmund J. James had tried to interest the University of Pennsylvania in the idea of dropping the freshman and sophomore years prior to his inauguration at Illinois in 1905. In his inaugural address he recommended modification of the work of the university by a "continued growth at the top and lopping off at the bottom." [36] Richard H. Jesse of Missouri and Andrew S. Draper of Illinois in the 1890's suggested in their addresses and publications the same university "amputation."

Before many years, the voices of David Starr Jordan, president of Stanford University, and Nicholas Murray Butler, president of Columbia University, were added to the growing group of university presidents who urged that the universities transfer lower division responsibilities.[37]

While these men did not participate directly in establishing junior colleges, their perspicacity and the prestige of their positions enabled them to contribute materially to the popularization of the junior college idea. In the history of the development of the junior college, two university men stand out. One was William Rainey Harper, president of the University of Chicago and called by many the "father of the junior college." [38] The other was Alexis Frederick Lange of the University of California.

William Rainey Harper

President Harper brought about the first real segregation of junior college and senior college with the opening of the reorganized University of Chicago in 1892. He organized the junior and senior years at the University of Chicago into what he called the "University College" and the freshman and sophomore years into an "Academic College." The names attached to the colleges continued in use until the academic year 1895–96, when "Junior College" was substituted for "Academic College" and "Senior College" for "University College." Harper apologized for the use of the word "junior college" but indicated that he used that term for lack of a better one.[39] The name "Junior College" was abandoned

---

[36] Eells, *The Junior College*, pp. 45–46.

[37] "Ancient History," *Junior College Journal*, II (October, 1931), 38; "Ancient History," *Junior College Journal*, II (November, 1931), 101–02.

[38] Eells, *The Junior College*, p. 47.

[39] William Rainey Harper, *The Trend in Higher Education* (Chicago: University of Chicago Press, 1905), p. 378.

in the reorganization of the university in 1931, when the lower division became "The College." [40]

President Harper also influenced a number of high schools to undertake "postgraduate" courses and some four-year colleges to concentrate on freshman and sophomore work. As early as 1903 he had expressed the need for clarity in the differentiation of levels of secondary, college, and university work, with subsequent improvement in the quality in each area.

"If, on the one hand," Harper wrote, "the academies and the high schools were elevated, and if, on the other hand, the scope of work done by many colleges were limited, and as a result institutions developed which would do that work thoroughly, there would come to be a recognized distinction between college and university which does not now exist." [41] Harper appreciated the excellent service rendered by the four-year colleges but nevertheless recommended the curtailment of the work of smaller, weaker senior colleges and suggested they concentrate on freshman and sophomore work.

Harper put into practical operation educational ideas that previously were incoherent and unorganized. For the first time in educational history, he built on the University of Chicago campus an integrated, corporate, and strong educational institution which he called a junior college.[42] He started a junior college at Morgan Park Academy that, during his lifetime, was a unit of the university. His influence reached outside the university as he encouraged the organization of junior colleges in connection with private academies. He also encouraged the establishment of pub-

[40]Eells, *The Junior College*, p. 47, and Ralph R. Fields, *The Community College Movement* (New York: McGraw-Hill Book Co., 1962), p. 19, indicate that Harper's use of the term was the first use of "junior college."

[41] William Rainey Harper, *The President's Report, July, 1898–July, 1899* (Chicago: University of Chicago, 1900), p. xxi.

[42] Eells points out that the distinction of being the first American institution to reach the decision to eliminate completely freshman and sophomore work belongs to the University of Georgia, where the plan was formally adopted by the trustees in 1859. The plan was not carried into effect because of the Civil War. The situation is described in E. Merton Coulter, *College Life in the Old South*, published in 1928. See Walter Crosby Eells, "Abolition of the Lower Division: Early History," *Junior College Journal*, VI (January, 1936), 193–95.

lic junior colleges and forecast their development in connection
with public high schools.

Alexis F. Lange

Contemporary with and subsequent to the work of Harper at
Chicago was the work of Lange, at the University of California,
that focused attention on the need for postgraduate work in the
public high schools. From 1906 to 1924 as head of the department
of education he influenced the development of the junior college
as part of the public school system of California.

Lange summarized the origin of the junior college movement
by referring to the legendary highwayman of Attica, Procrustes,
and his famous iron bed so ill-fitted to his victims. Lange suggested three questions: Shall the American university have its legs
cut off? Shall the American four-year high school be stretched?
Shall certain colleges have their heads cut off? [43]

Lange stressed the need for public support of more educational
opportunity for the youth of the country. He felt that a junior college education was important for the great mass of students not
seeking a four-year education beyond the high school. The junior
college should offer both general and vocational education as the
culmination of secondary education. Lange believed that the primary function of the junior college was vocational preparation.
He constantly admonished administrators of junior colleges to prevent the wrong persons from attempting to prepare for the transfer
requirements of most universities, when such additional training
would be harmful rather than helpful to them.

DEVELOPMENT OF THE JUNIOR COLLEGE

The history of the growth of the junior college has been similar
to that of other educational movements. A few junior colleges appeared; their programs and methods were imitated in other localities; and each one tried to prove that it was just as good as its
rival in some neighboring city. They had to secure recognition

[43] Alexis F. Lange, "The Junior College as an Integral Part of the Public School
System," *School Review*, XXV (September, 1917), 465.

from state universities and then win approval of some agency concerned with standards or accreditation. Both of these forces combined to compel this new institution to conform to the model of the traditional college. Here and there, in various sections of the country, a few daring souls ventured to do the unconventional by supplementing the "preparatory" or academic curriculum with a few terminal programs.

The first genuine example of this new educational species was probably Lewis Institute, founded in Chicago in 1896. Later it merged with Armour Institute of Technology and is now the Illinois Institute of Technology. While the claim of Lewis Institute was challenged in 1920 by the president of Bradley Polytechnic Institute, who declared that his institution was the first in America to be founded as a junior college when it undertook the junior college program in 1897, most historians of the junior college movement accept the claim of Lewis Institute.[44] Monticello College, in Alton, Illinois, has also claimed to be one of the early junior colleges, but this contention is hard to sustain. Russell T. Sharpe, former president of Monticello College, seems to believe that the original three-year program given by Monticello was not a junior college program.[45] Still another claim has been made by Susquehanna University, in Pennsylvania, which, as the Missionary Institute of the Evangelical Lutheran Church, opened its doors for instruction on June 14, 1858.[46]

It is generally accepted that the first public junior college was organized at Joliet, Illinois, under the leadership of J. Stanley Brown, who was inspired and encouraged by William Rainey Harper. While various authorities cite 1902 as the year of the founding of the Joliet Junior College, Elbert K. Fretwell, Jr., favors 1901 as the initial year of the college.[47] No matter what the

[44] Frederick Eby, "Retrospect and Prospect," *Junior College Journal*, VI (March, 1936), 279; James M. Wood, "Twenty Years' Progress," *Junior College Journal*, X (May, 1940), 511; Leonard V. Koos, "Rise of the People's College," *School Review*, LV (March, 1947), 142.

[45] Letters to Jesse Bogue, executive secretary of the AAJC, March 26, 1957 and April 4, 1957. AAJC Archives.

[46] Saul Sack, "The First Junior College," *Junior College Journal*, XXX (September, 1959), 13.

[47] Fretwell, *Founding Public Junior Colleges*, p. 11.

founding date was, by 1920 the junior college idea was definitely rooted in educational programs and was being implemented through the establishment of a variety of junior colleges.

TABLE I

GROWTH IN NUMBER OF PUBLIC AND PRIVATE
JUNIOR COLLEGES (1900–1960)

YEAR	NUMBER OF COLLEGES			PERCENTAGES OF PUBLIC COLLEGES
	TOTAL	PUBLIC	PRIVATE	
1900–1901	8	0	8	0
1915–1916	74	19	55	26
1921–1922	207	70	137	34
1925–1926	325	136	189	42
1929–1930	436	178	258	41
1933–1934	521	219	302	42
1938–1939	575	258	317	45
1947–1948	651	328	323	50
1952–1953	594	327	267	55
1953–1954	598	338	260	57
1954–1955	596	336	260	56
1955–1956	635	363	272	57
1956–1957	652	377	275	57.8
1957–1958	667	391	276	58.6
1958–1959	677	400	277	59.1
1959–1960	663	390	273	58.8

SOURCE: Edmund J. Gleazer, Jr., "Analysis of Junior College Growth," *Junior College Directory*, 1961, table 6, p. 41.

In 1900 there were no public junior colleges in the United States and only eight private junior colleges.[48] By 1961 there were 678 institutions, of which 405 were public and 273 private. Enrollment rose from 100 students in 1900 to 748,619 in October, 1961.[49]

From the beginning the junior colleges were urged to see their functions as broad rather than narrow. They were increasingly urged to become local institutions that would open their doors to

[48] Jesse P. Bogue and Shirley S. Hill, "Analysis of Junior College Growth," *Junior College Journal*, XX (February, 1950), 318.

[49] Edmund J. Gleazer, Jr., *The 1962 Junior College Directory* (Washington, D.C.: American Association of Junior Colleges, 1962), p. 27. See Tables I and II for detailed data.

the young and the old. The junior colleges grew in numbers and in influence as they developed a pragmatic educational program based on the needs of the whole community rather than on the ex-

TABLE II

JUNIOR COLLEGE ENROLLMENTS, 1900–1960

YEAR	TOTAL	PUBLIC	PRIVATE	PERCENTAGE PUBLIC
1900–01	100	0	100	0
1915–16	2,363	592	1,771	25
1921–22	16,031	8,349	7,682	52
1925–26	35,630	20,145	15,485	57
1929–30	74,088	45,021	29,067	61
1933–34	107,807	74,853	32,954	69
1938–39	196,710	140,545	56,165	71
1947–48	500,536	378,844	121,692	76
1951–52	572,193	495,766	76,427	87
1952–53	560,732	489,563	71,169	87
1953–54	622,864	553,008	69,856	89
1954–55	696,321	618,000	78,321	89
1955–56	765,551	683,129	82,422	89
1956–57	869,720	776,493	93,227	89.2
1957–58	892,642	793,105	99,537	88.8
1958–59	905,062*	806,849	98,213	89.1
1959–60	816,071*	712,224	103,847	87.3

* Cumulative Total. This total includes all students and gives some indication of the number of different people served by the college during the entire year.

SOURCE: Edmund J. Gleazer, Jr., "Analysis of Junior College Growth," *Junior College Directory*, 1961, table 7, p. 42.

clusive needs of students who planned to take their first two years of liberal arts courses in them.

AN EVOLVING AGENCY OF DEMOCRATIC EDUCATION

The junior college, offering two years of education beyond the secondary school, is a product almost entirely of the twentieth century. The junior college idea, however, is the result of centuries of philosophical and institutional struggle which influenced all of American education and developed an educational system with characteristics not to be found anywhere else in the world.

During the past three centuries higher education in the United

States has developed a variety of forms. Among these have been the New England hilltop college, the state college and university, the land-grant college, the municipal college or university, and the junior college. As these various types of institutions evolved, one feature characterized all of them: the concept of democracy. The American, because of his culture, changed the traditional system which he brought with him from the Old World. As a result of this transformation, the American people broadened and democratized these forms so that more and more individuals might have an opportunity to secure post-secondary training. They also increasingly sought to make higher learning both cultural and practical, more closely related to the daily concerns of the average American. Through the years there developed a growing demand for a form of schooling that would make provisions for those persons whose occupational, social, and economic level brought them somewhat above the training available within high school limits, yet somewhat lower than that of the four-year college graduate.

From the struggles to achieve equality of opportunity and to broaden the scope of higher education, the junior college idea was born. The idea took root in the soil of America's cultural, economic, and political heritage. It fed and grew on such concepts as equal opportunity for all and the desire to eliminate financial, geographical, and social barriers to higher education. It was nurtured by such educational leaders as Henry P. Tappan, William W. Folwell, David Starr Jordan, and William Rainey Harper, until by 1920 the junior college was accepted as an academic institution capable of offering the first two years of an approved baccalaureate program.

Between 1920 and 1945 another strain was added to produce a new hybrid form. At least two junior college leaders urged general acceptance by the junior colleges of an emerging trend, that of terminal and semiprofessional programs. Lange insisted that the first concern of the junior college "is with those who will go no farther." President William H. Snyder of Los Angeles Junior College established in 1929 fourteen terminal semiprofessional curricula at his institution.

Since World War II the junior college has emerged out of the mixture of these various strains as an institution which aims to meet the needs of the people in the locality in which it functions. In historical perspective, the junior college has become an institution which still offers the first two years of college education, but has added vocational curricula and an adult education program.

2

Foundation and Development
of the American Association
# of Junior Colleges

THE CATALYST that led to the establishment of the American Association of Junior Colleges was a conference of junior college representatives called by the U.S. Commissioner of Education, P. P. Claxton, in 1920. Dr. George F. Zook, specialist in higher education for the U.S. Bureau of Education, was in charge of the two-day meeting held June 30 and July 1 in St. Louis, Missouri.

Thirty-four members were present at this initial conference. More than a third of them were from Missouri; twelve other states were represented. President James M. Wood of Stephens College, Columbia, Missouri, was chairman of the meeting; Martha M. Reid, dean of William Woods College, Fulton, Missouri, was secretary.[1]

At the time of this initial conference there were probably 175 institutions in the entire country that might be designated as junior colleges. Their programs were diverse and their status often uncertain. The junior college had never been heard of in many places. Some looked upon it as a sort of last stand before the weak four-year college passed completely from the scene. Others dubbed it a "glorified high school." [2]

[1] See George F. Zook (ed.), *National Conference of Junior Colleges, 1920, and First Annual Meeting of AAJC, 1921,* Bulletin of the U. S. Bureau of Education, No. 19, Part II (Washington, D.C.: U.S. Government Printing Office, 1922).

[2] Doak S. Campbell, "After Sixteen Years," *Junior College Journal,* VII (December, 1936), 109.

The past forty-two years have seen many significant changes. The number of junior colleges has increased at such a rate that attendance at AAJC meetings today runs well over 350. During these years the American Association of Junior Colleges has gained recognition and status as spokesman and as leader of the junior college movement.

FOUNDING THE AAJC

Nineteen twenty saw many forces at work which led the Bureau of Education to call a junior college conference.

Forces for an Organization

There was James Madison Wood. By 1920 he was the moving spirit of the junior college movement. Wood, who was influenced greatly by William Rainey Harper, had assumed the presidency of Stephens College in Missouri in 1912, when it was almost a dead institution—a four-year college with a preparatory school attached to it and a total enrollment of 137 students. He convinced the Board of Trustees that he could save the institution by cutting off the bottom two years of the high school and the top two years of the college. By 1920 Stephens was a national success; Wood had made the junior college idea work successfully there.[3]

One reason for the conference in 1920 was the desire of Wood to bring together educators who were interested in furthering the junior college idea. He was anxious to find out if other struggling small colleges might be willing to try his Stephens program. Wood probably had a permanent organization in mind, but more important at the time were the national problems of developing an understanding of the junior college and of finding some means of saving many of the marginal colleges.

There was also Zook. He was aware of the nationwide problem of hundreds of struggling colleges about to give up the ghost. Zook was also aware that there were many national education associations and even more sectional and state education associations that were discussing questions affecting the future welfare of education in the United States. Very few that had been formed, however,

[3] Interview with Doak S. Campbell, former executive secretary of the AAJC, March 30, 1962.

were discussing the functions and the future of the junior college. It occurred to Zook and to the Commissioner of Education that it would be desirable for the Bureau of Education to "call a meeting of representatives from the junior colleges of the country for a full and frank discussion of their mutual interests and problems." [4]

The influence of Wood and Zook was instrumental in securing the organizational meeting in 1920. Wood's claim to the title of "Mr. Junior College" was validated when St. Louis, Missouri, in the home state of Stephens College, was chosen for this meeting.

Another factor that brought about the St. Louis meeting was the provision for accreditation in higher education, which began in the 1890's but did not begin to press the colleges until the first decade of the twentieth century. Accrediting associations set up standards and began to apply them. Whether or not one was on the accredited list was public information and could be enough either to save or to destroy marginal institutions.

For many colleges, a national organization was an ark of safety. Prior to the formation of the American Association of Junior Colleges the only hope junior colleges had for success was to have a friendly university indicate that it would accept transfer students. But such salvation was neither recognition nor accreditation— it was often charity. The formation of the AAJC offered a possibility for a national organization that could achieve respectability and win recognition for the junior colleges. Inviting four-year college educators to address the Association became policy at the annual meeting of the AAJC. The purpose of the invitations was to stimulate interest in the two-year college movement and to lend respectability to the organization.

The Association was born, then, out of the necessity to define and interpret the essence of the junior college and its potential. A great many people who ran the junior colleges did not understand the place of their institutions in the American educational pattern. Others, who understood, realized that they had to gain recognition. The needs were enough to bring people together to form an organization that would perform such functions.

Definition, leading to recognition, leading to status: this was the primary objective of the AAJC in the 1920's and the 1930's.

[4] Zook (ed.), *National Conference of Junior Colleges,* p. 1.

The Organizational Meeting, 1920

Zook, who took a leading role in the development of the American Association of Junior Colleges, said on many occasions that it took a good deal of courage to face the heat of midsummer in St. Louis in 1920, and "no little faith that the then vaguely defined institution called the junior college had a future sufficiently important to justify a conference." [5]

Thirty-four educators from twenty-two junior colleges located in thirteen states and the District of Columbia evidently had sufficient faith as they gathered on June 30 in the hot, muggy weather of St. Louis. Zook opened the conference and then introduced Wood, who spoke on "The Function of the Junior College" and acted as chairman for the remainder of the two-day meeting. [6]

Wood raised some interesting questions regarding the junior college that were illustrative of the differences of opinion which existed in 1920, and exist even today, about the nature of the junior college. Wood recommended a reorganization of education in America to allow for a four-year junior college and the awarding of a baccalaureate degree. He suggested reforms in curricula that would fit the needs of students rather than the needs of faculties to teach their specialties.

Others took issue with Wood and indicated that they would not like to see any degree granted to junior college graduates and that the junior college should merely concentrate on offering sixty hours. H. G. Noffsinger, "a quiet gentleman from the hills of Virginia, who didn't say much but thought a great deal," president of Virginia Intermont College at Bristol, remarked that he did not want to see the B.A. degree granted to junior college graduates but would like to see an Associate in Arts degree awarded to those who finished the two-year program. [7]

---

[5] George F. Zook, "The Changing Pattern of Junior College Education," *Junior College Journal,* XVI (May, 1946), 411.

[6] Zook (ed.), *National Conference of Junior Colleges,* p. 2.

[7] For the various discussions that took place at the organizational meeting in 1920 see Edward M. Bainter, "The Administration and Control of Public Junior Colleges," Merton E. Hill, "Vocationalizing the Junior College," David MacKenzie, "Problems of the Public Junior College," James M. Wood, "The Function of the Junior College," John W. Million, "Advantages of the Junior College," in Zook (ed.), *National Conference of Junior Colleges.*

Another theme at this first meeting was the relationship of the junior college to the secondary school and to the period of later adolescence. Several junior college administrators stressed that the freshman and sophomore years of the standard college course "are in subject matter much more of a continuation of the high school than a beginning of the specialized courses of the junior and senior years of the standard college course." David MacKenzie, dean of Detroit Junior College, differed and insisted that the high school and the junior college were different institutions. Some references —premonition of future debates—were also made to community functions and to the importance of providing vocational education.

A highlight of the conference was the presence of Commissioner Claxton. In his address he stressed that a national reorganization of education "would permit the secondary schools to continue their work to the completion of the general education in the school and the first two years of college." [8] Claxton saw the role of the junior college as that of a selective agency for the "higher institutions" and also as a means of preventing the state universities from being swamped with freshmen and sophomores.

Delegates to the St. Louis conference decided to organize a national association of junior colleges. Martha M. Reid read the report of the Committee on Permanent Organization, which had been appointed by Wood. The report recommended that a meeting of the organization of junior colleges be held in Chicago in February, 1921; that those junior colleges that were accredited by "recognized accrediting agencies" be admitted to membership; and that MacKenzie be nominated for president, T. W. Raymond for vice-president, and Miss Reid for secretary-treasurer.[9] The conference approved these proposals and levied a five dollar fee on

[8] P. P. Claxton, "The Better Organization of Higher Education in the United States," in Zook (ed.), *National Conference of Junior Colleges*, p. 30.

[9] Martha M. Reid, "Report of the Committee on Permanent Organization," in Zook (ed.), *National Conference of Junior Colleges*, p. 45. W. G. Bolcom, in 1920 superintendent of schools in Rochester, Minnesota, wrote to W. C. Eells on January 17, 1940, indicating that although it did not matter, he was elected the vice president of the temporary organization formed in St. Louis. In another letter, January 26, 1940, Bolcom wrote, "My own opinion is that the Secretary-Treasurer must have confused Mr. Raymond and me. My memory is somewhat hazy in regard to a number of things that took place, but I do remember that . . . I was elected vice-president." Eells papers (in the possession of the author).

each institution represented. The fee was to be used by the officers to promote and advertise the next meeting.

Thus the AAJC was born. It received support and approval from those in attendance because they saw the need for such an organization to provide professional leadership and direction for the junior college movement. Or perhaps it received approval because, as Zook said with tongue in cheek, the heat reduced everyone to a common mass so that they were all of one mind. "No one in the conference had the energy to object to anything on the program," said Zook, "including the report of the committee which recommended the formation of the new educational organization to be known as the American Association of Junior Colleges. You are entitled to this explanation as to the manner in which this organization got underway." [10]

Why didn't the junior colleges join with other higher educational institutions instead of starting their own national organization? The junior college had not become fully defined. The junior college leaders felt that they had the job of self-definition of their role in American education and this could only be done within their own organization.[11]

Definition and Standards

At the first annual meeting of the AAJC held in 1921, a formal constitution was adopted. The early meetings of the AAJC labored to define the junior college. The speakers at the first official meeting attempted to interpret this newcomer, which meant different things to different people.[12] Committees were appointed at the second meeting, in Memphis, Tennessee, to project an image of the junior college to accreditation societies and to the public. The AAJC defined the junior college as "an institution offering two years of instruction of strictly collegiate grade." [13]

At Memphis the Association also adopted its first standards

[10] George F. Zook, "The Past Twenty Years—The Next Twenty Years," *Junior College Journal*, X (May, 1940), 617.

[11] Interviews with Doak S. Campbell, March 30, 1962, and W. C. Eells, March 23, 1961.

[12] Zook (ed.), *National Conference of Junior Colleges*, part II.

[13] *Proceedings of the Second Annual Meeting of the AAJC*, 1922 [p. 2]. AAJC Archives.

dealing with definition, admission, graduation, equipment, faculty, support, and recognition. These goals were intended as a statement of aims, something toward which institutions could work; they were revised in 1925 and again in 1929.

Several of the early meetings of the Association were occupied with long and earnest debates on standards. Most junior colleges were anxious to maintain quality at least as high as that required by regional or state accrediting agencies. However, some of the standards imposed particular hardships on junior colleges. For the first two or three years after the organization of the AAJC, accrediting agencies insisted that junior colleges be separate from the high school. This was difficult for those junior colleges that had grown out of the high school organization. At the fourth annual meeting, Lewis W. Smith of Joliet spoke against the standard, insisting that there was no fundamental distinction between the junior college years and the senior high school years.

The adoption of standards by the Association in the 1920's did not mean that the AAJC was becoming an accrediting agency. In fact, from its inception the AAJC consistently avoided the function of accreditation. Arguments against the Association's assumption of this responsibility included:

1. The limiting effect which the time-consuming work of accreditation would have on the primary purpose of the AAJC—to study the professional problems associated with junior colleges.

2. The inability to assume the heavy cost of setting up and operating the machinery needed for accrediting institutions.

3. The existence of agencies supplying such service.

The Code of Ethics

As the junior college movement grew, institutions vied with one another to enroll paying students. This was especially true of some private junior colleges which utilized various means, some of them questionable, to attract students.

At the seventh annual meeting of the Association in 1927, Lucinda Templin of the University of Missouri protested inequitable tuition reductions, inaccurate advertising and publicity statements about their own and competing institutions, and unorthodox campaigns conducted by field secretaries.[14] Although the need for a code of ethics was quite evident, nothing was accomplished until 1934, when Richard G. Cox was appointed chairman of a committee to study the problem.

The fifteenth annual meeting in 1935 adopted a statement of principles or "Code of Ethics." The code required that statements and publications be accurate and truthful, that students known to have made formal application for enrollment at another school not be solicited, that all schools and representatives refrain from making derogatory remarks of any kind relative to any other college, and that, with certain exceptions, schools adhere to the published charges set forth in catalogues.[15]

ORGANIZATIONAL STRUCTURE AND LEADERSHIP

The founders of the AAJC faced so many obstacles when they started that it was no wonder that at times they doubted whether it would succeed at all. With no tangible inducements except the appeal of professional obligation, it was often difficult to persuade institutions to pay their membership dues. Finances were always a problem, and in the early organizational years there were sharp discussions and arguments over raising dues from $10 to $15 per year. In addition, there were divisive feelings between private institutions and public institutions. Diversity in types of organizations made more problematic than funny Walter Eells' classic statement that "the only way you knew whether an institution was a junior college was when it defined itself as such." [16]

The "Power Structure"

Analysis of the "power structure" of the AAJC indicates that a small group has guided the destiny of the organization since its establishment. Evidently, this is the pattern in the development of

[14] Lucinda Templin, "The Need of a Higher Code of Ethics in the Administration of Junior Colleges," *Proceedings of the Seventh Annual Meeting of the AAJC, 1927,* pp. 21–26. AAJC Archives.

[15] "Minutes and Committee Reports," Fifteenth Annual Meeting of AAJC, *Junior College Journal,* V (May, 1935), 468.

[16] Interviews with Doak S. Campbell, March 30, 1962, and Walter C. Eells, March 23, 1961.

voluntary associations.[17] During the 1920's the early executive secretaries and a handful of ex-presidents ran the affairs of the Association. Campbell, Wood, and Noffsinger were the leaders; Zook and Leonard Koos were the major speakers. The presidents of private junior colleges influenced the direction of the Association.

As the 1930's came to a close, the influence of private colleges began to wane. Private junior college representatives to AAJC meetings questioned whether their problems were receiving proper consideration by the national organization. Public junior college presidents, particularly from California, suggested that private junior colleges had too much to say in the councils of the AAJC.

For the sake of unity, efforts were made to democratize the power structure of the AAJC. This resulted in representation according to geographical location and balance between the private and public junior colleges in assigning leadership positions. A small group still controls the policy making of the Association. But since 1945 the executive powers have been defined and a hierarchy of executive officers, rather than a group of informal leaders, "run the show."

Structural Forms

Constitutional developments. The first constitution of the AAJC was adopted at the first regular meeting in 1921. The purpose of the Association stated in it was:

to define the junior college by creating standards and curricula, thus determining its position structurally in relation to other parts of the school system; and to study the junior college in all of its types (endowed, municipal, and state) in order to make a genuine contribution to the work of education.[18]

On March 4, 1939, the AAJC adopted a revised constitution which changed the stated purpose of the organization. It declared:

[17] See Louis Michael Vanaria, "The National Council for the Social Studies: a Voluntary Organization for Professional Service" (unpublished Ph.D. dissertation, Teachers College, Columbia University, 1958), chapter 4; also Stuart F. Chapin and John E. Tsouderos, "Formalization Observed in Ten Voluntary Associations: Concepts, Morphology, Process," *Social Forces*, XXXIII (May, 1955), 306–09.

[18] Article II, The First Constitution, in Zook (ed.), *National Conference of Junior Colleges*, p. 71.

the purpose of this organization shall be to stimulate the professional development of its members, to promote the growth of junior colleges under appropriate conditions, to emphasize the significant place of the junior college in American education, and to interpret the junior college movement to the country.[19]

The growth of the Association made it necessary to revise the 1939 constitution. A 1943 revision effort failed because of World War II. In 1945, following the resignation of Eells as executive secretary,[20] a new committee of twelve members from ten different states was appointed to draft a constitution. It presented a new constitution for approval at the annual meeting in January, 1946, and secured the membership's approval.[21] In its presentation, the committee pointed out that it was not a document designed to guard or protect any one group, "but it must govern all groups in the AAJC." [22]

The guiding principle of the reorganization under the new constitution was decentralization of the activities of the AAJC, with wider participation by the members. The flow of authority came from the membership to the elected and appointed officers rather than from the central authority down to the members. Many of the functions formerly performed by the central office in Washington were placed in the hands of various committees.

The University of Chicago was still interested in the junior college movement and offered its resources to the AAJC. The Executive Committee of the Association accepted the office space, the editorial services, and a cash contribution from the university.

The support given to the AAJC by the W. K. Kellogg Foundation and the new functions assumed by the central office warranted a new look at the structure of the AAJC. In the spring of 1962 a committee to revise the constitution began its work.[23]

[19] Article II, Constitution of American Association of Junior Colleges, adopted 1939, *Junior College Journal*, II (May, 1939), 556–59.

[20] See below, p. 42.

[21] The 1946 constitution was amended February 21, 1947; June 28, 1952; March 4, 1955; March 8, 1956; and March 4, 1960; but these amendments did not change the organizational structure.

[22] James L. Beck, "The New Constitution," *Junior College Journal*, XVI (May, 1946), 436–37.

[23] Edmund J. Gleazer, Jr., "Memorandum to the AAJC Board of Directors," April 23, 1962 (mimeographed). AAJC Archives.

Incorporation. The AAJC was incorporated on April 4, 1944, under the laws of the District of Columbia. The incorporators, as authorized at the annual meeting of the Association at Cincinnati in January, 1944, are the president, the vice-president, and executive secretary.

The principal advantages of incorporation were lending dignity to the organization; insuring permanency of succession under the corporate name; relieving the members and officers of personal liability; giving the organization legal standing in any necessary court procedures; facilitating such business transactions as those involved in the management of investment funds; and prescribing the process of dissolution of the organization and disposition of its remaining assets, if and when the dissolution might occur.[24]

The Board of Directors. The original constitution of the AAJC provided for a six-man Executive Committee of which the president was ex-officio member and chairman. Two members were elected at each annual meeting of the Association and were to serve for a period of three years. The Executive Committee determined policy for the Association. It cooperated with the president in planning and executing the program for the annual meeting.

The constitution of 1946 defined the structure of the present Board of Directors. It consists of the president, the vice-president, the immediate past president, and one director from each of six regional areas. The board is elected by a majority of the active members present at the annual meeting. It appoints the executive director, sets his salary, duties and term of office. The board approves all members of the Association and is required to report its actions for review by the Association delegates at the annual meeting.

Officers and elections. Officers of the Association have changed very little under the three constitutions. There have always been a president, a vice-president, and a secretary. The first constitution provided for a senior vice-president and a vice-president from each state represented. The constitution, however, failed either to state

[24] Walter C. Eells, "From the Secretary's Desk," *Junior College Journal*, XIV (May, 1944), 445.

how the senior vice-president and the state vice-presidents should be selected or to specify their duties. There is no record to show that any state vice-presidents were selected.

There has always been an attempt to rotate and distribute the offices of the AAJC to give representation to the various geographical regions of the country and to both private and public colleges. A Committee on Rotation and Distribution of Offices reported in March, 1954, at the annual meeting, that the offices of the Association by their very nature were neither geographical nor proportional but represented the entire Association. The committee recommended that the offices of president and vice-president should rotate between public and private junior colleges. For the sake of unity, the committee did indicate that these offices also should rotate so that each region could look forward to representation during a cycle of ten years.

The election of officers at the annual meeting has become formalized. A nominating committee, appointed in advance of the meeting by the Board of Directors, submits nominations for offices to be filled by election at the annual business meeting. Additional nominations from the floor are permitted.

The president usually has climbed the leadership ladder of the Association's structure. He comes up through the ranks as a member of the various committees and serves a term as vice-president before becoming president.

The executive secretary. The first secretary of the AAJC was Miss Reid, who served from 1920 to 1922. Campbell, president of Central College at Conway, Arkansas, succeeded her at the annual meeting of the Association in 1922. These two secretaries served without pay, "but received from nothing to $100 or so a year for secretarial and clerical help for getting out the minutes and keeping records of the Association." [25]

Campbell devoted sixteen years to this position. An oversized closet at Peabody College in Tennessee, where he became a professor of education, served for most of his tenure as the headquarters of the AAJC. When he became associate director of a

[25] C. C. Colvert and Henry Littlefield, "A Brief History of the Development of the AAJC," *Junior College Journal*, special Jesse P. Bogue Memorial Issue, XXXI (February, 1961), 38.

research project at George Peabody College and then dean of its Graduate School, Campbell relinquished his position as secretary of the Association. At the time of his resignation in March, 1938, the Association had grown from thirty to almost 330 members.[26]

Campbell had announced his intention of retiring from the secretaryship at the 1937 meeting of the AAJC in Dallas. A committee was appointed to plan the reorganization of the Association. It received a comprehensive statement from Walter C. Eells, editor of the *Junior College Journal,* which set forth his ideas about the reorganization of the AAJC. Eells indicated that in spite of the fact that the majority of junior colleges were in the Middle West and Far West, national headquarters should be in Washington, D.C., the educational headquarters of the country.

Eells listed as desirable activities research and survey activities, compilation and interpretation of statistical data, conferences, promotional work, and *Junior College Journal* editorial work. He concluded his statement by indicating his interest in the position of secretary for a two- or three-year trial period.[27]

As the 1938 meeting of the Association, the committee submitted a reorganization plan which was adopted unanimously. This provided for the opening of a national headquarters in Washington, D.C., in September and for the employment of an executive secretary who would also edit and manage the *Junior College Journal.* The annual membership fees of active members were increased from $10 to $20 in order to support this new program.[28]

Eells Becomes Executive Secretary

Walter C. Eells was offered the position of executive secretary on a part-time basis effective September 1, 1938, at a salary of $300 per month.[29] By 1940 he was working as full-time executive secre-

[26] Letter from Vera S. Bristow, secretary to Nicholas Ricciardi, President, AAJC, to Campbell, July 27, 1938, enclosing a release on the reorganization of the AAJC. Eells papers.

[27] Letter from Walter Crosby Eells, to Arthur Andrews, Col. A. M. Hitch, and Doak S. Campbell, the Committee on Reorganization of the AAJC, December 1, 1937. Eells papers.

[28] Doak S. Campbell, "AAJC, General Notice Regarding Plan of Reorganization Adopted at Philadelphia, March, 1938." Mimeographed notice sent to members of AAJC. AAJC Archives.

[29] Telegram sent to Eells, offering him position, by Nicholas Ricciardi, President, AAJC, June 2, 1938. Eells papers.

tary and served in such capacity until 1945. Eells was a scholar whose primary interests were historical research and editorial work. He thoroughly enjoyed editing the *Junior College Journal* and considered the publication the most important "unifying and interpretive element" of the AAJC.[30] During the war years he sent a weekly newsletter to junior college administrators at home and abroad which informed them of the latest events and government regulations pertaining to junior colleges.

However, Eells ran the Association as a "one-man show," often not heeding the Executive Committee. He was aware of resulting dissatisfaction, for he wrote to Henry Aldous Dixon, president of Weber College, Ogden, Utah, in 1945 that "fundamentally the criticism leveled at me seems to be that the Washington office is too strong, that I have been too effective, that it is too much a one-man show, that leadership and service should be decentralized, that the Executive Secretary should have his wings clipped."[31] Eventually the wings of Eells were clipped.

The resignation of Walter C. Eells. Warning came in 1942 that all was not as it should be. Financial difficulties plagued the AAJC. An indebtedness of several thousand dollars to printers had accumulated and they were pressing for payment. John W. Harbeson, president of Pasadena Junior College and president of the AAJC in 1942–43, called the Executive Committee together and recommended a meeting to consider organizing the AAJC office on a part-time basis. The Executive Committee at a special meeting held in Chicago on November 7 and 8, 1942, decided to abolish the Washington office of the Association no later than June 30, 1943. The Executive Committee also approved a recommendation empowering the president to move the office of the Association to a midwestern university and to make the executive secretaryship a part-time adjunct of a professorship at such a university.[32]

In protest against this decision and the methods by which it

[30] Interview with Eells, March 23, 1961.

[31] Confidential letter from Eells to Dixon, March 5, 1945. Eells papers.

[32] Walter Crosby Eells, *Wartime Letter No. 11,* Nov. 17, 1942. Also letter from Harbeson to author, March 1, 1962. Harbeson died in 1962 and this is one of the last letters he wrote setting forth his views of his year as President of the AAJC.

was reached, Eells submitted his resignation. The real problem, according to Eells, was not the current financial situation. He traced the difficulty to two men on the Executive Committee— W. H. Conley, dean of Wright Junior College, Illinois, and Byron S. Hollingshead, president of Scranton-Keystone Junior College, Pennsylvania. "Since 1940," wrote Eells to John Lounsbury, president of San Bernardino Valley Junior College in California, "I feel like I have been sitting on the lid trying to prevent an explosion. But it has finally come." [33] He accused Conley of constantly working for the removal of the Association offices to Chicago. "Conley, Leland Medsker, secretary of the Terminal Education Committee, and John Harbeson are all closely tied in with Leonard Koos and the University of Chicago," said Eells. "Robert Hutchins would like to influence or dominate junior college development, supported by Koos and the others. To get the office of the Association at Chicago, possibly with Koos as Secretary, would of course furnish the best possible opportunity for such influence." [34]

Eells also took issue with Harbeson's summary of the decisions reached at the Chicago meeting. "I regret to say," wrote Eells, "that I do not see how any man with any red blood in his veins or with any self respect [sic] could do otherwise than resign in protest in the face of such express and implied repudiation of his leadership and service as evidenced at the Chicago meeting." [35]

If the decision to move the office on a part-time basis to a university center had been carried out, it is most likely that the AAJC would have dissolved then and there.[36] Neither Harbeson nor the Executive Committee desired this. Eells was asked to withdraw his resignation pending the action of the forthcoming convention.

Weeks before the date set for the convention, the Office of Defense Transportation recommended cancellation of the annual meeting of the AAJC scheduled for St. Louis on February 23 and

[33] Letter from Eells to Lounsbury, Feb. 21, 1943. Eells papers.

[34] Letter from Eells to Lounsbury, Feb. 21, 1943, Eells papers; interview with James Reynolds, editor of the *Junior College Journal,* March 1, 1962.

[35] Letter from Eells to Harbeson, Nov. 18, 1942. Eells papers.

[36] Letter from Harbeson to author, March 1, 1962; also see "Annual Report of Executive Secretary," *Junior College Journal,* XIII (May, 1943), 445–46.

24, 1943. But the cancellation of the convention did not release the AAJC from its responsibility to deal with the problems which confronted it. Harbeson, in a special report to the members of the Association, reviewed the major events of his year in office. In it he disagreed with the way Eells had been operating as a one-man office and one-man Association. He insisted that Eells was usurping functions which were specifically vested in the Executive Committee.

Harbeson pointed out what he considered weaknesses in the AAJC. First, the Association was operating under loose business procedures. After the budget was approved by the Executive Committee its administration was left exclusively to the executive secretary. A second weakness was that it was relatively too much a pressure organization and too little a professional one. He indicated that a possible solution to this problem was the establishment of the Association offices in one of the leading institutions of higher learning. And third, the AAJC was built too much about a single office. "Now I concede," concluded Harbeson, "that if we are to be represented in everything by one and the same individual, no better person could be found for that purpose than our honored Executive Secretary. But certainly this is an exceedingly undesirable situation." [37]

Because the 1943 meeting was cancelled, it was decided to poll the membership of the AAJC on the following two questions:

1. For the duration of the war shall the Association headquarters be continued in Washington with a full-time executive secretary provided that adequate funds for its maintenance can be secured?

2. As an emergency measure shall the Association waive Sections 1 and 2 of Article IV of the constitution and increase dues? [38]

More than three-quarters of the membership voted and overwhelmingly approved both questions.[39] Jesse P. Bogue, president of the AAJC, commented that he hoped that the Association and its activities could now "go forward vigorously." He also expressed

[37] John W. Harbeson, "A Message to the Members of the AAJC," January, 1943 (mimeographed). AAJC Archives.
[38] Walter C. Eells, "From the Secretary's Desk," *Junior College Journal*, XIV (September, 1943), 43.
[39] *Ibid.*

hope that personal differences could be set aside.[40] The differences in the Association, however, were too deep to be set aside easily. Among other problems, there were sectional feelings. Eells deplored efforts to divide the Association and its activities on a sectional basis, emphasizing that each section of the country could learn from the others.[41]

Another divisive factor was the split between private and public institutions, which has existed from the first meeting of the Association to the present day. Early leadership in the Association rested primarily in the private junior college group. Through the years the number of private junior colleges decreased while the public junior colleges increased both in numbers and enrollments. Eells was accused of favoring the private colleges more than the public. At the twenty-fourth meeting of the AAJC Eells spoke out sharply against any effort "such as has been suggested in some quarters recently, to divide the Association into two organizations on the basis of publicly and privately controlled institutions." [42]

These disagreements came to a head on March 24, 1945, when Eells tendered his resignation as executive secretary of the AAJC. The resignation was accepted by the Executive Committee on April 18, 1945. The immediate cause for Eells' resignation was disagreement over the contract for his services. Eells wanted tenure, scheduled annual increments, provision for a retirement allowance, and provision for annual vacation. These were refused. In a letter Eells indicated that "the real issue is not the terms of a possible future contract, but whether the Executive Committee, to be more accurate two members of it, is more powerful than the entire Association and can refuse the Association the right to decide whether they wish a reasonable and professional contract to be entered into with their Executive Secretary." [43]

[40] Jesse P. Bogue and Walter C. Eells, *Letters to Members of the AAJC,* May 17, 1943 (mimeographed). AAJC Archives.

[41] Walter C. Eells, "Annual Report of Executive Secretary," *Junior College Journal,* XIII (May, 1943), 442. This awareness of sectional differences was expressed in interviews with Eells, Ingalls, Bishop, and Colvert, the latter three being past presidents of the AAJC.

[42] Walter C. Eells, "Annual Report of Executive Secretary to 24th Annual Meeting of AAJC," *Junior College Journal,* XIV (April, 1944), 349.

[43] Letter from Walter C. Eells to Alan S. Wilson, director of Hillyer Junior College, Hartford, Connecticut, May 10, 1945. Eells papers.

Eells had two long conferences with Lawrence L. Bethel, president of the AAJC, and two members of the Executive Committee. They agreed that the best way to bring matters to a head was for Eells to resign; Bethel would then ask the Executive Committee to authorize a referendum of the membership. Bethel took Eells' letter of resignation to the Executive Committee of the AAJC, which was asked to vote on several questions. They voted to accept Eells' resignation and not to offer him the sort of contract he desired. In addition, the committee declined to submit the questions to a referendum.[44]

The resignation engendered a bitterness that lasted until Eells' death. In letter after letter to his friends and associates, Eells referred to his repudiation by a group on the Executive Committee "who have been out to get me for sometime, and have finally succeeded."[45] Eells was convinced that the membership of the Association would have upheld him. However, according to the constitution, the executive secretary is responsible to the Executive Committee, not to the membership of the Association, and Eells knew that the Executive Committee was legally correct in not allowing a referendum on the matter. But legality did not lessen the hurt. To Lounsbury, Eells wrote that

I have quite determined that I will never be submitted to such humiliation again as last month with the Executive Committee. Life is too short, I am getting too old, and I have a little professional pride. If I can not be treated professionally, without constant petty sniping, I think it would be wiser for me to step out—and I could assure you it would be a great relief in many ways.[46]

Time has not healed the bitterness that existed between some of the leaders in the AAJC and Eells. After his resignation, Eells did not attend the meetings of the AAJC or continue activity in the junior college movement in America. His junior college interests and energies were expended on the movement in Japan.

[44] Lawrence L. Bethel, "Report of Executive Committee Ballot," April 30, 1945 (mimeographed), Eells papers; letter from Lawrence L. Bethel to Walter Crosby Eells, April 18, 1945, Eells papers. The votes on the three questions were 5–3, 6–2, and 5–3.

[45] Letter from Eells to Lounsbury, March 10, 1945. Eells papers.

[46] *Ibid.*

Jesse P. Bogue, Executive Secretary

The year 1946 was critical for the AAJC. Disagreements over basic policies in the Association had deepened into serious controversy. Several important alterations in the structure of the organization had been made, creating the usual uncertainties which novelty induces. The emotional atmosphere of the Chicago meeting of 1946 was highly charged. Prophets of doom were sufficiently vocal to make many of the participants wonder if this would be the last meeting of the AAJC.

In the midst of this situation, the office of executive secretary was vacant. Mrs. Winifred Long, assistant to Eells, had been appointed acting executive secretary, but only until a permanent choice could be made. The selection made by the Board of Directors was of critical importance. Their choice was Jesse Parker Bogue, president of Green Mountain Junior College, Poultney, Vermont, and former president of the AAJC. The wisdom of that choice is attested by the developments of the ensuing twelve years.

One of Bogue's first accomplishments was the alleviation of the pressure which had built up out of the existing controversy, permitting formerly diverse groups to find a common ground on which they might work constructively for the progress of the junior college movement. "Jesse Bogue was an expert public-relations man," said Dr. Roscoe Ingalls, a past president of the AAJC. "He traveled the country, pouring on the oil, and was able to unite people and areas." [47] Bogue also implemented a new set of organizational machinery. The speed with which this was done and the smoothness of the changeover are testimony to the leadership which Bogue provided.

During Bogue's term of office, the AAJC made attempts to interest foundations in the junior college movement. The Association undertook a public information project to cultivate an opinion favorable to the two-year colleges. Dr. Edmund J. Gleazer, Jr., president of Graceland College, Lamoni, Iowa, assumed the directorship of the project on December 1, 1956. He made contacts

---

[47] Interview with Ingalls, March 1, 1962. Walter C. Eells, when interviewed March 23, 1961, described Bogue as a promoter.

with the heads of foundations, business and industrial concerns, and publishers and editors of national magazines in order to tell the junior college story. After twelve years of service Bogue retired from the post of executive secretary, and Gleazer succeeded him on April 1, 1958.

Executive Director

Before Gleazer succeeded Bogue, the AAJC Constitution was amended, changing the title of executive secretary to executive director and indicating that the executive director would take a more active leadership role in the affairs of the AAJC.[48]

By 1959 it became evident that the duties of the executive director and the president of the Association overlapped and that it would be helpful to have on record a definition of the duties and responsibilities of all Association officers. In January, 1960, at the Board of Directors meeting, it was pointed out that the AAJC had grown to the point where the executive director required additional powers. He had to retain effective communication not only with the officers and Board of Directors of the Association but with foundations, other educational organizations and agencies, and the Federal Government. In March, 1960, at the fortieth annual meeting of the AAJC, a statement on the duties and responsibilities of the president and executive director was adopted by the Board of Directors. It was emphasized that the list of duties was merely illustrative and was not to be interpreted as inflexible.

The duties of the president include the following:

1. Chairmanship of the Board of Directors.
2. Appointment of members to all commissions and committees unless the Board of Directors provides a different method.
3. Presiding at business meetings of the Association and at general sessions unless he delegates to someone else.
4. Serving 'as an ex-officio member of all commissions and committees.
5. Acting as a spokesman for the AAJC and for the Board of Directors.
6. Working with the Executive Director and Finance Committee on the preparation of the budget.

[48] AAJC Board of Directors, *Minutes* (March, 1958). AAJC Archives.

The executive director is the agent of the Board of Directors and its chief executive officer and is responsible to it at all times. He is the professional leader of the Association. The duties and responsibilities of the executive director include the following:

1. Keeping the membership informed about junior colleges and related educational trends.
2. Providing leadership in junior college thinking.
3. Carrying out the policies adopted by the Board and the membership.
4. Administering the work of the Association central office.
5. Acting as a spokesman for the AAJC and for the junior college movement.
6. Making suggestions for appointments to the commissions and committees.
7. Preparing the agenda for Board meetings, the program for the annual meeting, and special conferences.
8. Working with other educational associations, foundations, and organizations in interpreting the junior college movement.[49]

The executive director is the most important officer in the AAJC. The Association's affairs and promotional activities require of the executive director an unusual combination of specialized abilities. He must understand business procedures and management. His duties and responsibilities, examined even in a cursory way, suggest that he possess some of the skills of an editor, writer, public speaker, accountant, personnel director, lawyer, publicist, salesman, educational consultant, fund raiser, and diplomat. Through its executive director the AAJC engages in a variety of activities to promote the specialized interests of junior colleges.

Central Headquarters and Staff

The office of the AAJC has moved several times during its history. Since 1939, however, it has been located in Washington, D.C.[50] The desire of the AAJC Board of Directors to have the Association housed in the same building with the American Council on Education led to arrangements in 1948 whereby the AAJC

[49] AAJC Board of Directors, *Minutes* (March 1–5, 1960). AAJC Archives.
[50] In 1939 the office of the AAJC was located at 744 Jackson Place. In 1940 the Association moved into the entire third floor of 730 Jackson Place and four years later moved once again to 1201 Nineteenth Street, N.W.

secured office space in the American Council on Education Building at 1785 Massachusetts Avenue, N.W. A grant from the W. K. Kellogg Foundation in 1960 resulted in the need for more space, and in 1961 the AAJC moved into a four-story building at 1777 Massachusetts Avenue, N.W.

The members of the present (1963) staff are William Shannon, assistant executive director, appointed in 1959; Thomas Merson, assistant director for commissions, appointed in 1960; William A. Harper, director of public information, appointed in 1961; Jesse R. Barnet, staff associate, appointed in 1961; Carol Bluford, information associate, appointed in 1962; and Roger Yarrington, editor, *Junior College Journal,* appointed in 1962.

Committees and Commissions

From the very beginning of the AAJC, committees have been an integral part of the administrative structure of the organization. The national office, however, has performed most of the work of the AAJC. An analysis of the "power structure" of the AAJC prior to 1946 indicates that a small group guided the destiny of the organization after its establishment, a not unusual situation in professional organizations. The early executive secretaries and a handful of ex-presidents "ran the show."

However, committees are devices that have enabled the AAJC to carry on important services inexpensively. Wesley has listed other reasons for having committees.

Why appoint a committee? Because it stops the debate. Because it postpones the issue. Because it seems like a solution. Because it provides time for consideration. Because it shifts responsibility from the whole group to designated individuals. Because some persons want to be appointed. Because it is a way of securing free service. Because it is kind of representative democracy.[51]

It is not surprising that the AAJC, following the pattern of earlier associations, quite early began to create a growing number of committees to deal with a widening range of activities.

At the seventh annual meeting, in November, 1926, the Association authorized the incoming president to appoint a research

---

[51] Edgar B. Wesley, *NEA: The First Hundred Years* (New York: Harper and Brothers, 1957), p. 292.

committee. Lewis W. Smith, president of Joliet Junior College, became chairman, and Wood and George F. Winfield, president of Lon Morris College in Jacksonville, Texas, were made members. The task of this committee was to contact individuals, institutions, and organizations that might undertake studies on junior colleges. It conducted many research studies in the junior college field. In 1928 the University of Chicago, at the request of the committee, surveyed the offerings of elementary economics at junior colleges. Another study conducted by the research committee analyzed attitudes of junior college graduates. In 1939, the committee sponsored a study on the function of administrative officers.

In 1933, Smith asked to be relieved of further work on the research committee. W. W. Carpenter of the University of Missouri replaced him. In his report to the fourteenth annual meeting, Carpenter and his fellow committee members indicated that the job of the research committee needed clearer definition.[52] This need also plagued other early committees of the Association. Clarity of purpose, however, could not be achieved because the members of the committees lacked the funds to hold meetings. Inability to consult except by mail caused overlapping as well as wasted effort.

The reorganization of the AAJC that occurred in 1946 involved overhauling the committee system. The purpose was to enlist participation on the widest possible basis of all sections of the country in research and service. Committees were composed of representatives of the junior colleges in all sections of the country. Membership rotated so that widespread interest would be created and "the genesis of ideas and projects kept close to the grass roots of the Association." [53] The new reorganization successfully halted the movement that threatened to divide the Association.

Five research and service committees were set up, with the vice-president of the Association as coordinator. These committees were slightly altered in 1953 and emerged as Administration, Legislation, Instruction, Curriculum, and Student Personnel.[54] A

[52] W. W. Carpenter, "Report of Research Committee to 14th Annual Meeting of AAJC," *Junior College Journal*, IV (May, 1934), 475.

[53] "Reports of Research and Service Committees to 29th Annual AAJC Meeting," *Junior College Journal*, XIX (May, 1949), 533.

[54] Colvert and Littlefield, "A Brief History of the Development of the AAJC," pp. 39–40.

director of research worked for all of these five committees under the vice-president of the Association and, of course, ultimately under the Board. When Koos retired as professor at the University of Chicago he became the first director of research under this new organization. He was paid by the University of Chicago as part-time editor of the *Junior College Journal* and part-time director of research for the Association. He served in both of these capacities until 1949.

The policy originally set in 1946 was that the research and editorial office was to be located at a university no longer than three years in succession. No doubt this decision was aimed at Koos. The supporters of Eells wanted to limit the influence of Koos and the University of Chicago on the AAJC. The Board of Directors of the AAJC favored living up to this policy, and in 1949 the research editorial offices were moved to the University of Texas. James W. Reynolds, professor of education, became editor of the *Journal,* and C. C. Colvert, professor and consultant in junior college education, became director of research. The universities paid the salaries of the professors who were the editor and the director of research. The cooperating university also paid the half-time salary of the associate editor and associate in research and paid half or more of a secretary's salary.

The University of Texas was once again granted the contract in 1952 even though renewal meant breaking the original policy of the AAJC to hold the research and editorial office at a university no longer than three years in succession. The contract expired June 30, 1955, and the University of Texas decided it wished to terminate the arrangement. The Association discontinued the research office but continued Reynolds as editor with a half-time associate editor and a half-time secretary paid by the Association. Colvert became coordinator of research under the vice-president of the AAJC until 1959, when another reorganization took place.[55]

By late 1950's dissatisfaction arose over the committee system. The chairmen of the committees reported that they felt that the effectiveness and value of the committee work had lessened in recent years and that the system needed rejuvenation. In July, 1958,

[55] *Ibid.,* p. 40.

at the summer Board of Directors meeting at Estes Park, Colorado, the committee chairmen recommended that the committees be continued as commissions directly responsible to the Board and that each commission be enlarged but maintain regional distribution of membership. The Association adopted a new plan devised by the Board of Directors at the annual meeting in Long Beach, California, in 1959.

There are now five commissions. Each is composed of sixteen members who are representatives from the six regional areas: New England, Middle Atlantic states, Southern, North Central, Northwest, and California. The sixteen members serve three-year staggered terms. A Council on Research and Service, composed of the chairman of each of the five commissions and the chairman of the Editorial Board of the *Journal,* coordinates the activities of the commissions, assists in the promotion of research and service programs, and recommends specific programs suggested by these commissions to the Board of Directors. It also seeks to identify emerging needs for research and service in American higher education with particular emphasis on junior college fields.

In general, the commissions (1) originate ideas, projects and proposals, including estimates of costs, (2) receive suggestions on research and service from the Council on Research and Service, (3) suggest special committees upon the advice of the Council on Research and Service, (4) prepare reports and release findings through the *Junior College Journal,* (5) execute approved plans of research and service, and (6) plan programs for the annual meetings as requested by the Board.[56]

Functions of the Commissions

The Commission on Administration concerns itself with projects in the following areas: administrative practices, organization, and structure; personnel; athletics; library; public relations; finance; and plant facilities and services.

The Commission on Curriculum directs its attention to various aspects of curriculum construction, evaluation, and coordina-

[56] AAJC Student Personnel Commission, "Conference Plan" (December 8–10, 1960), pp. 3–5 (mimeographed). AAJC Archives.

tion in junior colleges, such as general education, preprofessional education, terminal technical education, adult education, and articulation with high schools and other colleges and universities.

Responsibilities of the Commission on Instruction include the recruitment of teachers, professional education, in-service education, and improvement of instruction.

The Commission on Legislation is assigned responsibility for research and service in such matters as current developments in state and national legislation; evaluation and interpretation of such current developments as are essential to the junior colleges; investigations of issues of a legislative character, and of directives or regulations and the interpretations of these made by governmental agencies; dissemination of these evaluations to the membership in such a manner as the Board may approve; coordination of these activities and information with other agencies of higher education; and recommendations for new legislation.

Research and service by the Commission on Student Personnel are primarily in the fields of admission, testing, guidance, counseling, placement, follow-up for evaluation, student government, co-curricular activities of students, and technical aspects of student records.[57]

The most important work of the five AAJC commissions is to suggest and initiate research and service projects for the junior college movement. Special funds from the Kellogg Foundation of Battle Creek were given to the AAJC in 1960 to help the commissions perform their tasks.

However, as soon as the commissions began to function, leaders of the Association began to question the relative merits of the system. At the Board of Directors meeting held in Nassau in January, 1961, questions were raised in reference to changes needed so that the commissions might function more effectively. Would smaller commissions be more effective? Should regions be disregarded and leadership for the Association be developed and recruited where available? How could the funds allotted to the commissions be best spent for the greatest service to the Association and to the membership? [58]

[57] Conference Plan, p. 5.
[58] AAJC Board of Directors, *Minutes* (January 7–9, 1961). AAJC Archives.

To date, no change has been made in the commission system.

In addition to questioning the commission system, an attempt was made at the January 1962 meeting of the Board of Directors to do away with the Council on Research and Service and eliminate the position of the chairman of the Council. The motion to eliminate the Council was lost but a motion was passed that the executive director would serve in lieu of the chairman of the Council as liaison between the Council and the Board of Directors.[59]

FINANCIAL DEVELOPMENTS

In the first years of its development, the AAJC's only financial obligation was the national meeting. Speakers received no honorariums and the $10 membership fee covered expenses. The biggest financial outlays were for stenotype operators, printing of proceedings, and tips. Eventually honorariums were paid, and they took a good deal of the budget.

Early Struggles

When Campbell was executive secretary, the structure was simple. There was no financial problem because there were very few expenses. There were no expenditures for travel, research, or the *Journal,* which was being supported by Stanford University. The Association had not assumed a dynamic role but was serving as a forum for discussions and exchange of information.

As late as 1930 total receipts for the year were merely $2,323.15, while disbursements came to $2,154.32. By 1943 income had risen to $21,107.70 and expenditures to $19,335.37. Salaries in the latter budget accounted for approximately half the expenditures.[60] The Association based its financial practices on the age-old policies of sound personal finance, namely, to live within one's income and to lay by something each year against an unforeseen emergency. The

---

[59] AAJC Board of Directors, *Minutes* (January 6, 1962). AAJC Archives.

[60] "Financial Statement, November 5, 1930," *Junior College Journal,* I (February, 1931), 335; AAJC Report of Treasurer, January 1–December 31, 1943 (mimeographed). AAJC Archives.

Finance Committee of the Association continually recommended that these policies be followed.

At the close of 1942 there was $135 in the treasury and an old note of $2,575 hung around the neck of the AAJC "as a discouraging millstone threatening to sink the organization." By January, 1944, the financial picture had begun to look better. "This was due to the exceptional leadership of President Jesse Bogue, imbued with a Vermont spirit of New England thrift," said Eells.[61] It also reflected the fact that dues were increased and special contributions received by the AAJC. The AAJC had to increase membership dues periodically in order to meet expanding costs. The original $5 fee voted at the organizational meeting was increased to $10 in 1921, to $20 in 1938, and to $50 in 1946. This rise in dues continued until 1962 when a plan based upon a structure related to the size of member institutions took effect.[62]

As a result of thrift the Association was able to close its books throughout the 1940's and 1950's with a surplus. But the other side of this coin made it unable to carry out so many of the tasks it desired to perform in order to be a vigorous and effective professional organization.

So long as the view of the leadership of the AAJC was limited in scope the Association did not have to ask for support. If the role of the Association were merely one of administering an annual meeting, then the financial situation was fine the way it was. True, there were always struggles to raise the salary of the executive secretary to a point where it was somewhat comparable with that received by other educational executives, and the Finance Committee was constantly trying to find money to pay travel expenses for the officers of the Association. Despite these difficulties, the Association was able to perform its limited duties, but when it took unto itself the dynamic leadership of the junior college movement, it had to seek foundation support.

---

[61] Eells, "Annual Report of Executive Secretary to the 24th Annual Meeting," *Junior College Journal*, XIV, 350.

[62] AAJC Board of Directors, *Minutes* (January 6, 1962). Institutional size was determined on the basis of full-time equivalent student enrollment. Institutions with a full-time student enrollment under 349 paid $125; 350–999 students paid $150; 1,000–1,999 paid $175; and 2,000 and over paid $200.

Foundation Support of the AAJC

The General Education Board, an institution incorporated by a 1903 Congressional Act for the purpose of improving education throughout the United States, awarded the AAJC a grant which from 1940 to 1944 supported a study of terminal education.

From 1958 on, the United States Steel Foundation granted $10,000 annually to the AAJC, the money to be used "toward the attainment, by research and other means, of national objectives for the institutions below the four-year college level." [63] The Association used a portion of the 1960 grant to pay the expenses of its representatives on the Joint Committee on Junior and Senior Colleges. The Joint Committee consists of three representatives from the AAJC and three each from the Association of American Colleges and the American Association of Collegiate Registrars and Admissions Officers. Its major work at the present time is to sponsor activities which would lead toward more effective transfer of students from two- to four-year colleges.

Money from the U.S. Steel Foundation also supported participation by a representative of the AAJC in the Steering Committee on Minimum Data and Definitions, consisting of representatives of the American Association of Collegiate Registrars and Admissions Officers, American Association of Junior Colleges, American Council on Education, United States Office of Education, Association of University Evening Colleges, and the National University Extension Association. Under the chairmanship of James Hitt of the University of Kansas, the committee began to function in 1958. Its objectives were to identify and list the fundamental elements of specific data in higher education, to define and explain these, and to encourage colleges and universities to record these minimum elements of data and make this information available.

Further evidence of increased interest in the two-year college by foundations was the support given in 1955 to the AAJC by the Edward W. Hazen Foundation, the Danforth Foundation, and the Alden Trust to sponsor a conference on "Religion in the Junior

[63] Report by Edmund J. Gleazer, Jr., Executive Director, AAJC, to AAJC Board of Directors in AAJC Board of Directors, *Minutes* (August 11, 1959). AAJC Archives.

Colleges." The conference was held at Southern Methodist University in Dallas on April 5–7, 1955. This three-day conference brought together more than one hundred junior college administrators and teachers from every section of the country.[64]

In 1958 the Sears Roebuck Foundation granted the AAJC almost $6,500 to defray costs of publishing a brochure about the junior college and distributing it to secondary schools.

The AAJC benefited indirectly in 1960 when the Lilly Endowment gave $12,000 to the University of California at Berkeley. This financed a small invitational conference in December 1960 to discuss the junior colleges of the country. The American Association of Junior Colleges and the Center for the Study of Higher Education at the University of California at Berkeley co-sponsored the conference. Henry W. Littlefield, president of the AAJC at the time of this meeting, considered the conference an important event because "for the first time in the history of the Association we called a national conference to which were invited a cross section of American educators, industrialists, government representatives and foundation authorities. It is part of growing up when you lay yourself open and invite people to look at junior college education critically." [65]

Another more direct grant by the Lilly Endowment of $14,000 to the AAJC, in 1962, made possible the financing of a conference on the responsibilities of the private junior college in higher education held in 1963. Some of the money also financed an AAJC publications project. The General Electric Foundation in March, 1962, approved a grant of $2,500 to the AAJC.

Support came from other foundations. On October 31, 1957, Gleazer met with officers of the Fund for the Advancement of Education to discuss junior college education and the potential interest of the Fund in this field. On January 24, 1958, the Fund issued a check for $3,500 to the American Association of Junior Colleges to cover the costs of a conference held on February 17 and 18 in New York City. Papers presented at the con-

[64] *Proceedings, Conference on Religion in the Junior Colleges* (April 5–7, 1955), Southern Methodist University, Dallas, Texas, p. 3.

[65] Interview with Henry Littlefield, President, University of Bridgeport, former President of the AAJC, March 1, 1962.

ference discussed the central problems facing the junior colleges of the country.[66]

A National Science Foundation grant in 1960 of $28,100 made it possible for the AAJC to sponsor the visitation of a United States Technical Education Delegation to the Union of Soviet Socialist Republics. The visitation had recognition under the 1959 Cultural Exchange Agreement between the United States and Russia, which provided for an exchange of people and information in "scientific, technical, educational, and cultural areas." [67] The objective of the four-week visit during May, 1961, of the members of the United States Technical Education Delegation was to study the Soviet Technicum, a type of specialized secondary educational institution which prepares technicians for industrial work in the Soviet Union. The delegation viewed the programs, facilities, and personnel. They also visited Soviet industries to observe the utilization of the Technicum graduate.

Enter the W. K. Kellogg Foundation

Prior to W. K. Kellogg Foundation support of the American Association of Junior Colleges, all support had been helpful but certainly did not allow for the expansion of staff and professional services to junior colleges and to communities throughout the nation. In October of 1958 in Battle Creek, Michigan, Edmund Gleazer met with Emory W. Morris, president and general director of the W. K. Kellogg Foundation, and Maurice F. Seay, director of the foundation's Division of Education, to discuss the growing importance of the junior college in American higher education. The foundation had for many years been interested in continuing education and had spent two years studying the developments in community college education. They had concluded that the community college movement was important to community development programs and to continuing education. It was also of great importance in American education and was destined to become even more significant in the immediate years ahead.

[66] "Sequence of Events Leading to Appeal to W. K. Kellogg Foundation," p. B (mimeographed). AAJC Archives.

[67] *Report of the United States Technical Education Delegation to the Union of Soviet Socialist Republics, May 5–31, 1961* (Washington, D.C.: American Association of Junior Colleges, 1962), Foreword.

The study of the community college situation led to the approval of the proposal of the AAJC by the foundation. Seay asserted that, with all due credit to the value of other associations and with recognition of the need for junior college personnel to participate in them, no other educational organization would do for the junior colleges of the country what they must be able to do for themselves through the services of the Association.[68] In September, 1959, the Kellogg Foundation announced a five-year commitment of $240,000 to the American Association of Junior Colleges for the purpose of "strengthening and expanding professional services to junior colleges across the nation and to communities planning the establishment of these institutions." [69]

At the forty-first annual convention in Washington, D.C., the executive director of the AAJC reported to the Board of Directors that the Kellogg Foundation was interested in making still another commitment to the AAJC. A proposal for a grant extending from January 1, 1962, to December 31, 1967, was made to the foundation. The proposal stressed the fact that the junior college appeared destined to become the major development in post-high school education in this country and that the next ten years would be crucial in determining whether this social invention could actually respond with the quality of programs and tremendous expansion of plant and personnel sufficient to fulfill the expectations of growing numbers of state and national leaders. The proposal pointed out that there was no more important potential determinant nationally of what the junior college would be than its own professional organization.

The Association assured the Kellogg Foundation that it would not undertake activities which could be conducted more effectively by other agencies and organizations. The proposal indicated that the major emphases of the Washington office would be to provide "national leadership, stimulation, inspiration, encouragement, coordination and dissemination of information." [70] The Association summarized the objectives that it sought to achieve:

[68] Edmund J. Gleazer, Jr., "Memorandum to Members of the AAJC Board of Directors," May 22, 1959 (mimeographed). AAJC Archives.

[69] Edmund J. Gleazer, Jr., *Junior College Newsletter*, XV (September 23, 1959), 1.

[70] AAJC, "A proposal to the W. K. Kellogg Foundation," July 18, 1961, p. 2. Mimeographed. AAJC Archives.

1. Strong programs of pre-service junior college teacher preparation, in-service workshops and institutes, with the hope of attracting promising people to the field of junior college teaching.

2. Improved student personnel services with particular emphasis on counseling and guidance.

3. Well-conceived curricular offerings, especially technical and semi-professional education and community services.

4. Establishment of an accurate and positive image of junior colleges.

5. Development of sound legal bases for organization and support at local and state levels.

6. Establishment of effective relationships with high schools, universities, and accrediting agencies.

7. Strengthening of state and regional associations of junior colleges with productive liaison between these and the national organization.

8. Provision of increased number of competent junior college administrators.[71]

The proposal supplied a detailed budget for the additional personnel that would be needed as well as for travel, rent, publication, expansion of consulting services, and other expenses. The Kellogg Foundation was assured that by 1968 all activities would be self-supporting or terminated.

In September 1961 the Kellogg Foundation made an additional $337,600 commitment to the AAJC. These funds overlapped the five-year grant of $240,000, bringing the total commitment to the AAJC to $566,000. In his letter to Gleazer approving the Association's request for funds, Seay stated, "The program which you and your colleagues have described in your proposals is of tremendous importance to American education. We are glad to be able to cooperate with the Association in its efforts to expand its usefulness and effectiveness." [72]

DEVELOPMENT OF THE AAJC

The AAJC is primarily an organization of institutional members, and its growth has paralleled that of the junior college move-

[71] *Ibid.*, p. 15.
[72] Quoted in Edmund J. Gleazer, Jr., *Junior College Newsletter*, XVII (September 25, 1961), 3.

TABLE III

AAJC MEMBERSHIP BY STATES

STATE	1922	1930	1940	1950	1960
Alabama	1	1	5	7	6
Alaska	0	0	0	0	4
Arizona	0	1	2	2	2
Arkansas	2	5	6	6	3
California	1	20	36	47	60
Canal Zone	0	0	1	1	1
Colorado	0	1	4	8	8
Connecticut	0	3	9	8	5
Delaware	0	0	0	1	1
Dist. of Col.	0	2	10	6	6
Florida	0	0	4	7	24
Georgia	1	9	7	18	16
Hawaii	0	0	0	0	1
Idaho	0	2	3	3	3
Illinois	2	14	20	25	22
Indiana	0	2	1	1	2
Iowa	1	7	12	23	19
Kansas	0	8	14	18	20
Kentucky	3	8	11	13	8
Louisiana	0	3	2	3	1
Maine	0	1	4	3	2
Maryland	0	1	7	6	14
Massachusetts	0	4	16	20	20
Michigan	1	8	11	10	19
Minnesota	2	7	10	9	11
Mississippi	3	10	16	17	19
Missouri	6	12	18	18	18
Montana	0	0	3	2	2
Nebraska	0	4	4	3	5
New Hampshire	0	0	3	1	1
New Jersey	0	2	7	12	6
New Mexico	0	1	2	0	2
New York	0	4	7	21	32
North Carolina	1	9	17	20	20
North Dakota	0	2	3	3	4
Ohio	1	3	5	6	8
Oklahoma	0	7	14	14	10
Oregon	0	0	2	1	5
Pennsylvania	0	6	20	16	14
Puerto Rico	0	0	0	0	1
Rhode Island	0	0	0	2	1
South Carolina	0	0	4	4	5
South Dakota	1	1	1	2	3
Tennessee	2	8	8	9	6
Texas	10	32	22	47	42
Utah	0	4	4	4	4
Vermont	0	0	3	2	2
Virginia	3	9	13	13	11

TABLE III (continued)

STATE	1922	1930	1940	1950	1960
Washington	0	1	8	9	10
West Virginia	0	3	3	4	3
Wisconsin	0	0	2	1	4
Wyoming	0	0	0	1	4
TOTAL	41	225*	384**	477***	520

* Includes 15 Associate Members. Associate members exercise all rights and privileges of active institutional members except voting.
** Includes 36 Associate Members.
*** Includes 18 Provisional Members. A provisional membership is open to newly organized institutions and to others which have not yet received accreditation or equivalent recognition.

ment. A membership of thirty in 1921 grew to 519 institutional members and 122 individual members as well as ten honorary members in 1961.[73]

TABLE IV

PUBLIC AND PRIVATE MEMBERSHIP IN THE AAJC

YEAR	TOTAL	PUBLIC	PRIVATE
1922	41	7	34
1930	225	87	138
1940	384	171	213
1950	477	250	227
1960	520	312	208

Classes of Membership

Membership in the Association consists of five classes: active institutional, provisional institutional, organizational, individual, and honorary. Active institutional membership is open to regularly organized junior colleges that have been accredited by or have received equivalent recognition from a regional association, or from their state university, state department of education, or other recognized state accrediting agencies; and to separately organized units of similarly accredited four-year colleges and uni-

[73] *American Association of Junior Colleges, 1920–1961* (Washington, D.C.: American Association of Junior Colleges, 1961), p. 1.

versities which offer junior college programs. Active institutional members are entitled to one vote.

Provisional institutional membership is designed for newly organized junior colleges and for other junior colleges that have not yet been able to secure the necessary accreditation or equivalent recognition to qualify them for active institutional membership. The representative of a provisional institutional member may not vote or hold office in the Association.

Any organization or individual interested in the junior college movement may become a sustaining member. Junior colleges are not eligible for this type of membership. Sustaining members may not vote or hold elective office. Individuals who have performed outstanding service in the junior college movement may be elected honorary members of the Association upon nomination by the Board of Directors.[74]

Occasionally attempts have been made to change the constitution so that faculty members might become members of the Association. In 1953 more than one hundred letters were sent to college administrators who had played a prominent role in junior college affairs asking them if they thought teacher membership in the AAJC was a good idea. The responses expressed divided opinions, and no change was made.[75]

Location of Meetings

The location of the annual meeting was an important consideration, particularly during the early years of the Association. It was a major undertaking in 1920 to travel to meetings, in terms both of transportation convenience and of money. During the first ten years a major factor in determining the meeting place was the time and place of other national meetings. The first annual meeting of the Association was held in Chicago at the same time that the Department of Superintendence of the National Education Association was meeting. This allowed many educators to attend two meetings with a minimum of travel and expense.

During the next nine years the AAJC meeting was usually held

---

[74] AAJC, *Constitution and By-Laws,* January 18, 1946, Article III.
[75] "A Report to the AAJC Board of Directors on Possible Teacher Membership," July 15, 1953, Exhibit B. AAJC Archives.

a day or two preceding or following such meetings as the Southern Association of Colleges and Secondary Schools at Memphis in 1922, the annual meeting of the North Central Association of Colleges and Secondary Schools at Chicago in 1926, and meetings of the American Association of School Administrators.

It was not until 1929 that members of the Association felt that it was strong enough to meet independently of other organizations. The Committee on Nominations and Time and Place proposed "that in order to become more fully national the AAJC should hold its 1929 meeting either in the Atlantic or Pacific Coast regions." [76] The 1929 meeting was held in Atlantic City and that of the following year at Berkeley, California. However, in 1932 and 1936 the conventions of the Department of Superintendence of the NEA determined the locale of the annual meeting of the AAJC. [77]

Sometimes sentiment determined the site of a convention. One reason for the selection of Chicago for the twenty-first annual meeting in 1941 was the fact that the University of Chicago, which had been associated with the junior college movement since the days of William Rainey Harper, was celebrating its fiftieth anniversary. [78]

Finally, in 1947 the AAJC Board of Directors flexed its muscles and passed a motion stating that the Association had reached the stage of development which required meetings independent of other educational groups, "in cities which will cooperate fully and which have adequate hotel facilities for housing the delegates, the various meetings, and the exhibits." [79]

The Annual Meetings

The annual meetings provided an opportunity for junior college administrators to come together to exchange ideas and discuss

[76] Edgar D. Lee, "Report of Committee on Nominations," *Proceedings of the Ninth Meeting of the AAJC,* 1928, p. 144. AAJC Archives.

[77] Doak S. Campbell, "Across the Secretary's Desk," *Junior College Journal,* IV (December, 1933), 147; "Reports and Discussions," *Junior College Journal,* VI (December, 1935), 151.

[78] Walter C. Eells, "From the Secretary's Desk," *Junior College Journal,* XI (January, 1941), 276.

[79] AAJC Board of Directors, *Minutes* (February 18–22, 1947). AAJC Archives.

common problems. They regarded the Association as an agency for collective effort that would at the same time add status and prestige to their own institutions. Jesse P. Bogue, executive secretary of the AAJC, thought the national convention one of the most important projects of the members of the Association. "The breath of life for educators," said Bogue, "is a better idea, an advancing ideal, inspiration and encouragement caught from contacts with like-minded associates who seem to be gifted with a little clearer thinking and ideals, more profitable experiences and practices than we have." [80]

The early activities of the Association can be characterized as defensive. A small group of administrators came together to defend the junior college. Senior colleges, for the most part bound by traditional thinking, viewed the junior college of the 1920's with attitudes ranging from scepticism to virtual contempt. One of the major concerns of the Association was to win acceptance of junior colleges by other educational institutions. The meetings of the first decade of the AAJC were therefore devoted to interpretation and definition. Junior college administrators, particularly in the South and East, spent endless hours discussing problems incident to the transfer of junior college graduates to four-year institutions.

By the 1930's the defensive program of the AAJC became a promotional program. There followed conscious attempts to build conventions around central themes such as: "The Curriculum of the Junior College," "Social Adjustments of the Students," "Changes to Meet Expanding Needs," and "Should the Junior College Indoctrinate for a New Social Order?" [81]

A "Twentieth Anniversary" theme dominated the meeting held in Columbia, Missouri, in 1940. George Zook, one of the original founders of the AAJC, delivered the principal address. Many of the thirty-four educators who composed the original conference, and whom Eells labeled "the patriarchs," were guests of the Association.

[80] Jesse P. Bogue, "From the Executive Secretary's Desk," *Junior College Journal,* XXIII (January, 1953), 292.

[81] "Program of Fourteenth Annual Meeting of AAJC," *Junior College Journal,* IV (May 1934), 468–71; "Program of Sixteenth Annual Meeting of AAJC," *Junior College Journal,* VI (April, 1936), 396–98; "Program of Seventeenth Annual Meeting of AAJC," *Junior College Journal,* VII (May, 1937), 403–05.

The annual meetings of the 1940's were concerned with matters of national defense and the problem of returning veterans. "On again, off again, gone again, Flanagan" is an appropriate summary of the efforts of the Executive Committee to plan the conference of the Association in 1943. The meeting, set for February 23–24 in St. Louis, was cancelled at the request of the Office of Defense Transportation. Transportation conditions again made it necessary, at government request, to cancel the 1945 meeting.

A distinction that characterized the 1944 and 1946 conventions was the recognition by the President of the United States of the junior college movement and the AAJC. In 1944 President Roosevelt sent a message to the annual meeting in Cincinnati, Ohio, expressing the hope that the AAJC might devise ways "of serving most effectively the needs of American education and especially the post-war needs of ex-service men and women." He also indicated that these men and women "will wish, in many cases, terminal courses which assure a basic understanding of the issues confronted by them as American and world citizens. It seems possible that the junior college may furnish the answer to a good many of these needs." [82] The 1946 convention in Chicago received a message from President Truman in which he said that "the extension of general education and of terminal college grade vocational education represented by the junior colleges in this country constitutes a real contribution to democracy in education." [83]

Various events during the 1950's colored the meetings of the AAJC. The Korean War, the rising tide of students seeking a college education, and the outburst of congressional investigations of alleged subversives in colleges and universities were reflected in the conventions. Some AAJC meetings stressed the desire of the junior colleges to participate in defense efforts. At the 1951 meeting, in Des Moines, Iowa, a symposium examined the role of the junior colleges in national defense. At the same meeting Virgil M. Hancher, president of the State University of Iowa, analyzed the ideological struggle between democracy and Russian communism.

[82] "President Roosevelt's Message to the Twenty-Fourth Annual Meeting," *Junior College Journal*, XIV (April, 1944), 337.
[83] "President Truman's Message to the Twenty-Sixth Annual Meeting," *Junior College Journal*, XVI (May, 1946), 387.

Livingston L. Blair, vice-president of the American National Red Cross, delivered an address entitled "The Community in National Security." [84] The delegates to the 1953 convention endorsed a resolution that federal legislation on R.O.T.C. should include junior colleges.

Another recurrent theme was that junior colleges could offer educational opportunities to growing numbers of students who did not wish a four-year liberal arts program. The report issued in 1957 by the President's Commission on Higher Education substantiated the importance of the two-year college in meeting the educational demands of American youth. The discussions at the thirty-seventh annual meeting in Salt Lake City indicated four essential characteristics of educational opportunities beyond the high school which the United States must provide to meet the challenge of the future: quantity, quality, variety, and accessibility. The discussants indicated that the two-year colleges exhibited these characteristics "to an almost unique degree." [85]

The theme of the 1953 convention in Dallas, Texas was "Junior Colleges—Their Freedom, Integrity and Democracy," a subject which previously had received very little attention. The keynote address by Dr. Alvin C. Eurich, vice-president of the Fund for the Advancement of Education, expressed concern with the hysteria which had gripped the nation concurrent with the congressional investigations over civil liberties. Other speakers accented the need to maintain academic freedom.[86]

The meetings of the Association during the 1950's gave every indication that the AAJC had outgrown its adolescence. The delegates no longer spoke of the four-year college with reverence and awe. Convention themes such as "Diversity and Cooperation in Higher Education" and "That All May Learn" signified this maturity.[87] The financial contributions of the W. K. Kellogg Founda-

[84] "Proceedings of the Thirty-First Annual Meeting," *Junior College Journal,* XXI (May, 1951), 471–74.

[85] Elvis J. Stahr, Jr., "Your Theme—and The President's Committee," *Junior College Journal,* XXVII (May, 1957), 494.

[86] Francis H. Horn, "Convention Analysis and Critique," *Junior College Journal,* XXIV (September, 1953), 8.

[87] *Proceedings of Thirty-Eighth Annual Convention,* printed program of AAJC. AAJC Archives.

tion to the AAJC imbued the conventions of the 1960's with optimism for the future. Financial security gave the AAJC hope that its dreams could become realities.

The "Fortieth Anniversary" convention in 1960 considered the basic functions of the junior college and identified its three primary obligations as teaching, guidance, and community services.[88] The theme of the 1961 meeting in Washington, D.C., was "America's Stake in the Junior College." Discussion groups stressed that if society were to benefit from "America's stake in the junior college," there were certain musts for the junior colleges. These were:

1. The junior college must produce manpower with new competencies for a rapidly changing technological society.

2. The junior college must hold open the closing door of opportunity for college education.

3. The junior college must place higher education within financial reach of all qualified students.

4. The junior college must find means of interpreting the values of its services in accurate and effective ways.

5. The States must be given encouragement and guidelines toward establishing sound systems of junior colleges.[89]

The 1962 convention examined ways to increase teaching effectiveness in the junior colleges and to establish an institutional climate to promote qualities of moral responsibility. The climate of the convention indicated that the AAJC and the junior college movement were aware that they had come of age. The junior college was looked to as a powerful educational resource by local, national, and international agencies.

[88] Edmund J. Gleazer, Jr., "From the Executive Director's Desk," *Junior College Journal*, XXX (December, 1959), 234–35; "Proceedings of Fortieth Annual Convention of AAJC," *Junior College Journal*, XXX (May, 1960), 485–533.

[89] *Program of Forty-First Annual Convention*, printed program of AAJC. AAJC Archives.

3

"What Manner of Child?"[1]

THE DEVELOPMENT of junior colleges in the United States was evidence of a long overdue reformation in the stereotyped collegiate educational structure which had evolved from traditional educational attitudes. As the infant grew into manhood there arose the hostility and emotional outcries that often accompany educational change. In the attempt of the junior colleges to find an identity and a place in the educational hierarchy of the country, the AAJC functioned as a forum where educators could confer and seek this identity and this place, needed in order to speak to other educational and governmental agencies.

The AAJC also acted as a catalyst—prodding, promoting, and creating an image of the junior college as it was and as it could be.

THE SEARCH FOR AN IDENTITY

The junior college initially offered typical liberal arts college subjects to a few local students who wished to continue their education. From the beginning, however, many educators saw something bigger and better than such tradition.

But tradition is not an easy force to shake.

Status Symbols

In the minds of many, higher education has an element of magic, including a number system that invests only the numeral four with powers of higher education. The AAJC attempted to produce potions to counteract this and insisted that a two-year

[1] This title is taken from a speech delivered by Walter C. Eells to the eleventh annual convention of the AAJC, November, 1930.

education was part of the higher educational structure. Some of the potions used dealt with name and degree.

From the inception of the AAJC there was growing dissatisfaction with the name "junior" college. The search for a more suitable generic name consumed much time. In California many of the larger junior colleges were too impatient to wait for state or nationwide agreement on the issue. They either dropped the word "junior" or called themselves city colleges.

An analysis of the 1942 *Junior College Directory* showed that almost two-thirds carried the term "junior" in their titles. The term "college" without the "junior" qualifying adjective was used by a quarter of the colleges, while the remaining 14 per cent were scattered among "institute," "school," and a variety of other names.[2]

Many educators adopted the name community college as a more adequate description for the two-year colleges. In fact, in 1949 an article in the *Junior College Journal* suggested that the AAJC "adopt the more appropriate and more useful title [community college] instead of waiting until there are no junior colleges left that are willing to bear the name."[3] However, C. C. Colvert in 1955 disagreed with those who wished to change the name and argued that the term "junior college with all of its prestige, heritage, and good will, seems to be the best name for our colleges."[4]

The granting of titles, certificates, or degrees was an attempt to give dignity to the junior college program. From the organizational meeting in 1920 on, delegates to AAJC conventions were frequently asked to consider whether the degree awarded should be an "associate" degree or a full-fledged baccalaureate. The formal position eventually taken by the Association was stated in the 1925 report of the Committee on Standards: "No junior college shall confer a bachelor's degree."[5]

[2] Walter C. Eells, "From the Secretary's Desk," *Junior College Journal*, XIII (November, 1942), 168–69.

[3] William T. Boyce, "Wanted: A Family Name," *Junior College Journal*, XIX (April, 1949), 445.

[4] C. C. Colvert, "Why Not the Name 'Junior College'?" *Junior College Journal*, XXVI (September, 1955), 2.

[5] "Report of the Committee on Standards, adopted at the Cincinnati meeting, February 21, 1925," *Proceedings of the Fifth Annual Meeting of the AAJC*, pp. 44–46. AAJC Archives.

In 1942 Robert Hutchins and the University of Chicago unleashed a storm of debate when they announced a plan to confer the bachelor's degree at the end of the fourteenth year of study and put the eleventh and twelfth years in the college at Chicago. Six years later, James Bryant Conant, president of Harvard, agreed with Hutchins that the two-year junior colleges should grant a bachelor's degree. "This is the badge of respectability for most Americans," said Conant. "Indeed, the letters have almost mystical significance in the United States. To give the same degree as the four-year college (the A.B. or B.S.) would merely be confusing to all concerned. But a two-year degree of bachelor of general studies (B.G.S.) might well represent the final degree for a majority of college students." [6]

In 1942 the AAJC made an exhaustive study of the subject of degrees and recommended that junior colleges confer the associate degree upon their graduates.[7] Two years earlier Carl E. Seashore, dean emeritus of the Graduate School of the University of Iowa, had prophesied that in the practical world around us, "the Associate in Arts degree will be more common than the degree, Bachelor of Arts, and will carry a peculiar dignity of its own." [8]

It is fairly safe to predict that the junior colleges will cling to the associate degree, leaving the baccalaureate degree to represent four years of collegiate education.

Junior College Functions

The twentieth century has been an era of expansion, of changing goals, and of flexibility of education. In the course of these changes, higher education has been released from its aristocratic ideals, which one historian calls "the most dramatic fact about the course of American higher education in the twentieth century." [9] In their search for a *raison d'être*, the junior colleges contributed

[6] James Bryant Conant, *Education in a Divided World* (Cambridge: Harvard University Press, 1948), p. 201.

[7] Walter C. Eells, *Associate's Degree and Graduation Practices in Junior Colleges* (Washington, D.C.: American Association of Junior Colleges, 1942).

[8] Carl E. Seashore, *The Junior College Movement* (New York: Henry Holt & Co., 1940), p. 77.

[9] Frederick Rudolph, *The American College and University* (New York: Alfred A. Knopf, 1962), p. 442.

to the reexamination and redefinition of the purposes of higher education in America.

The AAJC, responding to the social and economic forces that had contributed to the development of the junior college idea, urged the two-year institutions to adopt broad rather than narrow functions. Discussions at conventions increasingly urged the junior colleges to open their doors to all students who desired further education as well as to encourage continuing education for adults. The AAJC pointed out the desirability of aiming for a comprehensive community college.

At the first meeting of the AAJC, Arthur Kyle Davis, president of Southern College, Petersburg, Virginia, identified three elements of the junior college curriculum. These were liberal arts courses, vocational courses, and courses "related to society as a social or finishing course." [10] Meetings since 1921 broadened the purposes of the two-year college. By the 1960's the AAJC favored the comprehensive community college as the institution to meet the educational demands of the twentieth century.

Probably the most significant function that the two-year college has identified for itself is the democratization of higher education, made possible through low tuition, nonselective admission, and geographic and social accessibility.[11]

Curriculum and Instruction

Coincident with the search for purpose were the very specific questions raised in regard to curriculum, teaching, and students. The proportion of courses in liberal arts and in specialized subjects in a student's program was one of the questions frequently discussed at AAJC conventions. How much and what kind of liberal education should the junior college offer?

Still another frequently debated topic was the nature of tech-

[10] Arthur Kyle Davis, "The Importance of Standardization and Coordination of Junior Colleges," in George F. Zook (ed.), *National Conference of Junior Colleges. 1920, and First Annual Meeting of AAJC, 1921*, Bulletin of the U. S. Bureau of Education, No. 19, part II (Washington, D.C.: U. S. Government Printing Office, 1922), p. 49.

[11] Both Leonard V. Koos in *The Junior College Movement* (Boston: Ginn and Co., 1925) and Walter C. Eells in *The Junior College* (Boston: Houghton Mifflin Co., 1931) stress this role as democratizer and popularizer of higher education.

nical education. How does this differ from vocational education? As we observed in Chapter One, technology produced major changes in American society and had very definite implications for the junior colleges. The major occupational trends in the twentieth century had increased the number of workers who required more education. The question was, should the junior college train these technicians?

Another matter which occupied the thinking of many junior college educators at AAJC conventions was the qualifications and professional training of teachers. Were teachers trained for high school positions proper teachers for the junior college? Did the junior college teacher need advanced degrees and if so, was it to be a Ph.D. or was a master's degree sufficient?

Who Should Go to the Junior College?

"To select or not to select" was another question discussed at meetings. The problem was to keep the doors open to higher education for growing numbers of students and at the same time to maintain standards. The advocates of a liberal admissions policy tried to convince everyone that the extension of opportunity did not necessarily mean mediocre education. On the other hand there were those who argued that the junior college was judged by the brightness of its students and therefore should have selective admissions.

One's view of the nature of the junior college determined the answers on the issues debated at the meeting of the AAJC.

SECONDARY OR HIGHER EDUCATION

The leaders of the AAJC were aware of the fact that the junior college was in a difficult if not unique position, wedged between the high school and the university. Was the junior college part of secondary education or was it part of the collegiate picture? On this there was wide disagreement from the very moment that the AAJC was organized.

At the third annual meeting one of the leading proponents of

the four-year junior college, Leonard Koos of the University of
Minnesota, as well as Charles H. Judd of the University of Chicago
defined the junior college as secondary in nature.[12] In 1924 in
Chicago, Superintendent L. W. Smith of Joliet, Illinois, decried
the attempts of the accrediting agency in Illinois to separate the
junior college from the senior high school. It required that the
junior college be housed in a separate building or in a portion of
a building isolated from the high school; that the junior college
have a library separated from that of the high school; that teachers
be assigned exclusively to junior college work; and that they not
be permitted to teach in both the junior college and senior high
school. The agency assumed that junior college work was fundamentally different from that done in the last years of the high
school, a view to which Smith said he could not subscribe.[13]

In immediate response from the floor, Colonel Louis C. Perry
of Texas Military College, Terrell, Texas, contended that Smith
made a fundamental error in his presentation, "for he makes the
Junior College a high school, not a college." [14] Heated discussion
followed. Smith responded to the discussion by indicating that the
freshman and sophomore classes at all colleges and universities
were essentially in the field of secondary education, not in university or college education. "It is this fundamental distinction,"
he concluded, "that we have to fight out and it is by such meetings
as these, we are doing it." [15]

Walter C. Eells entered the fray in 1931. His position was that
the junior college was essentially secondary but this did not mean
high school. Eells claimed that the meaning and implications of
the term secondary had been misused. He declared that secondary
education meant general education, preliminary to university
specialization and professional study. Taken in this context, there
should be no objection to designating the freshman and sophomore college years as secondary. One could think of the educa-

---

[12] Leonard V. Koos, "The Place of the Junior College in American Education,"
Proceedings of the Third Annual Meeting of the AAJC, pp. 25–35. AAJC Archives.
Charles H. Judd, "Psychological Background of the Junior College," *Proceedings of
the Third Annual Meeting*, pp. 40–45.
[13] L. W. Smith, "The Public Junior College," *Proceedings of the Fourth Annual
Meeting of the AAJC*, 1924, pp. 6–8. AAJC Archives.
[14] *Proceedings of the Fourth Annual Meeting*, p. 9.
[15] L. W. Smith, "The Public Junior College," p. 19.

tional field as consisting of elementary education, secondary education, and higher education.[16]

Eells thought it was unfortunate that many people had carelessly assumed that high school and secondary were synonymous. This led to an erroneous concept in thinking of the junior college years as "merely some more high school." Eells preferred the use of the term collegiate and believed that the junior college was neither an appendix to the high school nor a prefix to the university, "but that it can and should have an individuality and personality of its own." [17]

The debate continued. Some insisted that the junior college was the fulfillment of the high school, "not the stepchild of the university"; others that the junior college be recognized as part of higher education rather than as a "glorified high school." [18]

The attempt to define the junior colleges has continued to this day. This has not been an easy task, for the junior college has an ambiguous status in the American educational system. In states such as California, Florida, Texas, and a good many others, it is defined as a part of secondary education. In effect, however, the junior college is a part of the enterprise of higher education. The multiple functions that the junior college performs and the diversity of the student body also tend to blur the image.

By the 1960's leaders of the AAJC stressed that it was not important to define the junior college as either secondary or higher. What was important was that it perform certain functions. Marvin C. Knudson, President of the AAJC, stated that

the time has long since passed when we ought to debate the proposition of whether we are secondary or higher educational institutions. Whatever the theoretical considerations, the fact remains that in the popular American concept, higher education begins after the completion of the 12th grade. The junior college has broadened the concept of what might be included in 'education beyond the high school!' [19]

[16] Eells, *The Junior College*, p. 657.

[17] *The Junior College*, p. 658.

[18] Robert Gordon Sproul, "Certain Aspects of the Junior College," *Junior College Journal*, I (February, 1931), 278; "Glorified High School," *Junior College Journal*, III (November, 1932), 102; William Martin Proctor, "Time to Take Account of Stock," *Junior College Journal*, II (March, 1932), 303.

[19] Marvin C. Knudson, "Tell the Story," *Junior College Journal*, XXX (December, 1959), 186.

Reorganization of American Education

Since the late nineteenth century, criticism has been leveled at the traditional school system of eight elementary, four high school, and four college years. Agitation for reorganization resulted in fundamental changes in the educational structure.

In the late 1880's President Eliot of Harvard urged the high schools to dip down and include two years of elementary school work. In 1902 President Harper of the University of Chicago urged the organization of six-year high schools to extend upward and include two years of college work.

Various committees of the National Education Association, especially the "Committee of Ten" in 1892 and the "Committee on the Reorganization of Secondary Education," whose first report appeared in 1913, gave careful consideration to the many problems of interrelation and articulation and were strong influences in hastening experiments in reorganization.[20]

Dr. J. H. Baker, chairman, and Dr. Henry Suzzallo of the National Council on Education Committee on Economy of Time in Education, reported that the period of general education could be shortened. "Economy in the selection of subjects and topics and in methods," said Suzzallo, "will save approximately two years in the whole period of general education; with greater efficiency in the earlier periods the college course may well end nominally at 20 instead of 22." [21]

There were many efforts to shorten the college course during the late nineteenth and early twentieth centuries. At stake was what William Rainey Harper dubbed the "four-year fetish." [22] This acceleration movement advanced the idea that a student could telescope his college years and arrive earlier at the upper levels of university training.

At Johns Hopkins a student could complete the collegiate program in two years, three years at the most. At Columbia, Nicholas

[20] Eells, *The Junior College,* pp. 649–50.
[21] U. S. Bureau of Education, *Report of the National Council of Education on Economy of Time in Education,* Bulletin No. 38 (Washington, D.C.: U. S. Government Printing Office, 1913), p. 9.
[22] William Rainey Harper, *The Trend in Higher Education* (Chicago, University of Chicago Press, 1905), p. 89.

Murray Butler developed the "professional option" plan whereby after two years of college a student could enter any of the professional schools except law. Harvard's President Eliot was a persistent advocate of shortening the traditional college course. From 1883 to his retirement in 1909 he promulgated the idea of a three-year bachelor's degree for well-prepared and professionally motivated students—in other words "four years for the dawdlers and three for the young men who knew where they were going." [23]

In addition to the acceleration movement there were attempts to separate the freshman and sophomore years from the rest of the college. These proposals to bisect the college conceived the first two years as different in character from the latter two. In this concept were the seeds of the four-year junior college.

Presidents Andrew D. White and Charles Kendall Adams of Cornell University were among the first to suggest the union of the freshman and sophomore college years and the last two years of high school, thereby forming a new type of four-year college. Presidents Butler of Columbia and David Starr Jordan and Ray Lyman Wilbur of Stanford advocated bisection of the college and awarding the A.B. degree at the end of the sophomore year.[24]

While the outstanding educational leaders of America clearly recognized the serious faults in the liberal arts college, none were able to effect permanent and widespread change. The collegiate way with its mores of class loyalties, societies, and athletics was too strong. The acceleration movement had not recognized that "higher education rested on what happened outside the classroom. College was too much fun, too socially rewarding, too clearly effective as a means of getting ahead in the world, for people to be sure that a whole year could be surrendered." [25]

The Four-Year Junior College

Out of the various attempts to reorganize the standard college came the plan for the four-year junior college. This involved transfer of the seventh and eighth grades from the elementary to the

[23] Rudolph, *The American College and University*, p. 447.
[24] John A. Sexson and John W. Harbeson, *The New American College* (New York: Harper & Brothers, 1946), p. 17–18.
[25] Rudolph, *The American College and University*, p. 448.

lower unit of the secondary school, thus creating a four-year junior
high school. It also formed an upper four-year secondary unit of
the junior and senior years of high school and the freshman and
sophomore years of college.

Credit for the first clear statement of the four-year junior college plan and for its popularization must go to George A. Merrill,
director of the Wilmerding School of Industrial Arts of San Francisco. In a 1908 report to the president of the University of California, and again in 1910, Merrill delineated his design for a reorganized school system.[26]

A long list of distinguished educators advocated the 6-4-4 plan.
President James M. Wood of Stephens College outlined this plan
for the North Central Association in 1919 and for the national
Junior College Conference in 1920. In succeeding years Koos,
George F. Zook, William M. Proctor, Frederick Eby, John A.
Sexson, and John W. Harbeson joined the ranks of the four-year
junior college advocates.

The AAJC and the 6-4-4 plan. The AAJC debated whether the
junior college should be a two-year or a four-year institution. At
the third meeting in 1923 Koos presented a paper in which he gave
evidence of "tremendous and inevitable forces at work" which
were bound to alter the amount of time spent in collegiate liberal
education. Koos showed the extent to which high school and college work overlapped. He informed the delegates that the proper
plan was to make the junior college period "the culminal portion
of a senior high school" covering the 11–14 years of the school
system. Beneath this would be a junior high school including the
seventh through tenth grades.[27]

At the same meeting Charles H. Judd of the University of
Chicago lauded G. Stanley Hall, who in his book *Adolescence* attacked the 1893 report of the Committee of Ten. Hall had averred
that if anything were to be done to make education effective, one
had to take into account not only the subject taught but also
the human material that went into the teacher's hands; the two
must be adapted to each other.

[26] National Education Association, *Proceedings* (Boston: 1910), p. 756.
[27] Leonard V. Koos, "The Place of the Junior College in American Education,"
Proceedings of the Third Annual Meeting, pp. 25–35. AAJC Archives.

Judd stated that if you observed the school system and studied its continuity from the point of view of the maturation of the students, then you would begin to realize that "it is periods of maturity, not subject matter of instruction, which determines the different levels of educational organization." If you then organized schools to match the development of pupils, you would combine the eleventh through fourteenth grades into a new unit of school instruction which would "bring children forward to a type of course which is now artificially postponed by our stereotyped school organization." [28]

The Committee on Standards of the AAJC reported to the fifth annual convention in 1925. Discussion centered around the first standard which defined the junior college. The Association turned down a recommendation that it go on record as favoring the ultimate organization of a four-year junior college. It adopted the standard defining the junior college as an institution "offering two years of instruction of strictly collegiate grade." [29]

A year later the annual meeting devoted most of its debates to defining the type of institution the junior college was to be. L. W. Smith, vice-president of the AAJC, opened the session and indicated he regarded high school and the junior college as one unit. This view was supported by a private junior college administrator who insisted that "a four-year Junior College, following a four-year Junior High School, is the logical answer to the educational demands of the time." [30]

J. Thomas Davis, of John Tarleton Agricultural College, Stephenville, Texas, raised the problem of Southern Association accreditation and pointed out that in order to receive accreditation, there must be a separation between the high school work and the college work. Davis asked the AAJC to endorse the policy of overlapping in the four-unit system, and to present the matter forcibly to the standardizing agencies of the country, and to urge their recognition of the combined high school and junior college.

The papers presented at the sixth meeting of the AAJC empha-

[28] Judd, "Psychological Background of the Junior College," p. 44.
[29] *Proceedings of the Fifth Annual Meeting*, pp. 44–51.
[30] Sister M. Ignatius, "The Junior College—A Two, Four, or Six Year Institution?" *Proceedings of the Sixth Annual Meeting of the AAJC*, 1926, p. 6. AAJC Archives.

sized that the junior college could do better work if it permitted its teachers to work in both college and preparatory departments. A resolution introduced at this meeting was debated at length and finally adopted. It called on the regional accrediting agencies to study the four-year junior college as a distinctive unit in education. Hugh Noffsinger, President of the AAJC, summarized: "This recommendation says to the accrediting agencies that this is the direction in which we are looking, and won't you look in that same direction with us, and see if our vision is correct?" [31]

The case for the 6-4-4 plan. The proponents of the plan based their case upon a number of specific arguments.

The first two years of college were essentially secondary in nature. The problems of articulation causing great concern among American educators would diminish through the consolidation of the three units involved in the three-three-two plan into the two units of the four-four plan.[32] Frederick Eby of the University of Texas indicated to the ninth annual convention of the AAJC that there was nothing sacred about the 8-4-4 plan of educational organization. As a matter of fact, he claimed that it arose chiefly in an accidental way and was confined to the American continent. It had neither scientific nor historical reasons for existence and had been condemned soon after it was organized because it wasted two years or more for students going through college.[33]

Another argument in favor of the 6-4-4 plan was that the span of grades eleven through fourteen was more psychologically homogeneous than other possible groupings. Davis addressed the seventh annual meeting and pointed out that adolescence covered the

[31] Hugh G. Noffsinger in *Proceedings of the Sixth Annual Meeting*, p. 64.

[32] The U.S. Office of Education listed forty-three different types of organizational pattern in 1931. Eight of these were distinct types and of interest to the junior colleges. These were: (1) eight-four-two plan, the traditional type with eight years of elementary, four high school, and two of junior college; (2) eight-six type, proposed by William Rainey Harper in the early years of the century and flourished for a time in a few localities as the six-year high school; (3) six-three-three-two, which includes six of elementary, three of junior high, three of high and two of junior college, the most common reorganized type in existence in the 1930's; (4) six-two-four-two; (5) six-six-two; (6) six-four-four; (7) five-four-four; and (8) seven-four-two, the southern variant of the eight-four-two.

[33] Frederick Eby, "The Four-Year Public Junior College," *Proceedings of the Ninth Annual Meeting of the AAJC*, 1928, p. 64. AAJC Archives.

eleventh through fourteenth grades and that to break this period in half was psychologically unsound.[34] Eby stressed the same point at the ninth annual meeting and reminded the assemblage that the most fundamental assumption of twentieth-century educational philosophy was that the processes of human growth condition education. He declared that development takes place in special stages and that this fact of stages or levels has dominated the organization of our schools in the grouping of grades. "The junior high school has been organized to minister to that stormy and changeful period of puberty," said Eby, "from 11 or 12 to 15 or 16. That leaves middle adolescence from about 16 to 20 to be divided between the senior high school and junior college."[35] He felt that it was not wise to divide the latter period.

There were many other arguments for this "new American College" by the proponents of the 6-4-4 plan. There would be economies in administration. The time of the student would be conserved. The 6-4-4 organization would enable the upper unit to render distinctive educational service not satisfactorily performed in the schools, namely education for the semi-professions. The four-year junior college would attract a better faculty than the traditional high school and enable the gifted student to progress more rapidly. The four-year junior college would enhance a college spirit.

Eells voices disapproval. Many leaders in junior college education were committed to the 6-4-4 plan when Eells presented his paper, entitled "What Manner of Child Shall This Be?" at the eleventh annual convention of the AAJC in November, 1930. Eells was particularly outspoken in his disapproval of the four-year junior college plan. He informed the convention that the prevailing type of organization was the two-year junior college and that therefore in order to justify a change the burden of proof rested upon the four-year advocates.

"After a careful study of all the arguments," said Eells, "that burden is a considerable one." Eells asked all friends of the junior

---

[34] J. Thomas Davis, "Adolescence and the Junior College," *Proceedings of the Seventh Annual Meeting of the AAJC*, 1926, pp. 63–65. AAJC Archives.
[35] Eby, "The Four-Year Public Junior College," pp. 67–68.

college movement "regardless of whether they see through two-year spectacles, four-year spectacles, or tinted educational glasses of other hues, to unite in the sincere search for truth." [36]

Eells pointed out that the arguments offered for the 6-4-4 plan were not unique but just as valid for other organizational forms. He listed the disadvantages of the 6-4-4 plan. These were (1) the difficulty of intercollegiate athletic competition; (2) difficulty of adjustment to existing administrative practice; (3) difficulty of adjustment to varying geographical conditions; (4) difficulty of too great variety in age of students; (5) difficulty of adjustment of instruction to different levels; and (6) the danger of stopping school at compulsory age limit.[37]

The two-year unit, according to Eells, had the following advantages:

1. Could easily adjust to existing administrative and geographical conditions.
2. Offered students new contacts.
3. Offered advantages in transition from high school to college.
4. Offered advantages for vocational preparation and the advantage of age homogeneity.
5. Had a distinctive collegiate atmosphere.
6. Would be in tune with the psychology of the American people.[38]

Eells predicted that experience and experiment, not theory, ultimately would decide the entire matter.

Growth of the 6-4-4 plan. As Eells joined battle with Wood, Koos, and Eby, the disputants were at a disadvantage since their discussions were almost purely speculative. Only Stephens College in Columbia, Missouri, a private institution for women, had experimented with the new plan. Soon, however, two cities were to lead in the development of the four-year junior college. One was Pasadena, California, and the other, Hillsboro, Texas.

The Pasadena public school system had supported junior college instruction as an extension of its high school program since

---

[36] Walter C. Eells, "The Junior College—What Manner of Child Shall This Be?" *Junior College Journal,* I (February, 1931), 327–28.

[37] *Ibid.,* pp. 318–19.

[38] *Ibid.,* pp. 319–321.

1924. In 1926 Frank Hart and L. H. Peterson of the University of California conducted a survey of the school building needs of the Pasadena schools. In the course of their report they recommended the adoption of the 6-4-4 plan of organization. Superintendent John Franklin West endorsed their recommendation and the Board of Education concurred. The new form of organization went into effect at the beginning of the school year 1928–29.

Coincident with the establishment of the new plan was the election of a new superintendent, John Sexson, who had been a superintendent in a small city in Arizona and came to Pasadena with little or no familiarity with the 6-4-4 plan which the Board had recently adopted.[39] He set out, however, to inform his community of the advantages of the new system as he learned them. Sexson worked tirelessly to make the new system effective. He knew that its success in Pasadena would be influential in its acceptance elsewhere. The educational literature of the 1930's and 1940's abounds with articles by Sexson and his associates which described in enthusiastic terms the progress of the 6-4-4 plan in California.

In 1937, following the adoption of the 6-4-4 plan in Compton and Ventura, the California State Legislature amended the Educational Code to provide for the organization of four-year junior colleges upon the approval of the governing boards of all affected high school districts.[40] The total number of systems known to be operating on the 6-4-4 plan during the school year 1940–1941 was ten.[41] In 1944 the Educational Policies Commission of the National Education Association endorsed the plan.[42] In 1946 Sexson and Harbeson published *The New American College,* a "comprehensive apologia for the four-year junior college." [43] The future looked bright indeed and on the occasion of the dedication of the

---

[39] Stephen B. Reichert, Jr., "The End of the Four-Year Junior College in California," *Junior College Journal,* XXIX (February, 1959), 308.

[40] Sexson and Harbeson, *The New American College,* pp. 34–35.

[41] Leonard V. Koos, *Integrating High School and College* (New York: Harper & Brothers, 1946), p. 7.

[42] National Education Association, Educational Policies Commission, *Education for all American Youth* (Washington, D.C.: Educational Policies Commission, National Education Association, 1944).

[43] Reichert, "The End of the Four-Year Junior College in California," p. 312.

newly established John Muir Junior College in Pasadena on September 15, 1946, A. M. Turrell, principal of the new institution, proclaimed that the new American college had come of age. "The 6-4-4 plan is no longer an experiment, a fad, an academic fancy," said Turrell.[44]

Yet within ten years not a single four-year public junior college remained.

The decline of the 6-4-4 plan. The Compton Junior College district was the first of the communities to abandon the plan. Ventura was the next. The beginning of the end of the 6-4-4 plan in Pasadena dates from the retirement of Sexson in 1948. By 1953 the abandoment of the 6-4-4 plan was under active consideration in Stockton.

By 1955 the four-year junior college plans came to an end in California and those national debates came to an end in the meetings of the AAJC. Theoretically the plan was sound. Arguments for it made good sense, but it fought a losing battle. As Eells had predicted, the four-year junior college had the problem of living in a world of reality, not theory. Interscholastic athletic competition was a reality and the four-year junior college did not readily fit into existing patterns. Another reality was tradition, which was a powerful factor in impeding reorganization of the standard college. Still another reality was the vested interests of administrators. A system organized on the 6-4-4 plan required a smaller administrative staff than one set up on the 6-3-3-2 plan.

A member of the faculty of Pasadena City College attempted to analyze why the four-year college movement ended in California. He concluded that of the seven communities which abandoned the plan "not one did so for purely educational reasons." [45]

Today the AAJC does not discuss the four-year or the two-year plan of organization for the junior college. Rather the Association is attempting to clarify and promote public understanding of the functions of junior colleges, to stimulate and assist junior colleges to develop comprehensive curricula with special attention to tech-

[44] A. M. Turrell, "The New American College," *Junior College Journal,* XVII (January, 1947), 172.
[45] Reichert, "The End of the Four-Year College Movement in California," p. 443.

nical education and community services, to assist the states to develop sound and orderly systems of junior colleges to serve the major part of the population in each state, and to promote more effective relationships between junior colleges and the high schools on one hand and the senior colleges and universities on the other.

The "New American College" seems unlikely to achieve the magnificent growth predicted for it, and the two-year junior college flourishes as the typical institution of the 1960's.

4

Spokesman for the
Junior College Movement

REPRESENTATIVES of the American Association of Junior Colleges have made important and continuous contacts with various educational and lay organizations. Through these personal contacts the AAJC has been able to present the position of the junior colleges in a manner that individual colleges never could. When a representative of the AAJC spoke, he spoke for hundreds of institutions, and other organizations listened. Thus the Association acted as spokesman—telling the junior college story to government, to educational organizations, to the public, and to its own administrators and faculty.

THE AAJC AND THE GOVERNMENT

Early in its existence, the AAJC presented its position to the federal government in order to achieve legislation favorable to the junior college movement. The AAJC had to convince the federal government that higher education included the institutions it represented. Time and again the AAJC Board of Directors passed resolutions authorizing the executive secretary to make special efforts to bring about changes in the wording of national legislation so that junior colleges would be eligible to receive educational funds. There were successes and there were failures. Notwithstanding, the AAJC was the organization that spoke for the hundreds of junior colleges in America.

Federal Aid For Private Junior Colleges

In 1934 an AAJC Committee conferred with U.S. Commissioner of Education George F. Zook to decide on the best procedure to draw the attention of Congress and the administration to the need for federal assistance and relief for "strategically located, soundly organized and administered junior colleges." [1] In 1936, at the urgent request of the presidents of six private junior colleges, the AAJC endeavored to revive interest in the Walsh–Guyer bills. These provided the machinery to give specific junior colleges federal aid for amortization of their debts. The Association sent a letter to the presidents of forty private junior colleges urging them to take the matter up with their representatives in both the House and the Senate. The junior college presidents acted; but the bill did not get out of committee. [2]

Wartime Activities

When World War II broke out, the AAJC made it very clear to the agencies of the federal government that it wished to cooperate in the effort to win the war as well as the peace. On July 30, 1941, the AAJC sent representatives to a Washington conference called by the Subcommittee on Military Affairs of the National Committee on Education and Defense. Representatives of eight national educational associations convened with representatives of defense agencies of the federal government to discuss what colleges and universities could and should do in the defense program. The college representatives learned of the dearth of men both with needed technical training and with broad training in business and commerce. The agencies especially emphasized the need for leadership and direction in the development of proper morale and the organization of civilian defense.

During the war years Walter Eells represented the junior colleges in meetings with government agencies. In April, 1942, he sent out a newsletter stating that the U.S. Office of Education Wartime Commission had asked for information regarding shortages

[1] E. E. Cortright, "Federal Aid For Private Junior Colleges," *Junior College Journal*, IV (May, 1934), 423.
[2] E. E. Cortright, "Report of Legislative Committee," *Junior College Journal*, VI (May, 1936), 466.

of instructors in junior colleges, particularly in science and mathematics; and he had had no data available. Eells asked the presidents of junior colleges to inform him if they faced such difficulty so that he could relay the information to the Wartime Commission or the Manpower Board.[3] Eells also told the AAJC membership that he had been able to secure a ruling from the Selective Service System regarding the favorable consideration for deferment of junior college engineering instructors in one large state where the state director had ruled that no such consideration could be given junior colleges.[4]

After conferences with Eells, the United States Marine Corps, the Navy, and the Coast Guard interpreted their requirements for admission to Officers Candidate School to include junior college students. The AAJC was not fully satisfied, since the Armed Forces would not publish a general policy; but at least in specific cases the Armed Forces removed discrimination against junior colleges.[5]

The AAJC, through the tireless Eells and its Washington staff, kept a close watch on government activities to make sure that junior college interests were protected. Eells sent a letter to each of the chief state school officers suggesting that junior colleges be represented adequately in state meetings on wartime problems.[6] During 1942 and 1943 Eells conferred continually, and with some success, with officials of the War Department, Navy Department, War Manpower Commission, National Youth Administration, United States Office of Education, American Council on Education, and the National Education Association to secure rulings favorable to junior colleges.[7]

Eells in his *Wartime Letters* assured the AAJC membership that he was trying to see that Congress did not overlook or forget junior colleges. In February he reported that two important pieces of legislation under consideration had been so drawn as to exclude junior colleges, but those responsible for the plans had assured him that they would correct the oversight.[8] In that same month the Ex-

[3] Walter C. Eells, *Wartime Letter No. 2*, April 30, 1942. AAJC Archives.
[4] *Ibid.*
[5] For Eells' contacts with the Armed Forces see *Wartime Letter No. 20*, May 8, 1943; *Wartime Letter No. 25*, September 25, 1943; and *Wartime Letter No. 2*.
[6] Walter C. Eells, *Wartime Letter No. 7*, September 12, 1942.
[7] Walter C. Eells, *Wartime Letter No. 14*, January 9, 1943.
[8] Walter C. Eells, *Wartime Letter No. 15*, February 10, 1943.

ecutive Secretary of the AAJC became a member of the National College Work Council of the National Youth Administration, the chief advisory and policy-forming body for the college phases of the N.Y.A. program.

Junior colleges were running into difficulties with reference to deferment of students in scientific and technical fields, while senior colleges were not. In one state the Selective Service state director ruled that the junior college was not a recognized college or university. In another the local board said that Bulletin No. 33 (which covered such cases) did not include junior colleges. Eells took the matter to Selective Service and received assurances that a clarifying interpretation would be issued. Eells suggested to all junior colleges that if they had difficulty with a local board, they write directly to Selective Service Headquarters in Washington and send him a carbon of the letter. He promised that he would get action on the matter.[9]

Vocational rehabilitation was a field in which the junior colleges could offer significant service, particularly through their terminal curricula. Eells found the officials of the Rehabilitation Division of the Federal Security Administration unaware of the possibility of using junior colleges for rehabilitation work. However, they were interested in receiving information, and the AAJC was very happy to furnish it. After August 1943 the junior colleges were considered eligible to participate in all rehabilitation.[10]

By 1944 innumerable bills before Congress proposed educational benefits for returning servicemen and women. Congress finally passed the "omnibus" or "G.I." Bill, formally known as Public Law No. 346 or the Servicemen's Readjustment Act of 1944. This act provided a wide variety of benefits for returning servicemen. The Washington office of the AAJC informed the membership on all aspects of the bill. There were some initial difficulties during the early months of the law's operation, for the Veterans Administration's rulings at times prevented payment of tuition to public junior colleges. Eells had many conferences with

[9] Walter C. Eells, *Wartime Letter No. 18,* April 7, 1943.
[10] Walter C. Eells, *Wartime Letter No. 15,* and *Wartime Letter No. 24,* August 20, 1943.

responsible officials of the Veterans Administration and straightened out this matter.[11]

National Defense

The Korean War brought uncertainty again to the junior colleges of the country. At the AAJC Board of Directors Meeting on July 27–29, 1950, discussion centered on the war situation. The Board offered the Association's services to the government and authorized the executive secretary, Jesse Bogue, to ascertain the needs of the government and the actions each junior college could take.

At the annual meeting in 1951, the AAJC adopted a plan for national defense, a program differing from that issued by the Pentagon. At the Senatorial hearings in Washington, Eugene B. Chaffee, president of the AAJC, voiced the position of the junior colleges. The plan called for placing the junior colleges on an equal footing with senior colleges and universities relative to the utilization of facilities and participation in national defense. Discrimination against junior colleges and general reference to them as non-degree-granting institutions were vigorously opposed. The AAJC recommended passage of S. 325 and H. R. 1168, leading to an expansion of the R.O.T.C. program and making junior colleges eligible to sponsor senior units of the R.O.T.C. The AAJC called for legislation to establish a National Defense College Training Program in which junior colleges might participate directly without being subcontractors for senior colleges. The Association also called for the establishment of accredited cadet-training programs for nurses, laboratory technicians, medical secretaries, and others essential to national defense.[12] The AAJC indicated that the junior colleges were opposed to universal military training but were in favor of combining education and military training.[13]

[11] Walter C. Eells, *Wartime Letter Nos. 38–41,* June 17, 1944, through August 16, 1944.

[12] Jesse P. Bogue, "A Suggested Plan for National Defense," *Junior College Journal,* XXI (January, 1951), 263–68.

[13] From 1944 on the AAJC was opposed to compulsory military training. In April, 1948, the AAJC stated its position before a Senate Committee as being opposed to "universal military training as a permanent peacetime policy for our national security can be attained and maintained by a better method." See "Report of the Advisory Committee on National Defense," *Junior College Journal,* XXI (May, 1951), 518–20.

United States Office of Education

For years the U.S. Office of Education has been interested in the junior college. Since 1919 it has produced a steady flow of valuable and useful information describing and promoting junior colleges. The Office performed these functions as a by-product of the execution of other services identified more directly with the usual divisions of the American school system—elementary, secondary, and higher education. But in 1948 junior college relationships with the federal government reached a high point. The United States Office of Education appointed William Henry Conley, dean of the School of Commerce, Loyola University, Chicago, as specialist in junior colleges.

Conley and his successors, William Wood, Homer Kempfer, and S. V. Martorana, furthered junior college education. The AAJC worked with these men, invited them to meetings, and supplied them with information when they asked for it (and sometimes when they didn't). The Office of Education has consulted with the AAJC before selecting a new appointee to ascertain whether he and the AAJC leadership would be in harmony.

Technical Education

One activity of the AAJC has been the attempt to induce the federal government to pass legislation which would advance the terminal technical programs of the junior colleges. At the seventeenth annual meeting, in February, 1937, the AAJC decided to press for revision of the George–Dean Act, which provided federal funds for vocational education, to read "of less than senior college grade," rather than "of less than college grade." [14] Nothing came of these efforts.

When hearings were held in 1945 before the Senate Committee on Education and Labor on the Vocational Education Bill (S. 619), Henry Littlefield, then assistant to the president, Junior College of Connecticut, represented the Association. The phrase that particularly disturbed the junior colleges was that funds would be given to programs "of less than college grade." Littlefield told the Senate

[14] "Minutes and Committee Reports, 17th Annual Meeting of AAJC," *Junior College Journal,* VII (May, 1937), 488.

Committee that the AAJC recognized the need for vocational education and was convinced that consideration should be given to a plan for federal subsidy. However, the AAJC felt that if S. 619 were passed in its present form, it would retard rather than accelerate the total development of vocational education. The bill had too much of the language of the Smith–Hughes Act of 1917, an act which thought of and discussed vocational education in terms of high school youth. Said Littlefield,

> But now, and in the future, this type of education must be thought of as a vital part of the various levels of post high school education as well as high school. We must think of vocational education, not in terms of any particular grade level, but as a program which cuts across all levels from the high school to the university.[15]

Again no progress was made.

The AAJC interest in technical education bills continues to the present day. The Board of Directors in 1948 authorized Jesse Bogue to work with the proper persons to revise the Smith–Hughes and similar acts so that junior colleges and technical institutes and adult educational institutions would be eligible for participation in federal aid for collegiate-level technical education.[16]

In 1960 the AAJC presented its position to Congress on the National Defense Education Act and requested support for junior college technician training programs. The AAJC averred that training for technicians called for college-level programs. Title VIII of NDEA states that funds shall be appropriated for the training of individuals to fit them for useful employment as highly skilled technicians; it also stipulates that programs receiving these federal funds must be "less than college grade." This phrase causes difficulty for a large number of junior colleges and technical institutes because many states legally define junior colleges as institutions of higher education and are not able to classify pertinent programs as "less than college grade." Thus NDEA funds support programs in some states and not in others.[17]

The Association's latest trip "to the Hill" in regard to technical education was in June, 1962, to testify in favor of the Brademas

---

[15] Walter C. Eells, *Wartime Letter No. 53*, May 8, 1945.

[16] AAJC Board of Directors, *Minutes* (July 26–28, 1948). AAJC Archives.

[17] AAJC memorandum to AAJC Board of Directors and Officers, April 7, 1961; AAJC statement on NDEA, November 15, 1960. AAJC Archives.

Bill.[18] This bill calls for federal support of collegiate technical-training programs. Despite the efforts of the AAJC the bill did not get out of committee.

THE AAJC AND OTHER ORGANIZATIONS

The AAJC is vitally interested in its rapport with other educational agencies. Over and over it has encouraged the executive secretary and the president to meet as often as possible with as many agencies as possible "to make certain that the junior college point of view is presented and defended if necessary in long range educational planning." [19]

The NEA

The National Education Association increased its interest in the junior college movement in the 1930's. Eells addressed the 1932 and 1939 meetings of the NEA and helped interpret the junior college to the Department of Secondary School Principals. Zook also spoke about the junior college at NEA conventions.

In 1938 Nicholas Ricciardi, president of the AAJC, proposed affiliation with the National Education Association. Byron S. Hollinshead, AAJC president in 1939, proposed affiliation again; negotiations were entered upon in January, 1941, but never reached fruition. However, the AAJC always felt that the Association for Higher Education, a department of the NEA, was an important contact and encouraged AAJC members to work closely with it.

American Council on Education

The American Council on Education, founded in 1918, is an organization of institutional members and national educational associations serving as a center of cooperation and coordination for the improvement of education at all levels, with particular emphasis on higher education. The AAJC became a constituent member of the ACE on May 5, 1927.

In 1951 Jesse Bogue contacted Arthur S. Adams, president of the ACE, and told him that there was insufficient junior college

---

[18] H.R. 10396.
[19] AAJC Board of Directors, *Minutes* (March 6, 1956). AAJC Archives.

representation on ACE committees. Adams assured Bogue that he would remedy this situation. Today the executive director of the AAJC, Edmund J. Gleazer, Jr., is the secretary of the American Council on Education. Bogue in 1948, 1952, and 1956, and Gleazer in 1960 edited the *American Junior College Directory,* a companion volume to *American Universities and Colleges.* Both of these are ACE publications. The AAJC is housed in a building contiguous to and owned by the American Council on Education.

Committee on Junior–Senior Colleges

In 1957 the AAJC and the Association of American Colleges organized the Committee on Junior and Senior Colleges to improve relations between the two. In March 1958 the American Association of Collegiate Registrars and Admissions Officers joined the committee.

In the summer of 1958 the committee prepared a statement of principles to guide the transfer of students from junior to senior colleges. It urged senior colleges to consider junior college transfer applicants as they do transfer applicants from senior colleges. The committee recommended that junior and senior colleges make continuing studies of the academic success of transfers. The joint committee also urged that a study be made concerning factors affecting performance of students who transfer from two- to four-year colleges. Such a project is going on at the Center for the Study of Higher Education at the University of California at Berkeley with financial support form the U.S. Office of Education.[20]

Other Contacts

The AAJC spoke for the junior college movement to many other organizations. It negotiated with the American Association of University Professors which, after many years, opened its membership to instructors in junior colleges on the same basis as to instructors in senior colleges. In 1941 the AAJC negotiated with three other national organizations for recognition of junior colleges.[21]

During World War II the medical schools of the country, act-

[20] *Junior College Newsletter,* XV, no. 6, February 23, 1960.

[21] Walter C. Eells, "Executive Secretary's Report to the 21st Meeting of the AAJC," *Junior College Journal,* XI (May, 1941), 509.

ing through the Council on Medical Education of the American Medical Association, reduced entrance requirements from three or more years of college work to two years. The AAJC was unable to secure a statement which would make it clear that this action included junior colleges. For weeks Eells negotiated with the American Medical Association, the War Department, and the American Council on Education. He finally received a statement from the Secretary of the Council on Medical Education and Hospitals of the AMA which he characterized as "not entirely satisfactory but it is much better than nothing, and I trust may solve some of the difficulties." [22]

The AAJC strengthened its relations with other associations and agencies through staff and member representation on important committees and at major educational meetings.[23] In all these contacts the AAJC obtained recognition of junior colleges—their programs, faculty and students.

HONORS AND ATHLETICS

Honor Societies

Junior colleges in Missouri had organized honor societies since the early 1900's. One society in particular, Phi Theta Kappa, had achieved some prominence.

At the 1926 annual AAJC meeting Rose Lisenby, dean of Christian College, Columbia, Missouri, requested that the Association recognize Phi Theta Kappa. At that time the AAJC merely went on record as approving honorary societies in principle.[24] Two years later Phi Theta Kappa again asked for recognition. This time the AAJC referred the petition to an *ad hoc* Committee on Honor Scholastic Societies.

[22] Walter C. Eells, *Wartime Letter No. 24.*

[23] In 1943 Eells became the junior college representative on the National Conference of Christians and Jews Commission on Educational Organizations. In 1946 Lawrence L. Bethel, AAJC president, represented the Association on the National Committee on Educational Rehabilitation in War Devastated Countries. In 1961 Gleazer became a member of the Defense Advisory Committee on Education in the Armed Forces.

[24] Rose Lisenby, "Honor Scholarship Societies for Junior Colleges," *Proceedings of Sixth Annual Meeting of the AAJC,* 1926, pp. 59–60. AAJC Archives.

The Committee formulated a constitution for honor scholarship societies, and the AAJC approved it at the 1929 annual meeting. Phi Theta Kappa accepted this constitution and the Association officially recognized the society as its national scholastic honor society.[25] In 1931 the AAJC designated Phi Rho Pi as the national forensic honor society. In 1942 the Association approved a third honor society— Alpha Pi Epsilon (for the field of secretarial training).

In 1960 the Board of Directors of the AAJC decided to review Association policy on recognition of honor societies. The Board asked its Student Personnel Commission to study this matter and to determine whether the function of approval of such organizations should continue to be a responsibility of the Board of Directors. On the recommendation of the Student Personnel Commission the Board adopted the following resolution in January, 1961:

Beginning January 1, 1961, it is the policy of the Board of Directors of the AAJC to no longer endorse sororities, fraternities, and societies.[26]

The director and other leaders of Phi Theta Kappa immediately wrote to the Board of Directors of the AAJC and insisted that the Board had no authority to cancel Association support of Phi Theta Kappa. These protests and a perusal of the proceedings of the 1928 and 1929 conventions persuaded the Board to rescind its resolution and pass a new motion that it be the policy of the Board of Directors of the AAJC in the future "not to receive and consider requests for endorsement from student groups or outside organizations." [27]

Athletics

Junior colleges opposed the one-year rule regarding athletic participation, which prevented a junior college graduate who transferred to a senior college from participating in intercollegiate

[25] For the complete text of the recommended constitution for Phi Theta Kappa as proposed by the Junior College Honor Scholarship Society Committee, see *Proceedings of Tenth Annual Meeting of the AAJC*, 1929, pp. 165–71. AAJC Archives.

[26] AAJC, Board of Directors, *Minutes* (January 8, 1961). AAJC Archives.

[27] AAJC Board of Directors, *Minutes* (July 17, 1961). AAJC Archives.

sports until he had been in residence for one year. Coaches did not wish to spend time and effort training a man who could play for only one year. At the 1928 annual meeting the AAJC passed a resolution which urged athletic conferences to remove the one-year rule for junior college graduates. In 1930 the Southern Intercollegiate Athletic Conference and three years later the Southwestern Athletic Conference amended their rules and allowed junior college graduates two years of eligibility.[28]

The AAJC was instrumental in developing a set of guiding principles for intercollegiate junior college athletics. The National Junior College Athletic Association in the late 1940's told the AAJC that it would like to have a working agreement with the Association. Because of the opposition of the North Central Association of Junior Colleges and some irregularities in the operation of the National Junior College Athletic Association, the Board of Directors of the AAJC withheld approval of the NJCAA at its 1950 meeting. The Board also indicated that the AAJC would make no attempt to organize a national athletic program. It took the position that the AAJC did not regard sponsorship of any athletic association as one of its functions. It did, however, recommend that the AAJC appoint a committee to formulate a set of principles for guidance in the organization and operation of junior college athletic conferences throughout the nation.[29]

In 1951 and 1952 the executive committee of the NJCAA expressed its desire to be incorporated into the AAJC and allow the latter organization to supervise and direct athletic activities on a national scale, but the Board of Directors decided that the AAJC should not become closely affiliated with NJCAA or any other outside group.[30]

An *ad hoc* subcommittee of the Committee on Administration studied the entire problem of intercollegiate athletics in accordance with the vote of the Board in March, 1950, and formulated a statement of guiding principles which it released at the thirty-third annual convention in 1953. The AAJC then urged each

[28] James L. Beck, "Report on Intercollegiate Athletics," *Junior College Journal,* VII (May, 1937), 495–97.

[29] AAJC Board of Directors, *Minutes* (March 26–29, 1950). AAJC Archives.

[30] AAJC Board of Directors, *Minutes* (June 28, 1952). AAJC Archives.

junior college to use these principles in the conduct of junior college intercollegiate athletics.[31]

CONSULTING SERVICES

A steadily growing service of the AAJC makes resource personnel and materials available to members. In 1960 the superintendent of public instruction of the state of Ohio used the AAJC to help plan a statewide junior college system. Gleazer met with the State Board of Education Committee of Ohio and sent them publications prepared by various Commissions of the AAJC.[32]

In December, 1960, Gleazer wrote to Virgil M. Hancher, president of the State University of Iowa, once again presented the place of the junior college in the total structure of education, and offered suggestions for a legislative program for the establishment of a junior college system in Iowa.[33]

The AAJC became increasingly aware that certain information could be provided adequately only on a personal basis—by individuals having professional competence in a specific area of junior college education. The Board of Directors adopted the idea of a field-service advisory program, from which emerged the Program of Professional Advisory Services, financed by a special grant from the W. K. Kellogg Foundation. Advisors are available in such areas as finance and development, legislation, student personnel, administration, curriculum, construction and design of facilities, instruction, and community relations.[34]

THE AAJC AND THE PUBLIC

One of the major functions of the Washington office of the AAJC is communication—with the press, with prospective junior

[31] Roscoe C. Ingalls, "Report of Committee on Resolutions to 33rd Annual Meeting of AAJC," *Junior College Journal*, XXIV (October, 1953), 105; also AAJC Board of Directors, *Minutes* (June 28, 1952).

[32] Letters from Edmund J. Gleazer, Jr., to Dr. E. E. Holt, Superintendent of Public Instruction, State of Ohio, December 29, 1960, and to Edward C. Ames, Public-Relations Director, Owens-Illinois, Ohio, December 29, 1960. AAJC Archives.

[33] Letter from Edmund J. Gleazer, Jr., to Dr. Virgil M. Hancher, president, State University of Iowa, December 29, 1960. AAJC Archives.

[34] AAJC, *A Program of Professional Advisory Services* (Washington, D.C.: American Association of Junior Colleges, 1962).

college students and their families, as well as with the agencies already mentioned. The establishment of an identity for junior colleges has been the essence of these communication efforts.

Lawrence Bethel, president of the AAJC, pointed out in 1945 that potential students and their parents did not understand the functions of the junior college, particularly the terminal function. Bethel called for constructive and positive steps toward the establishment of an identity which would reveal the true purposes of junior colleges, for "as long as we do not give ourselves an identity, other organizations must give us one of their own choosing." He stressed that the junior colleges need not all be alike but "we must be something and not just everything or something less than." He emphasized that the AAJC had to work with the public to bring about a recognition of the purposes of the junior college, and also must find means for obtaining recognition by other associations, by government agencies, by state legislatures and by the national Congress.[35]

"We must be heard," said Bethel.[36] And heard they were—in the newspapers and magazines of the nation. In 1959, International News–United Press published a feature on junior college education which appeared in newspapers from coast to coast. The *New York Times,* the *Christian Science Monitor,* and the *Wall Street Journal* gave a significant amount of space to discussion on the value of junior colleges. The *Reader's Digest, Changing Times, Newsweek, Time* and *U.S. News and World Report* were a few of the magazines that carried articles on this subject. The AAJC staff spent a considerable amount of time providing information to these newspapers and magazines and answering many resulting inquiries with personal letters.[37]

And the junior colleges were heard at annual meetings of professional organizations. "Telling the Junior College Story on the National Level" was the theme of a junior college seminar at the annual meeting of the American College Public Relations Asso-

[35] Lawrence L. Bethel, "What Are 'These Institutions?' ", *Junior College Journal,* XVI (November, 1945), 105.

[36] *Ibid.*

[37] AAJC Board of Directors, *Minutes* (March, 1959). AAJC Archives.

ciation held in New York in June, 1954.[38] They were heard too at chambers of commerce, PTA's, and labor organization meetings. By 1961 they were heard in the far corners of Africa, Europe, and Latin America.[39]

In order to be heard still more clearly and effectively, the AAJC at the close of 1961 established an office of public information and employed William A. Harper as Director of Public Information. The 1963 budget supported an independent National Education Policies Commission composed of representatives from industry, labor, government, and education. This commission reports periodically to the public, to the AAJC, and to the two-year colleges its suggestions for desirable directions and procedures for the junior college movement.

THE JUNIOR COLLEGE JOURNAL

In order to accomplish its purpose the AAJC had to speak not only to many outside groups and agencies but to its own. It had to find a satisfactory means for dissemination of information and for interchange of opinion among junior college faculty, junior college administrators, and other interested junior college workers. To supply this means the *Junior College Journal* was born.

From the fourth annual meeting members proposed, year after year, the creation of an official publication, but the AAJC was cautious. It did not wish merely to add another periodical, and the Annual Proceedings seemed a sufficient medium for the dissemination of information. However, the rapidity with which the junior college movement was developing, the increasing number of calls for information, and the lack of any news medium specifically for junior colleges, finally convinced the officers and the membership of the Association that there was a definite need for a junior college publication.[40]

---

[38] Alfred T. Hill, "Report of the AAJC Section Meeting," *Junior College Journal,* XXV (October, 1954), 73.

[39] "Edmund J. Gleazer, Jr., Report to AAJC Board of Directors, calendar year 1961." Mimeographed. AAJC Archives.

[40] Doak S. Campbell, "The Association and the *Journal,*" *Junior College Journal,* I (November, 1930), 61.

At the tenth annual meeting the Stanford University Press presented, and the AAJC approved, a plan for the publication of a periodical under the joint editorial control of the AAJC and the School of Education at Stanford University. Stanford provided offices, clerical help, and a professor, part-time, as editor. Eells, then a professor at Stanford University, became the first editor of the *Junior College Journal*. The first issue came out in October, 1930.[41]

Educators throughout the country received the first issue of the *Journal* with favor. Eells published all the kudos he received and stated the guiding principles which governed the editing of the publication. He stated that the *Journal* would be "sanely progressive and progressively interpretive of the best in the junior college movement." [42] Eells loved his work as editor of the *Journal*, which he considered the most important single contribution of the AAJC to the junior college movement.[43] There were many who didn't share this feeling. A major criticism of the *Journal* during the 1930's was that it suffered from a malady called "California-itis." [44] It also suffered from lack of funds.

Eells remedied the first; and on the whole the contents of the *Journal*, during the first five years at least, adequately fulfilled its function as the means of expression of junior college education in America.[45] Universities attempted to remedy the lack of funds. First Stanford, then the University of Chicago, and finally the University of Texas, subsidized the *Journal*. In 1938 Eells reported that the deficit borne by the Stanford University Press during eight years of publication of the *Journal* had exceeded $7,000; the deficit payments of the AAJC for the same period were $4,000.[46]

In 1938, when Eells indicated that the editorial work was dif-

[41] Agreement between Stanford University Press and the AAJC, 1930. AAJC Archives.

[42] Walter C. Eells, "The *Junior College Journal*," *Junior College Journal*, II (May, 1932), 505.

[43] Interviews with Walter C. Eells, March 23, 1961, and December 27, 1962.

[44] Walter C. Eells, "The *Junior College Journal*, Editorial Report," in "Minutes and Committee Reports to the 13th Annual AAJC Meeting," *Junior College Journal*, III (May, 1933), 483.

[45] Harold W. Leuenberger, "The *Junior College Journal*: An Analysis," *Junior College Journal*, VI (February, 1936), 253–54.

[46] Eells, "*Junior College Journal*," p. 483.

ficult because of his "heavy burden of administrative and research work in the educational field," the AAJC combined the secretary-ship of the Association and the editorship, and appointed Eells to the position.[47]

Eells made no major changes in the *Journal* until the World War II years. Regulations related to shortage of paper, and budgetary considerations related to shortage of cash, led to a reduction of the *Journal* from sixty-four to forty-eight pages in 1942. Each month he published one or two major articles dealing with wartime issues, and others with little or no direct reference to war conditions. A separate department, "Wartime Activities," reported what various institutions were doing to aid the war effort.[48] Eells served as editor of the *Journal* until his resignation as executive secretary of the AAJC in 1945. Winifred R. Long, who took over as acting executive secretary, edited volume sixteen of the *Journal*.

From 1946 until 1949, while Leonard V. Koos edited the *Journal* at the University of Chicago, it served as an outlet for the five AAJC research and service committees. In response to suggestions made by junior college administrators, Koos increased the amount of news published in the *Journal* about individual junior colleges and junior college personalities. He also published more articles of interest to junior college teachers.[49]

In 1949 the AAJC moved the editorial office from the University of Chicago in accordance with the original policy of limiting to three years the location of the research and editorial office. James W. Reynolds, professor of education at the University of Texas, became the editor and continued in that capacity until January, 1963.[50]

[47] *Ibid.*

[48] Walter C. Eells, "Policy of the *Journal* in Wartime," *Junior College Journal,* XIII (September, 1942), 3.

[49] Leonard V. Koos, "Policies and Pleas," *Junior College Journal,* XVII (October, 1946), 43–44; Roy W. Goddard, "Appraising the *Junior College Journal,*" *Junior College Journal,* XIX (September, 1948), 3–7.

[50] The research and editorial office was moved to the University of Texas in 1949. Texas was once again granted the contract in 1952, breaking the original policy of the AAJC. In 1955 the Association discontinued the research office but continued Reynolds as editor.

Editorial Board

When the Association began publication of the *Journal* in 1930 it set up a National Advisory Board of eleven men. This Board had little or no responsibility in determining the policies of the *Journal,* held no official meetings, and took no part in editing the publication. Its contribution was to lend members' names and thus give prestige to this new educational endeavor. Bogue, as president of the AAJC, induced a significant change in editorial policy in 1943. He appointed a new six-member board, each of whom represented a geographical region, which was to act in an advisory manner and aid in securing and suggesting articles for publication.[51] But the new arrangement had little effect.

When Koos became editor of the *Journal* in 1946 he met with the Board to formulate policies to govern the relations between the editor, the editorial board, and the executive secretary. Although they adopted some policies, the function of the Editorial Board was a controversial question in the AAJC for many years. The Board of Directors in 1947 voted unanimously that the Editorial Board is "responsible to the Board of Directors and recommends to it policies governing the promotion, publication, and evaluation of the *Journal.*" [52]

The *Journal* has been and remains largely the responsibility of the editor. The Board of Directors of the AAJC sets fundamental policies; the editor determines minor policies as they arise. In 1960 the Editorial Board once again requested clarification of its role by the AAJC Board of Directors. By 1963 it had its answer: the Editorial Board was abolished.

Content and Evaluation

One thing the *Journal* has never suffered is lack of evaluation. In 1936 Harold W. Leuenberger analyzed the subject distribution of major articles which had appeared in the first five volumes. The most frequent item was curriculum and instruction, followed by articles on the history and administration of junior colleges and

---

[51] Walter C. Eells, "Annual Report of Executive Secretary," *Junior College Journal,* XIV (April, 1944), 345–55; also "From the Secretary's Desk," *Junior College Journal,* XIV (October, 1943), 90.

[52] AAJC Board of Directors, *Minutes* (August 2, 1947). AAJC Archives.

articles on student personnel.[53] In 1944 Eells listed the major articles that had appeared in the past fourteen years; the curriculum
category again led the field followed by articles on developments
in special regions and states, guidance and personnel, and objectives and functions of junior colleges.[54] A doctoral dissertation at
Teachers College, Columbia University, in 1953 added to the list
of appraisals of the *Journal*.[55] In that same year Reynolds, editor
of the *Journal*, indicated that the field of curriculum and instruction still led the list, followed by student personnel articles.[56]

Through the years, then, few changes occurred in the fundamental policies which governed the *Journal* or in the subjects
discussed in its pages. The editor and guest writers continued to
write the editorials. The major portion of the publication has been
used for articles from contributors, with emphasis on articles of
interest to both administrators and teachers. Two features, "Junior College World" and "From the Executive Director's Desk,"
continued until January, 1963, when the features were combined
and called "AAJC Approach." These departments function as
media to keep readers posted concerning current developments of
significance to the junior college and to provide news about individual junior colleges and junior college personnel.

A New York advertising agency made the most recent evaluation of the *Junior College Journal* in the summer of 1960. The
criticism was direct and frank. The report indicated that the dress
of the journal "is lackluster and dull. The layouts have a stuffy,
old-fashioned air about them." [57] The editorial content also came
in for criticism. "One not acquainted with the editorial policies
of the Journal gets the distinct impression," said the report, "that
the magazine is not vital, challenging or incisive as it might be.
It does not sound enthusiastic about education, about junior col-

[53] Leuenberger, "The *Junior College Journal*," *Junior College Journal*, VI, 251.
[54] Walter C. Eells, "*Journal* Articles Worth Reading Again," *Junior College Journal*, XV (September, 1944), 28–30.
[55] Albert Anderson, "An Appraisal of the *Junior College Journal*, 1946–1953" (Unpublished Doctor of Education project report, Teachers College, Columbia University), 1953.
[56] James W. Reynolds, "Report on the *Junior College Journal*," *Junior College Journal*, XXIV (September, 1953), 29–31.
[57] Memorandum from Edmund J. Gleazer, Jr., to Officers and Board of Directors of the AAJC regarding N. W. Ayer & Son, Inc., comments on the *Junior College Journal*, September 6, 1960. AAJC Archives.

leges, or even about itself." [58] The evaluation indicated that if the junior college movement were the fastest growing phase of education, then some of the attendant excitement ought to be reflected in the pages of the *Journal*. "In brief," concluded the report, "the magazine should grasp its opportunity to be the authoritative voice of a responsible movement." [59]

This evaluation, and a burgeoning awareness by the Board of Directors of the AAJC that the *Journal* needed a full-time editor, led to the termination of the publishing contract with the University of Texas. As of January 1, 1963, the AAJC assumed direct responsibility for publication of the magazine with a full-time editor appointed to work out of the Washington headquarters. Roger Yarrington, managing editor of Herald House, a national church publishing house, became the new editor of the *Junior College Journal*.

OTHER PUBLICATIONS

The AAJC carries on an extensive publication program, including, in addition to the *Journal,* books, pamphlets, reprints, a newsletter, and the *Junior College Directory*. These media report the results of research projects, significant developments and news of the junior college world, editorial comment and opinion, and developments in the nation which may affect the future of the junior colleges.

[58] *Ibid.*
[59] *Ibid.*

5

Professional Leadership: Curriculum

EDUCATORS FROM other lands have always found it difficult to understand or to accept the fact that the United States has a decentralized system of education. They have tried in vain to find a ministry of education that controls school programs and instruction. When they cannot find such centralized control they mistakenly think that there is no coordination in the development of educational institutions.

As a matter of fact, voluntary associations, which are characteristic of American education, provide the coordination; they have made it possible for individuals to work together for the advancement of common objectives. The American Association of Junior Colleges was one of the hundreds of educational organizations which appeared on the American scene shortly after World War I.[1] Committed to "the professional development of its members," the Association, through research, discussion, and dissemination of information, attempted to improve the services of the college to its various constituents. Like other educational associations, it was interested in curriculum development, technical aspects of teaching methods, teacher education, student personnel practices, and the area of administration.

CONFLICTING CURRICULAR TRADITIONS

Higher education in the United States has been influenced and molded by a variety of historical forces. On one hand there are the traditions of higher learning which came over from Western Eu-

[1] United States Bureau of Education, "Handbook of Educational Associations and Foundations in the U.S.," Bulletin No. 16 (Washington, D.C.: U.S. Government Printing Office, 1926).

rope; on the other, there are native American conditions that affected and modified the development of the transplanted heritage.

Liberal Education

The tradition of liberal education can be traced to Greece. The ancient Greeks confined liberal studies to those fields of knowledge which involved the political and intellectual life of free citizens. A liberal education did not include activities which involved earning a living through manual labor. Plato and Aristotle gradually tended to prescribe only certain kinds of studies as leading to "the good life" and helped create a dualism between knowledge and action. In his *Republic* Plato prescribed a course of study for his prospective "philosopher-kings," while Aristotle insisted that a liberal education was appropriate only to the free citizens who were politically and intellectually free as well as wealthy. After Roman scholars adopted Greek culture, a liberal education became associated more and more with non-physical, non-commercial, and non-political activities.

The medieval university adopted the liberal arts curriculum that had been determined and limited by educational philosophers in ancient Greek and Roman times and by the medieval Christian Church. The liberal arts curriculum became prescribed "because the church desired its clergymen and teachers to be orthodox in belief and educated in the literary and philosophical studies inherited from Greco-Roman culture." [2]

Higher education in America reproduced the prescribed curriculum, which became extremely tenacious in the colleges of the country. By the end of the eighteenth century, however, forces released by the Enlightenment and the American Revolution were at work that challenged and changed the curriculum. A highly industrialized society demanded education for professions and vocations that gradually modified the early focus on intellectual concerns.

Technical Education

The vocational concept in education can be traced to a respectable past in the United States. William Penn as early as 1682

[2] R. Freeman Butts, *The College Charts Its Course* (New York: McGraw-Hill Book Co., 1939), p. 30.

desired that his children be taught "the useful parts of mathematics, as building houses or ships, measuring, surveying, navigation, but agriculture is especially in my eyes; let my children be husbandmen and housewives, it is industrious, healthy, honest, and of good example." [3]

In 1685 Thomas Budd, also a Quaker, made a very interesting proposal for vocational training.[4] He argued not only that boys and girls should learn the most useful arts and sciences but also that the boys should learn a useful trade and the girls should receive instruction in spinning, knitting, needlework, and straw work.

Benjamin Franklin, "the apostle of practicality," [5] set forth the most elaborate plan for utilitarian education in the colonial period. In 1749 he published *Proposals Relating to the Education of Youth in Pennsylvania* which recognized the importance of the learned languages and the classics but also stressed the practical and vocational aspect of education.[6]

Many new types of colleges, dedicated to special purposes, made their appearance in the nineteenth century. "Among these," say Brubacher and Rudy, "none was more attuned to the utilitarian spirit of the booming Republic than the technological college or institute." [7] Although some colonial colleges and the United States Military Academy gave instruction in what may be termed "technical education," it was not until 1824 that Rensselaer Polytechnic Institute in Troy, New York, the first distinct and separate technical school in the United States, was set up. Once the technical movement got under way, it rapidly gained momentum.[8]

Much of the educational ferment of the past half century has

---

[3] Samuel M. Janney, *The Life of William Penn* (Philadelphia: Friends' Book Assn., 1882), pp. 198–203.

[4] Thomas Budd, *Good Order Established in Pennsylvania and New Jersey*, ed. Frederick J. Shepard (Cleveland: Burrows, 1902).

[5] R. Freeman Butts and Lawrence A. Cremin, *A History of Education in American Culture* (New York: Henry Holt and Co., 1953), p. 77.

[6] Thomas Woody (ed.), *Educational Views of Benjamin Franklin* (New York: McGraw-Hill Book Co., 1931).

[7] John S. Brubacher and Willis Rudy, *Higher Education in Transition* (New York: Harper & Brothers, 1958), p. 61.

[8] Brubacher and Rudy, *Higher Education in Transition*, point out that the first use of the word "technology" in America is to be found in Jacob Bigelow's textbook, *Elements of Technology* (Boston: Hilliard, Gray, Little & Wilkins, 1831).

grown from the controversy between academicians and vocational educators as to the nature of the knowledge that is suitable for college students—a controversy which has been described as the conflict between "culture and cash." [9]

The Association was sensitive to the conflicting educational traditions.

GENERAL EDUCATION

A college curriculum is significant in part because it reveals "the educated community's conception of what knowledge is most worth transmitting to the cream of its youth." [10] Because the curriculum is a product of the society in which it operates, educators have to analyze society and develop programs that respond to societal demands. Speakers at the conventions of the AAJC repeatedly reviewed the purposes of society and the related functions of the junior college.

Origins and Purposes

Though the term "general education" has been traced back to the early years of the nineteenth century,[11] the general education movement developed most rapidly after World War I. Since that time it has been a major curriculum concern of higher education in America.

Several developments helped spark the interest in general education. Following World War I, Columbia College introduced its "Contemporary Civilization" courses; a decade later the University of Chicago started its program in general education. Antioch, St. John's at Annapolis, Sarah Lawrence, and Bennington developed general education programs, and the results of their experimental work began to make an impact by 1933.

The National Society for the Study of Education in 1939 pub-

[9] Butts, *The College Charts Its Course*, p. 358.

[10] Richard Hofstadter and C. DeWitt Hardy, *The Development and Scope of Higher Education in the United States* (New York: Columbia University Press, 1952), p. 11.

[11] Russell Thomas, *The Search for a Common Learning: General Education, 1800–1960* (New York: McGraw-Hill Book Co., 1962).

lished a yearbook on general education;[12] in 1942–43, at the request of the Armed Forces, the American Council on Education produced a report on the same subject.[13] The most widely discussed and perhaps most influential publication that helped stimulate the developing interest in general education was the celebrated Harvard Report.[14]

Why all this excitement and concern? There was considerable dissatisfaction with existing college curricula and with overspecialization by undergraduates. There was lack of adequate connection between undergraduate programs and the real problems of students and society. There was an influx of a new type of student in the 1930's—men and women who before the depression never would have gone to college at all; they did not respond to existing courses and programs. A good deal of new knowledge about youth and their problems began to emerge. There also existed an impending sense of social crisis, and the desire that higher educational institutions of the country prepare their students to cope with it.[15]

Another factor, and perhaps the most important, was the need to work with other peoples of the world for the betterment of mankind. The movement for curriculum change was a quest for "unity with diversity."

General education has been defined in many ways and with differing emphases. "General education," declares a publication of the American Council on Education, "refers to those phases of nonspecialized and nonvocational education that should be the common possession, the common denominator . . . of educated persons as individuals and as citizens in a free society." [16] The American Historical Association Commission on the Social

[12] Guy Montrose Whipple (ed.), *General Education in the American College*. Thirty-Eighth Yearbook of the National Society for the Study of Education, Part II (Bloomington, Illinois: Public School Publishing Company, 1939).

[13] American Council on Education, *A Design for General Education* (Washington, D.C.: ACE, 1944), Series I, No. 18.

[14] Harvard University, Committee on the Objectives of a General Education in a Free Society, *General Education in a Free Society: Report of the Harvard Committee* (Cambridge, Mass.: Harvard University Press, 1945).

[15] For a discussion of the agitation for curriculum reform see Thomas, *The Search for a Common Learning*, pp. 61–91.

[16] American Council on Education, *A Design for General Education*, p. 7.

Studies wrote about the development of "rich, many-sided personalities." [17] Earl J. McGrath defined general education as "that
which prepares the young for the common life of their time and
their kind. It is the unifying element of a culture." [18]

No matter what the definition, those who advocated reexamination of the curricula of the colleges of the country were responding to a growing realization that our student population was
increasing and changing in character; higher education was not
preparing youth to make decisions concerning the critical issues
of our time. It required the shocks of a first world war, a depression, growing fascism, a second world war, threat of atomic de-
struction, and the challenge of Communism to force reexamination of college curricula.

Educators began to understand that some of the most critical
problems they had to deal with were social rather than physical in
character. Such problems as achieving world peace in a world of
conflicting ideologies and strengthening our political and economic institutions within a framework of democratic values required major surgery on the curricula of the colleges rather than
the mere treatment of symptoms.

The literature that has been published on this subject is stag-
gering.[19] It not only reflects the amount of time and energy that
has been devoted to the concept of general education but also
reveals a diversity of opinion about both ends and means. Through
the *Junior College Journal,* its research bulletins, and its Commission on Curriculum, the AAJC has contributed to the vast amount
of literature and discussion.

AAJC Debates

Discussions of curriculum improvement and the role of the
junior college in developing programs of general education have
been on the agenda of the meetings of the AAJC since its incep-

[17] Charles A. Beard, *A Charter for the Social Sciences in the Schools,* A Report
of the Commission on the Social Studies (New York: Charles Scribner's Sons, 1932),
Part I, pp. 3, 96.

[18] Earl J. McGrath, *et al., Toward General Education* (New York: The Macmillan Co., 1949), pp. 8–9.

[19] Walter C. Eells, "Adjustments in the Junior College Curriculum," *Junior
College Journal,* III (May, 1933), 401–02; see Thomas, *The Search for a Common
Learning.*

tion.[20] The thirteenth annual meeting of the Association, in 1933, paid a great deal of attention to the junior college curriculum and the importance of general education. This conference followed on the heels of the report of the Carnegie Foundation Commission on State Higher Education in California, dealing with organizational, administrative, financial, and curricular aspects of junior colleges, teachers colleges, and university education in the state. The Carnegie report was one of the first significant and authoritative statements to suggest adjustments of the curricula in junior colleges. It criticized these institutions for permitting the majority of their students to take courses "which should be reserved for the higher ranges of intelligence in preparation for a life devoted to research, scholarship, or teaching." [21] It went on to recommend that general education be the main emphasis of the junior college.

The report recommended five types of curricula for the junior college, the first and most significant of which it designated as a "Curriculum for Social Intelligence." The others were vocational, preprofessional, preacademic, and adult curricula. The social intelligence curriculum was described as

a curriculum devised to give the student about to complete his general education a unitary conception of our developing civilization. It should be the most important curriculum, inasmuch as it aims to train for social citizenship in American civilization . . . The courses will tend to organize knowledge and intelligence for effective social behavior rather than for the intense and detailed mastery required for professional or avocational scholarship.[22]

The concept of a curriculum for "social intelligence" was adopted by many leaders of the junior college movement. Convinced that the preparatory function of the junior college was not the primary one, speakers at meetings of the AAJC and writers in the *Junior College Journal* called upon administrators to pay greater attention to the needs of those students who would not transfer to four-year institutions. The alternative was not voca-

[20] C. S. Boucher, "Curriculum and Methods of Instruction in the Junior College of a University," *Proceedings of Eighth Annual Meeting of the AAJC,* 1928, pp. 24–31; William S. Gray, "Educational Readjustments at the Junior College Level," *Proceedings of Ninth Annual Meeting of the AAJC,* 1928, pp. 39–46. AAJC Archives.

[21] Carnegie Foundation for the Advancement of Teaching, *State Higher Education in California* (Sacramento: California State Printing Office, 1932), pp. 35–36.

[22] Carnegie Foundation, *State Higher Education in California,* p. 36.

tional preparation but rather a terminal program in general education.

Despite these ample warnings by educators and the clarion call to throw off the yoke of the traditional college and meet new responsibilities, the junior colleges continued to emphasize the traditional liberal arts courses rather than to experiment with general education programs. However, the AAJC continued to maintain a definite concern for general education. The new constitution adopted in 1945 made provision for a reorganized Committee on Curriculum and Adult Education. Fired with the enthusiasm that new people bring with them, the reorganized committee outlined eight major areas that required study. Leading the list was the area of general education for all.

At the thirty-first annual meeting, in March, 1951, general education was considered by three groups which formulated definitions that, while differing in detail, agreed in emphasizing "ministering to the common needs of human beings in contemporary democratic society." [23] It was relatively easy to get agreement on the ends of general education. It was almost impossible to get agreement on the means to these ends. The discussants recognized, however, that general education was needed by all junior college students.

Blocks and Doubts

The group deliberating at the annual meeting in 1952 concluded that the main obstacle to developing and maintaining an effective general education program was lack of faculty awareness and understanding, a natural outcome of traditional preparation for college teachers in subject matter specialization.[24] Earlier in 1950 James Reynolds, professor of education at the University of Texas and editor of the *Junior College Journal*, found evidence which made him doubt that junior colleges had well-defined policies for the general education of their students. Reynolds noted not only the admission requirements of senior institutions but the re-

---

[23] Karl W. Bigelow, "Report on the Discussion Groups," *Junior College Journal*, XXI (May, 1951), 494.

[24] Francis H. Horn, "Convention Analysis," *Junior College Journal*, XXIII (September, 1952), 40.

luctance of increasing numbers of terminal students to take general education programs and the lack of conviction of administrators and faculty members. The latter he ascribed to a background of training which produced a disproportionate respect for specialized subject-matter programs.[25]

Doubts about the general education movement were summarized by McGrath in the *Journal of Higher Education* when he warned that the success of the movement was by no means assured.[26] He pointed to three social and educational factors which would condition the future developments in general education:

1. The conditions of American life generally and the attitudes of the American people.

2. The values, the purposes, and the practices of the teaching profession, particularly in institutions of higher education.[27]

3. The leadership among administrative officers in colleges and universities.

By the 1960's semiprofessional and adult education had replaced general education as the field of main concern for the once again reorganized Commission on Curriculum of the AAJC.

If this trend on the part of the Association is part of a growing number of signs in recent years that might be construed as a disenchantment with the whole area of general education, then it seems to be a reaction to a name rather than to a basic educational idea. The fundamental principle for which the term has traditionally stood does not appear to have been rejected, for the members of the Curriculum Commission and administrators of individual junior colleges continue to speak of the "broad foundation of

[25] James W. Reynolds, "General Education and the Junior College," *Junior College Journal*, XX (January, 1950), 239–40.

[26] Earl J. McGrath, "The Future of General Education," *Journal of Higher Education*, XXIV (March, 1953), 121–26.

[27] McGrath was voicing a concern that he was to spell out in a later publication, that the future of general education would in large measure be determined by the faculty and that in turn the teachers would be influenced by the graduate schools. Oliver C. Carmichael put it this way: "not until the graduate school has set its house in order as the provider of college teachers can we hope to effect needed reform in the colleges." See Earl J. McGrath, *The Graduate School and the Decline of Liberal Education* (New York: Bureau of Publications, Teachers College, Columbia University, 1959); Oliver C. Carmichael, President's Report, *The Carnegie Foundation for the Advancement of Teaching: 46th Annual Report for the Year ended June 30, 1951.*

learning," or "the common body of knowledge" that they indicate should be a part of every student's experience.[28]

TECHNICAL AND SEMIPROFESSIONAL EDUCATION

During their developmental years the junior colleges had difficulty in defining their purposes and functions. It was one thing for administrators of junior colleges to verbalize in addresses to local groups and national meetings their belief in both transfer and terminal functions. It was quite another to get these implemented in the programs and accepted by the faculty and public.

Early Recognition

The junior colleges of 1920 confined their work largely to the traditional freshman and sophomore courses found in the four-year colleges. There was some recognition, however, of the significance of the terminal function as both general education and preparation for an occupation. Harper in 1900 hinted at this function when he indicated that "many students who might not have the courage to enter upon a course of four years' study would be willing to do the two years of work before entering business or the professional school." [29]

Another early advocate of terminal education for the junior colleges was C. L. McLane, superintendent of the school system in Fresno, California. In his May, 1910, circular to the board of education, prior to the founding of California's first public junior college, McLane set forth as an aim of the Fresno Junior College the provision for terminal programs in "agriculture, manual training, domestic science, and other technical work." [30] By 1916 Lange, director of the School of Education at the University of California, insisted that "probably the greatest and certainly the most original contribution to be made by the junior college is the

[28] AAJC, Commission on Curriculum, *Minutes* (December 27–29, 1960, and December 26–28, 1961). AAJC Archives.
[29] William R. Harper, "The Small College—Its Prospects," National Education Association, *Addresses and Proceedings*, 1900, p. 83. Reprinted under the title *The Prospects of the Small College* (Chicago: University of Chicago Press, 1900).
[30] C. L. McLane, "The Fresno College," *California Weekly*, II (July 15, 1910), 539–40.

creation of means of training for the vocations occupying the middle ground between those of the artisan type and the professions." [31]

Other leaders in the junior college movement attempted to temper the liberal arts attitude of the junior colleges. For example, William H. Snyder, superintendent of schools at Los Angeles, introduced technical programs at Los Angeles Junior College when he took over the junior college program in 1929. He inaugurated a successful program for bankers. Other junior colleges in California added technical programs, and the state took the lead in the development of such curricula.

The Depression and Terminal Education

In addition to such forces as changes in the nature of the school population, the growth of technology, and urbanization, an important factor at work during the 1930's that gave impetus to the interest in terminal education was the economic depression. A majority of junior colleges reported increased enrollments, particularly in the number of local students.[32] As a result of the depression, many high school graduates who normally would have gone away to college found it impossible to raise sufficient funds to pay even nominal fees in addition to the cost of room and board. The depression did not reduce the desire of young people for college education but shifted the enrollment from higher- to lower-cost institutions. It also brought to the attention of many people the fact that the development of the junior college movement was more than a matter of low cost. The junior college thrived through the depression years from the accumulating need for an educational system better adapted to a rapidly evolving civilization.

AAJC Assumes Leadership

The AAJC early recognized the importance of the terminal function. At the 1920 organizational meeting the principal of the Chaffey Union Junior College of Agriculture in California insisted

---

[31] Alexis F. Lange, "The Junior College—What Manner of Child Shall This Be?" *School and Society*, VII (February 23, 1918), 211–16.

[32] Doak S. Campbell, "Effects of the Depression," *Junior College Journal*, III (April, 1933), 381–82.

that the junior college "must prepare young men and women for the most important vocations of their community."[33] The address immediately brought forth comments that clearly delineated the future discussions on terminal education and the junior college: Why couldn't the high school handle vocational courses and why should the junior college be responsible for all of this? Should the junior college offer merely vocational courses or should there be a certain amount of general education in the program? The third annual meeting of the Association raised still another issue; the need for recognition of a level between the vocations and the professions—namely, the area of semiprofessional training.[34] It is important to note that these questions are still being debated today.

Hardly a meeting of the Association throughout the 1920's and 1930's failed to discuss terminal education. The old problem of preparation for college versus preparation for life, long a prominent factor in the articulation between the secondary school and the college, now made its appearance in the relationship between the junior college and the upper classes of the four-year college. Despite all the speeches at the meetings of the AAJC on the importance of technical education, the junior colleges of the country continued to demonstrate that exhortation was the poorest means to secure change and continued to emphasize liberal arts programs at the expense of technical education.

The AAJC was aware that it had to take a leadership role in directing the movement for terminal education. The relative merits of the terms "vocational" and "semiprofessional" as applied to junior college education had come in for much discussion at meetings of the Association. There was confusion as to the distinction between the two; and there was the all-important question of which type of education was a legitimate function of the junior college. More and more it had become clear that students who entered the junior college were primarily interested in preparing

[33] Merton E. Hill, "Vocationalizing the Junior College," in George F. Zook (ed.), *National Conference of Junior Colleges, 1920, and First Annual Meeting of AAJC, 1921,* Bulletin of the U. S. Bureau of Education, No. 19, Part II (Washington: U. S. Government Printing Office, 1922), p. 19.

[34] Leonard V. Koos, "The Place of the Junior College in American Education," *Proceedings of the Third Annual Meeting of the AAJC,* 1923, p. 29. AAJC Archives.

to make a living and that they expected the junior college to mark the completion of their formal full-time education.[35]

The membership of the AAJC was also aware that two federal agencies, the Civilian Conservation Corps and the National Youth Administration, were spending large sums of money in attempting to meet some of the problems of American youth during the 1930's. C. C. Colvert in a presidential address was to admonish junior college educators for not performing their duty and thus forcing the national government to set up a separate agency, the N.Y.A., to educate the young people of junior college age.

Had not we of the junior college been so busy trying to offer courses which would get our graduates into the senior colleges instead of working and offering appropriate and practical courses—terminal courses— for the vast majority of the junior college students, we might have thought to ask for, and as a result of having asked, received the privilege of training these young people.[36]

The AAJC responded and at its meeting in March, 1939, the Committee on Vocational Education defined principles for terminal education and submitted recommendations for action by the Association. The report, adopted unanimously, stated in no uncertain terms that the membership felt that the Association and the junior colleges should encourage semiprofessional programs. First the committee tried to define terms. "Vocational education in the junior college," it said, "is best described by the word 'semi-professional' to distinguish it from professional or strictly trade training." [37]

The first recommendation of the committee stated that the Association should "actively encourage the amendment of existing state laws defining the function of the junior college so as to make easily possible the establishment of semi-professional curricula of a vocational type to meet the needs of youth as determined by

[35] Walter C. Eells, "Junior College Terminal Education," *Junior College Journal*, X (January, 1940), 244.

[36] C. C. Colvert, "Terminal Education and National Defense," *Junior College Journal*, XI (May, 1941), 496.

[37] Roscoe C. Ingalls, *et al.*, "Report of the Committee on Vocational Education in the Junior College," *Junior College Journal*, IX (May, 1939), 450–51.

modern social and economic conditions." [38] Another recommendation charged the Association with defining the public image of the junior college as a "community institution," and indicated that the community college should not imitate the first two years of the four-year college but create an effective program of vocational curricula of the semiprofessional type. The Association was asked to push for the amendment of the Smith–Hughes law so as to make federal money available to junior colleges offering technical education. The crux of the matter in the Smith–Hughes Act, from the junior college standpoint, is the stipulation that in order to obtain funds the education shall be less than college grade.

Commission on Junior College Terminal Education

Following the unanimous approval of the 1939 report, Byron S. Hollinshead, president of the Association, created the Committee of Eleven on Policy that later became the Commission on Junior College Terminal Education. The Policy Commission met in Atlantic City on September 1–2, 1939, to discuss and select the research that would be of greatest benefit to the junior colleges of the country, and also to give some attention to the formulation of plans for the development of such a study and to decide upon ways and means of carrying it out. Part of the impetus for the project very properly grew out of the belief over the years on the part of the members of the Association that there had been all the discussion that was necessary in regard to the place of the junior college in American higher education. What was needed now was an impressive study that would reveal something about the curricula of junior colleges.[39]

Campbell was unanimously selected as chairman of the meeting, and Eells was selected as secretary. Campbell indicated that the procedure for the deliberations of the Committee would be a consideration of junior college problems as a whole, followed by discussion of a specific problem with reference to a grant from a foundation. The agenda included the following topics for consideration for possible research:

[38] *Ibid.*, p. 451.
[39] Interview with Doak Campbell, March 20, 1962.

1. Conditions under which junior colleges should be organized
2. Financing of junior colleges
3. Adult education in the junior college
4. Preparatory function
5. Terminal education in the junior college
6. Preparation and qualifications of staff
7. Methods of instruction
8. Standards for evaluation and accreditation[40]

In the course of the discussion, personnel and guidance, organization and administration, and public relations were added to the above list.

The list is an interesting illustration of the fact that these are the very same problems that have been considered by the Association from its inception until the present day. The problems have not changed; the emphasis has.

After discussion each member of the Policy Committee was asked to vote for the three studies listed which he thought were most needed at the present time. Terminal education was judged by far the most important, with eleven first-place votes. Personnel and guidance services was the second choice and adult education was the third.[41] The three areas that ranked highest were receiving the least amount of attention in the junior college programs.

Exploratory Study of Terminal Education

Robert J. Havighurst attended the meeting in Atlantic City in 1939. He represented the General Education Board, an institution incorporated by an act of Congress in 1903 with the stated object of promoting education within the United States.[42] The board had been sympathetic to the junior college movement and to the work of the Association. Campbell had entree to the General Education Board, and taking the beaten path to its offices in New York City had almost become standard procedure for the Association.

[40] AAJC, Policy Committee, *Minutes*, Atlantic City, New Jersey (September 1–2, 1939). AAJC Archives.
[41] *Ibid.*
[42] A. H. McDannald (ed.), *The Americana Annual* (New York: Americana Corporation, 1940), p. 329.

Havighurst, director of general education for the General Education Board, was impressed by the tentative proposals of the Association and made a favorable recommendation to the General Éducation Board. The board made a grant to the AAJC of $25,000 for a one-year exploratory study of terminal education in the junior college to begin January 1, 1940. The commission employed Eells to direct the project.

As early as July, 1940, however, it became evident to the Administrative Committee for the Commission on Terminal Education that a continuation study of junior college terminal education was necessary. The General Education Board finally approved a new grant for the continuation study although Eells, who envisioned an elaborate study costing a good deal of money, was unhappy with the project and insisted that he had been repudiated by the Association.

The study done on terminal education may be divided into two parts: a one-year exploratory study in 1940, and a three-year continuation study beginning in 1941. Out of the exploratory study came three publications.[43]

Another major activity of the exploratory year consisted of a series of twenty-four one-day state and regional conferences located so as to be accessible to most of the 600 junior colleges in the country at the time. The object of these conferences was to "report progress and findings to date, solicit suggestions for continued development of the study, and promote an understanding through press releases, by parents and the public of the important nature of terminal education in the junior colleges." [44]

The year of exploratory study did more than produce the publications and conferences. It raised some very important questions as to the nature of terminal programs in the junior college as well

[43] Lois E. Engleman and Walter Crosby Eells, *The Literature of Junior College Terminal Education*, contains classified and indexed references to some 1,512 books, articles, monographs, and studies dealing with phases of junior college terminal education during the years 1900 to 1940. Eells, *Present Status of Junior College Terminal Education*, and Eells, *Why Junior College Terminal Education?* complete the trilogy. A fourth monograph was published which did not deal directly with terminal education. This was Eells, *Associate's Degree and Graduation Practices in Junior Colleges*.

[44] Walter C. Eells, "Executive Secretary's Report," *Junior College Journal*, XI (May, 1941), 503.

as to the functions of junior colleges. In addition it engendered great interest on the part of individuals and organizations throughout the country. Once again, it raised the very fundamental question—is terminal education to be vocational or semiprofessional? It was the fundamental difference between the California approach and the approach of the junior colleges in the East.

The Continuation Study

The three-year continuation study allocated $60,000 directly to nine individual colleges for special experimental studies and made a grant of $45,500 to the Association to carry on activities in 1941–43. The General Education Board designated the institutions to participate in the study.[45] The Association used a good part of the grant for workshops for junior college instructors and administrators. Army officials warned educators to speed up training and to offer more short terminal courses to help the all-out war effort of the nation. In order to help foster such programs, workshops were held on three campuses in the summer of 1941. One hundred and twenty-nine faculty members representing ninety-seven junior colleges located in thirty states were able to to attend the programs at the University of California at Berkeley, the University of California at Los Angeles and George Peabody College for Teachers at Nashville.[46] The war effort gave increased interest to terminal education and added a sense of urgency to these workshops. In the summer of 1942 conferences were held at Harvard University, the University of Chicago, and the University of California.[47]

Any attempt to evaluate the results of these workshops is extremely difficult. Leland L. Medsker, secretary of the Administrative Committee, Commission on Junior College Terminal Education, indicated at the twenty-second meeting of the AAJC that

[45] These institutions were: Bakersfield Junior College, Los Angeles City College, Pasadena Junior College, San Francisco Junior College, all in California; Meridian Municipal Junior College, Mississippi; Rochester Athenaeum and Mechanics Institute, New York; Scranton-Keystone Junior College, Pennsylvania; Weber College, Utah; Wright Junior College, Illinois.

[46] AAJC Commission on Junior College Terminal Education, Second Annual Report, *A Report on Terminal Education in Junior Colleges* (Washington, D.C.: American Association of Junior Colleges, 1942), p. 9.

[47] *Ibid.*, p. 65.

there "were certain definite values gained from the workshops held in 1941." [48] One of these values was that the participants brought with them individual problems on which they wanted to work, and these problems were followed through successfully. A second result was that these workshops gave impetus to terminal education as a legitimate function for the junior colleges.

"Inspirational and general values" were reported by participants in the workshops as results of their experience. [49] Probably few of those attending the 1941 summer workshops anticipated that the country would be at war even before the close of the coming fall semester. But whether they did or not, they found their workshop experience decidedly helpful in meeting the new and sudden, sometimes even drastic, adjustments necessitated by the war. Many of their once transfer-minded students now wanted terminal courses, and the adjustments had to be made. In those institutions less in sympathy with terminal education, the main problem for the workshop participants as they returned home seemed to be one of converting the faculty and administration to the terminal point of view; in those institutions already terminal minded, returning workshop participants could obtain more tangible results such as the inauguration of new courses and procedures.

In addition to these workshops, four regional conferences for junior college administrators were held from August 14 to November 22, 1944. Approximately 280 administrators attended these conferences. [50] Their purpose was to offer an opportunity for groups to get together and think through the problems which would face them in planning terminal education programs after the war, and to devise some plan which would be helpful in bringing about a more rapid adjustment to postwar needs.

The Southern Regional Conference, held in Atlanta, Georgia, pointed out the growing need for technicians as compared with the number of professionally trained personnel. [51] The Western

[48] Leland Medsker, "Reports on Study of Terminal Education," *Junior College Journal,* XII (March, 1942), 399.

[49] *Ibid.,* p. 26.

[50] Doak S. Campbell, "Report of Commission on Terminal Education," *Junior College Journal,* XVI (September, 1945), 27–29.

[51] C. C. Colvert (ed.), *Report of Terminal Education Conferences, Southern Region,* October 16–20, 1944. AAJC Archives.

Regional Conference, held in Boulder, Colorado, recognized that war made it necessary for the two-year colleges to engage in narrow job training but recommended renewed emphasis in the postwar period upon a broader program of terminal education providing social sensitivity and efficiency, as well as vocational proficiency. A recommendation made at this Western Conference (almost as if the participants could foresee one of the real problems in the next two decades) was that the junior colleges solicit the cooperation of teacher education institutions to provide an appropriately trained supply of teachers who would participate in and contribute to an adequate program of terminal education.[52]

Dr. H. L. Smith, vice-president of the North Central Council, summarized the North Central Regional Conference held in Chicago: "the junior college should serve the whole community and not simply a small fraction of the adolescents of college age. . . . It remains to be seen whether the currently established schools can achieve sufficient flexibility to meet the changing needs of today or tomorrow or whether new schools will have to be brought into existence." [53] The conference held at Rye, New York, for the Eastern Region completed the group of conferences.

The final stimuli to the growing interest in the terminal education movement at this time were the nine institutional studies sponsored by the Terminal Education Study. The nine institutions were selected by the General Education Board because of the progress that each of them had already made in the field for which it was chosen. The studies were subsidized by direct grants from the General Education Board, the institution itself making an additional subsidy.[54]

Growth of Technical and Semiprofessional Programs

What did all this work accomplish in terms of terminal education and the junior college movement? It is impossible to ascertain the number of junior college educators who were affected either

[52] Walter C. Eells, "Report and Discussion," *Junior College Journal*, XV (November, 1944), 130.

[53] Walter C. Eells, "Report and Discussion," *Junior College Journal*, XV (February, 1945), 272.

[54] For details of the institutions and the studies see Commission on Junior College Terminal Education, *A Report on Terminal Education in Junior College*.

way by these studies. Generally speaking, those who identified the junior college with secondary education were able to accept the technical function for the junior college. This was particularly true in California. Those who felt that the junior college was basically an institution of higher education looked askance at the terminal function.

The issues identified as a result of these studies pointed out directions for the junior colleges to follow. Graduate institutions were asked to train teachers who could teach technical subjects in the junior colleges. Evidently graduate institutions were not impressed with this plea for to date there are very few programs of this nature. Eells felt that the most important phase of the terminal education study and the one with the most far-reaching and lasting effects was the definite and systematic interpretation of the junior college movement to the public.[55]

While the studies called attention to the need for occupational education at the junior college level, the entrance of the United States into World War II unfortunately decreased their effect. However, the war replaced and reinforced them with two other developments. During the early part of the war effort, the junior colleges participated in defense training. These programs affected the colleges by giving them equipment, facilities, experienced personnel, and—perhaps most important—a favorable attitude toward this kind of education.

One of the defense programs that the junior colleges and the AAJC became involved with was the Civilian Pilot Training program. During the first year of operation under the Civilian Pilot Training Act of 1939, 150 junior colleges in thirty-five states trained over 5,000 students.[56] The AAJC had a national committee on aviation, and this committee took the lead in promoting aeronautical education in the junior colleges, helping to lobby for the extension of the Pilot Training Act when it ran out in 1944. The junior colleges also adapted their program to maintain a continuous flow of welders, riveters, lathe workers, machine operators, and other necessary workmen into the war industries.

[55] Eells, "Executive Secretary's Report," *Junior College Journal*, XI, 506.
[56] Walter C. Eells, *Wartime Letter No. 18*, June 17, 1944. AAJC Archives.

The enrollment of veterans in junior colleges was the second reinforcing element in the development of terminal education. At the beginning of the 1945 fall semester over 6,000 ex-servicemen entered junior colleges.[57] These were mature students who wanted to get their education over with in a hurry. Many of them felt that after spending two or three years in the service they could not afford four more years of educational preparation. The terminal programs of the junior colleges attracted a good number of them.

Two important studies in the 1940's gave the technical-terminal movement a real boost. The influential Educational Policies Commission of the National Education Association suggested in 1944 the desirability of providing in all states "one or two years of vocational education in technical and semi-professional fields combined with continuing civic and cultural education." [58] Three years later came the report of President Truman's Commission on Higher Education:

As one means of achieving the expansion of educational opportunity and the diversification of education offerings it considers necessary, this Commission recommends that the number of community colleges be increased and that their activities be multiplied.[59]

The role of semiprofessional training, the report continued, "can make a significant contribution to education for society's occupational requirements." [60]

It became increasingly apparent that a very sizeable percentage of the youth who went to college did not complete a full four-year course. The President's Commission observed that two-year graduates gained more from a terminal program specifically planned to meet their needs than from the first half of a four-year curriculum. The Commission therefore recommended that junior colleges emphasize terminal education programs.

The postwar years witnessed the quickening pace of technology

[57] Walter C. Eells, *Wartime Letter No. 3*, November 21, 1945.

[58] National Education Association, Educational Policies Commission, *Education for All American Youth* (Washington, D.C.: Educational Policies Commission, National Education Association, 1944), p. 326.

[59] United States President's Commission on Higher Education, *Higher Education for American Democracy* (New York: Harper & Brothers, 1947), pp. 67–68.

[60] *Ibid.*

and the intensification of the demand for highly trained personnel. Much of the recent concern with scientific and technical manpower, it is true, resulted from reports on the Soviet Union's emphasis on the training of scientists and engineers rather than from the work done by professional associations. Sputnik, not speeches, made acceptable the concept of highly trained manpower, particularly technical personnel, trained in post-high school situations, in order to meet the nation's needs.

A growing population, coupled with rising living standards, an increasingly complex society, and the technology that is so much a part of it, are the basic forces responsible for the changing occupational trends occurring in the United States. Studies by the dozens indicate that the most significant changes in the labor force, and in society in general, have occurred at the level of the semi-professional and technical, the managerial, the business and sales, and the highly skilled jobs. Various statistical projections state that these jobs, taken together, will account for over 50 per cent of the labor force by 1970.[61]

The Challenge of the '60's

The issue today is in clear focus. The challenge is clear that higher education must provide the means by which individuals in our society may keep pace with the modern world. Congressman John Brademas of Indiana introduced a bill into the House of Representatives in 1962 which called for federal support of technical training in colleges.[62] At the forty-second annual meeting of the AAJC in February, 1962, Brademas told the Association membership that it was essential to start "a program to stimulate the training of greatly increased numbers of engineering technicians, people with the equivalent of two years of college level training, to assist our engineers and scientists and to multiply their effectiveness." [63] The congressman pointed out that the vocational

[61] For a discussion of occupational trends and their implications see Ralph R. Fields, *The Community College Movement* (New York: McGraw-Hill Book Co., 1962), pp. 287–95.

[62] H. R. 10396, introduced on February 26, 1962, 87th Congress.

[63] John Brademas, "Education, Manpower, and National Needs," p. 3. Mimeographed transcript of remarks made by Brademas in a film made exclusively for the 42nd annual convention of the AAJC, February 27–March 2, 1962, Denver, Colorado. AAJC Archives.

training and trade schools at the high school level could not train the required technicians.

The leadership of the Association supports the principles of the Brademas Bill. The present executive director, Edmund J. Gleazer, Jr., has emphasized that vocational training beyond the high school interwoven with general education is, and ought to be, a major concern of the junior college.[64]

Norman C. Harris, associate professor of technical education at the University of Michigan, in March, 1962, lent support to this point of view by insisting that today's high school education does not give adequate preparation for the technical jobs that will exist by 1970. He pointed out that "these are the jobs for which liberal arts colleges and universities are increasingly denying any responsibility. These are the jobs, and these are the demands of our society, for which . . . the community junior college is uniquely fitted." [65]

The forces arrayed against the Brademas Bill are basically two. First there is the group that feels that the support given to vocational education of less than college grade, through such acts as Smith–Hughes and George–Barden, is sufficient to meet the manpower needs of the country. They fail to understand that developments in science and technology in the past twenty-five years have been so rapid that we need persons trained for new jobs for which vocational or trade education in the high schools is inadequate.

The other force is a much more powerful one. It is the tradition which decrees that only the academic-minded are educationally worthwhile. There is a tendency to look down on education for work. American parents have desired for their children upward occupational and social mobility which they consider obtainable only through liberal or professional education. University curricula and their equivalents still have a halo and glamor for a

[64] Interview with Edmund J. Gleazer, Jr., Executive Director, AAJC, May, 1962, Washington, D.C.; Edmund J. Gleazer, Jr., "Facing Up to Basic Ideas in the Junior College Field," an address before the third annual Summer Work Conference for Community and Junior College Administrators, Teachers College, Columbia University, June 18, 1962.

[65] Norman C. Harris, "The Community Junior College—A Solution to the Skilled Manpower Problem," p. 4. Mimeographed paper presented at the 17th National Conference on Higher Education, sponsored by the Association for Higher Education, Chicago, Illinois, March 5, 1962. In the possession of the author.

vast majority of students and their parents; and one should not underestimate the desire for a four-year degree. Professional education is looked to as a short cut to fortune and fame.

Through the Commission on Curriculum the AAJC again has attempted to give direction to junior college technical education, identified as the field most in need of study in the next decade.[66] Representatives of the Curriculum Commission and of industry and government met at a conference in New York on July 10, 1962, to consider junior college programs in technical education designed to meet the specialized manpower needs of industry. The Curriculum Commission then took upon itself the task of studying the technician, his education and training, what industry requires of him, and the various jobs open to him.[67]

The success of the AAJC in achieving public and junior college acceptance of technical education in institutions of higher education will determine whether the prophecy that H. L. Smith made in 1945 to the North Central Regional Conference will come true. He had indicated that either the community colleges would be flexible enough to adopt technical education as their legitimate function, or another group of schools would be created to meet these needs.

The vocational education group is waiting eagerly in the wings for its cue.

TECHNICAL NURSING EDUCATION

Junior colleges have participated in nursing programs in a variety of ways for many years. At a meeting of the Association of Colleges and Universities of the Pacific Southwest in 1933, Ray Lyman Wilbur, president of Stanford University, speaking of the school economy controversy, stated that Los Angeles County had saved $150,000 by letting the junior colleges train nurses instead of training them in the public hospitals.[68] In 1937 the National League

[66] AAJC, Commission on Curriculum, *Minutes* (December 26–28, 1961). AAJC Archives.

[67] *Junior College Newsletter*, XVII (July, 1962), 1.

[68] Walter C. Eells, "Reports and Discussions," *Junior College Journal*, IV (October, 1933), 48.

for Nursing Education stated that two years of education beyond the high school was essential to nursing education. By 1943 more than 200 junior colleges offered pre-nursing curricula.[69] All this activity, however, was directed at programs which were typical transfer programs and not specifically developed for nursing.

Response to War Needs

War gave impetus to the training program for nurses. On June 15, 1943, President Roosevelt approved the Bolton Act, which provided liberal federal funds to train 65,000 new nurses who, it was conservatively estimated, had to begin their training in that year to meet only the minimum needs in the field.[70] The Bolton Act established the U.S. Cadet Nurse Corps, which offered junior college students and graduates an opportunity to train with pay. It recognized that the girl who had at least two years of college background in addition to her training as a nurse would be better equipped to make rapid professional advancement.

The executive secretary of the AAJC encouraged junior colleges to bring to the attention of their students the advantages of the nursing profession and the advantage of membership in the Cadet Nurse Corps. He also urged junior colleges to offer their instructional facilities to nearby schools of nursing.[71] Eells represented the AAJC during the war years at many emergency meetings which attempted to find a place for the junior colleges in the education of nurses. In 1943 the National Nursing Council for War Service invited Eells and Jesse Bogue, then President of the AAJC, to attend a two-day institute in New York. They were the only men at the meeting, an experience recalled by Eells as both "novel and not unpleasant." [72]

The executive secretary of the Association in 1944 attended meetings of the newly appointed National Committee on Recruitment of Student Nurses. The committee of twenty members, rep-

[69] Compiled by Eells from reports furnished for publication in *American Junior Colleges* in 1940; supplemented by special reports received in Autumn, 1943. "Junior Colleges Offering Pre-Professional Nursing Curricula," December 31, 1943. Mimeographed. AAJC Archives.

[70] Walter C. Eells, *Wartime Letter No. 23*, July 28, 1943.

[71] *Ibid.*

[72] Walter C. Eells, *Wartime Letter No. 26*, October 9, 1943.

resenting various nursing, medical, and educational organizations, had as its immediate objective the recruitment of at least 65,000 urgently needed new student nurses.[73] Eells worked with the National Nursing Council for War Service to coordinate the visits of a selected group of nursing representatives to junior college campuses in order to begin a long-range program of counseling and education.

These activities indicate the interest of the junior colleges and their Association in nursing education. In addition, the agenda of the twenty-fourth annual meeting of the Association included Marion G. Howell, dean of the Frances Payne Bolton School of Nursing at Western Reserve University, who spoke on nursing education.[74]

While all these efforts were responses to emergency war needs, C. Maud Lynch, consultant in public information of the National Nursing Council for War Service, voiced the thoughts of the AAJC when she indicated that junior college administrators had expressed hope that they and their students would continue to be in touch with the needs and opportunities in nursing. "They have come to feel," she said, "that nursing is no longer a step-child among professions for college women, nor is it merely an emergency profession. They regard it as an expanding profession in which their graduates may find useful and successful post-war careers." [75] The same attitude was revealed at a meeting held in Chicago in the fall of 1945 where heads of junior college regional associations met in an all-day conference with representatives from the field of nursing education.[76]

Nursing Education Reform

One can trace the demands for educational reform in nursing education to the establishment of the first schools of nursing in

[73] Walter C. Eells, *Wartime Letter No. 33* and *Wartime Letter No. 37*, March 9 and June 7, 1944.

[74] Marion G. Howell, "Nursing Education for Junior College," *Junior College Journal*, XIV (April, 1944), 339.

[75] C. Maud Lynch, "The Junior College—A Source of Nurses," *Junior College Journal*, XV (April, 1945), 367.

[76] Dorothy M. Bell, "Nursing Education," *Junior College Journal*, XVI (November, 1945), 130.

1873.[77] A study by Josephine Goldmark in 1923 pointed out the difficulties of operating schools under hospital management and also suggested the possibility of reducing the training period. A later study confirmed Goldmark's findings.[78] These studies, and other reports published in 1948 [79] and 1950,[80] called attention to the need for a re-examination of hospital-controlled nursing schools and recommended the development of more nursing programs in institutions of higher education. Coupled with the demands for reform of nursing education were studies that indicated the growing need for nurses.[81]

This set of circumstances made it almost inevitable that the junior colleges of the country would become involved in experimentation in education for nursing. The demand for such experimentation was present. In addition, such experiments as that conducted in Canada under the auspices of the Canadian Nurses' Association by the Metropolitan School at Windsor, Ontario, as well as evidence in the United States in connection with the Cadet Nursing Program during World War II, demonstrated that one could prepare capable nurses in less than three years.[82] Add the fact that the President's Commission on Higher Education had focussed attention upon the junior college as a source of personnel for new and rapidly developing occupations, and the results could be foretold.

Joint Nursing Committee

The junior colleges for years had attempted to find a place for semiprofessional programs in their curricula, and their interest in

[77] For a discussion of the history of nursing education see Walter E. Sindlinger, "Experimentation in Education for Nursing at Orange County Community College" (unpublished Doctor of Education project report, Teachers College, Columbia University, 1956), chapter 1.

[78] Committee on the Grading of Nursing Schools, *Nursing Schools Today and Tomorrow* (New York: Committee on Grading of Nursing Schools, 1934).

[79] Esther Lucile Brown, *Nursing for the Future* (New York: Russell Sage Foundation, 1948).

[80] National Committee for the Improvement of Nursing Services, *Nursing Schools at the Mid-Century* (New York: National Committee for Improvement of Nursing Services, 1950).

[81] Mildred L. Montag, *Community College Education for Nursing* (New York: McGraw-Hill Book Co., 1959), p. 12.

[82] Walter E. Sindlinger, "Experimentation in Education for Nursing at Orange County Community College," pp. 35–37.

nursing was of long standing. The increased involvement of junior colleges led in 1949 to a proposal by the National League for Nursing Education to the AAJC that the two organizations form a committee to explore ways in which junior colleges could participate more effectively in nursing education.[83]

The Joint Nursing Committee met early in March, 1950, and reached agreement that the preparation of nurses should be a responsibility of the school system of the nation. They further agreed that the junior college was a logical place for this preparation to take place. In concluding its report, the Joint Nursing Committee recommended the establishment of a national advisory committee composed of representatives of junior colleges and national nursing organizations. The job of such a committee would be: (1) to develop guides for experimental programs in junior colleges; (2) to study the problems of an adequate program and staff; (3) to obtain funds for a consulting service to those junior colleges interested in the establishment of experimental programs in nursing; and (4) to study the problem of students who transfer from junior colleges to collegiate schools of nursing.[84]

The Board of Directors of the AAJC adopted the report and presented it to the members of the Association at the annual convention in March, 1950. The endeavors of the Joint Committee helped nursing educators understand the philosophy and characteristics of educational programs leading to associate degrees "and to envision the potentialities of associate degree programs in nursing." [85] Although the AAJC and many junior college administrators wished to start experimental nursing programs, the need for guides to help plan the proposed nursing program was soon apparent.

Mildred L. Montag, professor of nursing education at Teachers College, Columbia University, in 1951 proposed a nursing curriculum designed specifically for junior colleges.[86] In her report Mon-

[83] National League for Nursing, *Report on Associate Degree Programs in Nursing* (New York: National League for Nursing, 1961), p. 1.

[84] AAJC Board of Directors, *Minutes* (March 26–29, 1950). AAJC Archives.

[85] National League for Nursing, *Report on Associate Degree Programs in Nursing*, p. 1.

[86] Mildred L. Montag, *The Education of Nursing Technicians* (New York: G. P. Putnam's Sons, 1951).

tag stated that the nursing technician could be educated and trained in two academic years and then proceeded to show how to do it. Montag also believed that the junior college could best accomplish the preparation of the nursing technician.

The Joint Committee, in order to implement these recommendations, sought research funds from private foundations for the establishment of experimental programs in nursing. The Kellogg Foundation was interested but did not award a grant. This foundation, and others, believed that a university and not the Joint Committee was a proper agency to conduct organized research. In addition, the Kellogg group indicated that experimental programs in junior colleges were not kinds of projects it wished to support.

Cooperative Research Project

A coordinated program of research was assured in 1952 when the Division of Nursing Education of Teachers College, Columbia University, received a $110,000 grant from Mrs. Nelson Rockefeller.[87] The project, known as the Cooperative Research Project in Junior and Community College Education for Nursing, was to run for five years, from 1952 to 1956, and was placed under the direction of Mildred Montag. The purpose of the project was to see if junior colleges could develop programs which would prepare "bedside nurses who could qualify for licensure as registered nurses and who could meet the institution's requirements for an associate degree." [88]

Teachers College appointed an advisory committee early in 1952 composed of college administrators and nursing educators. The AAJC nominated junior college representatives to the committee. The AAJC, through its Curriculum Committee on Nursing, worked closely with the Cooperative Research Project at Columbia University. At the annual meeting of the Association in 1952, members of the staff of the project reported the progress of experimentation with the two-year nursing program. The Board

[87] AAJC Board of Directors, *Minutes* (January 11, 1952). AAJC Archives.
[88] National League for Nursing, *Report on Associate Degree Programs in Nursing*, p. 1; for more detailed information about the project see Montag, *Community College Education for Nursing.*

of Directors of the Association endorsed the project, promised continued support by providing opportunities for reports and discussion at the annual meetings and by issuing progress reports in the *Junior College Journal,* and approved the continuation of the Joint Committee on Nursing Education. It also authorized the committee to develop a set of guiding principles for nursing education in junior colleges subject to final approval by the board.[89] The membership of the AAJC had always guarded their right to control their own educational programs.

The Joint Committee continued to meet annually and to coordinate the development of nursing programs. The exciting years of developing a new concept in nursing education faded into history. By 1962 the period of experimentation was over. Two major foundations were supporting the development of nursing programs.[90] The nursing issues raised at the AAJC meetings in the 1960's were of small import. What is important, however, from the point of view of the history of the AAJC, is that in response to societal demands a voluntary organization teamed up with another national group to experiment in an area of curriculum development. Not only did the AAJC help establish guidelines and standards for this program but also it suggested an approach that other areas of curriculum development could use.

CONTINUING EDUCATION

The 1960's have witnessed a great deal of emphasis on the concept of continuing education. In a 1962 Valentine's Day press conference, President Kennedy reported that automation had become such a pervasive factor in modern life that we will have to find 25,000 new jobs every week for the next ten years for people displaced in business and industry by machines. "This state of affairs," he said, "constitutes the major domestic challenge of the sixties." [91] According to W. Willard Wirtz, Secretary of Labor, the

[89] AAJC Board of Directors, *Minutes* (March 10, 1954). AAJC Archives.
[90] The Kellogg Foundation and the Sealantic Fund.
[91] "President Ranks Automation First as Job Challenge," *New York Times,* February 15, 1962, p. 1.

President underestimated. The figure should have been 35,000. James Reston of the *New York Times* pointed out that one of the most remarkable things about these pronouncements is that hardly anyone has paid any attention to them.

Early developments

Some attention has been paid to adult education. While the concern here is not with the historical details of the adult education movement, it might be meaningful to suggest some of its historical forerunners. The first forms of adult education in this country were probably clubs, lecture series, public forums, and the like, rather than organized classes. Lyceums, correspondence schools, women's clubs, and "chautauquas" are early examples of adult education. William Rainey Harper drew upon his experiences at the original Chautauqua Institution when he instituted summer sessions and correspondence courses at the University of Chicago.[92]

A factor in the early development of adult education was the "Americanization" classes developed to meet the demands for acculturation of the great number of immigrants, and also as a response to a growing spirit of nationalism aroused by World War I.

Nineteen twenty-six was a turning point in the adult education movement. In that year adult education "ceased to be a combination of sporadic and scattered impulses and began to take shape as an organized pattern within both our public school system and many of our urban collegiate institutions." [93]

Junior Colleges and Adult Education

While the adult education movement picked up momentum, the junior colleges did not see this phase of education as their responsibility. One of the earliest studies of the junior college, made by McDowell in 1920, did not even mention the adult education

[92] Lyman Bryson, *Adult Education* (New York: American Book Co., 1936), pp. 20–21.

[93] *Ibid.*, p. 24.

function, nor did studies made in the following decade.[94] At last, the October 1934 issue of the *Junior College Journal* carried an editorial which pointed out that one of the greatest opportunities for significant service by the junior college was the challenge to originate a workable program for adult education.[95] At the fifteenth annual meeting of the AAJC in 1935, Eells concluded that

adult education should be considered an integral part of the total program of the junior college, not an incidental adjunct to be curtailed or discontinued as an unnecessary frill at the first need for financial retrenchment.[96]

Junior colleges were somewhat belated in accepting responsibility in this field of work. Yet when given the opportunity to do so, administrators of junior colleges verbally supported the idea of adult education. The AAJC Committee on Junior College Adult Education sent a questionnaire to 610 junior colleges in 1941 and received replies from 457. It asked the administrators to express their opinions on a number of questions related to whether the Association should undertake a comprehensive national study of junior college adult education. Eighty-five per cent responded affirmatively to the question as to whether there was a need for such a study. Seventy-five per cent indicated that the results of such a study would be of value to their institutions.[97]

Forces Fostering Increased Interest

Several forces were at work to foster increased interest and enrollment in adult education in the junior colleges. First, junior colleges had been realizing increasingly that they were community-serving institutions. As they oriented their work to the community rather than to senior colleges and universities, it became clear that

[94] F. M. McDowell, *The Curriculum of the Junior College,* U. S. Bureau of Education, Bulletin No. 19, part I (Washington, D.C.: Government Printing Office, 1922); Leonard V. Koos, *The Junior College Movement* (Boston: Ginn and Co., 1925), pp. 16–28; Doak S. Campbell, *A Critical Study of the Stated Purposes of the Junior College* (Nashville, Tenn.: George Peabody School for Teachers, 1930); Walter C. Eells, *The Junior College* (Boston: Houghton Mifflin Co., 1931), pp. 190–350.

[95] E. G. Brothers, "The New Deal and the Junior College," *Junior College Journal,* V (October, 1934), 2.

[96] Walter C. Eells, "Adult Education as Carried on by California Junior Colleges," *Junior College Journal,* V (May, 1935), 448.

[97] Joseph Hackman, "Report on Adult Education to 21st annual meeting of the AAJC," *Junior College Journal,* XI (May, 1941), 571.

the education of adults fell definitely within their sphere of operation. Second, the years of depression during the 1930's stimulated interest with clear-cut needs that had to be met. It was necessary for institutions to provide training for the young men and women who graduated from high school annually but who could not afford to enroll in day classes. Third, World War II brought far-reaching demands for specialized training. Many mature men and women, high school graduates and nongraduates, needed more training; and they felt that they could profit most if the work were on the college level. Fourth, the efforts of the AAJC and other organizations kept the junior colleges aware of the part they could play in adult education. The American Association of Adult Education, of which the AAJC is a member, and the President's Commission on Higher Education encouraged the expansion of programs for older students and looked to the junior colleges to help in this area.[98]

Despite the growing interest, only a small group discussed adult education at the 1952 AAJC convention; the convention analyst felt that it contained only those persons who were fully committed to the importance of continuing education and its place in the program of junior colleges.[99] Though many junior colleges were doing a remarkably effective job, many others were not aware of their responsibility and opportunity to provide education for adults.

The Curriculum Commission in recent years has recognized the importance of adult education and has made this one of its priority projects. While it is not the peculiar responsibility of junior colleges, those two-year institutions that are truly oriented to community service should perform a major share of the nation's total program for adults. With the increased emphasis on the value of education throughout life, with more leisure time, and with the increased need for retraining, continuing education is a new frontier in American education.

[98] Walter C. Eells, *Wartime Letter No. 37;* AAJC, *Minutes of the Thirty-First Annual Meeting* (March 4–8, 1951). AAJC Archives.
[99] Horn, "Convention Analysis," p. 36.

6

Professional Leadership:
Teachers and Students

THE CHIEF FUNCTION of the university is the discovery of truth. The chief function of the college, and especially of the junior college, is the transmission of truth and the training of youth. Therefore the training of members of the faculty for the university and for the junior college may be expected to differ somewhat in pattern and emphasis.[1]

With this editorial Walter Crosby Eells raised the question of the proper preparation of junior college instructors; and it has been a concern of the American Association of Junior Colleges ever since.

PREPARATION OF INSTRUCTORS

It is undoubtedly as true now as formerly that a college may consist of a teacher on one end of a log and a student on the other; but surely the success of the meeting of the minds depends on the type of teacher sitting on the log. An educational institution can be no stronger than its faculties; and the nature of the discussions that occurred at AAJC conventions indicates that the leaders of the junior college movement were aware of this truism.

Committee on Teacher Preparation

A Committee on Teacher Preparation was formally established by the AAJC in 1941. The Committee's report analyzed questionnaire returns from one hundred and five junior colleges repre-

[1] Walter C. Eells, "Preparation of Junior College Instructors," *Junior College Journal,* VII (November, 1936), 55.

senting seventy-two different institutions. In order to find out whether junior college administrators were satisfied with current candidates, the questionnaire had asked "do prospective instructors, newly from graduate schools, show characteristics of poor physical, mental, or emotional health that in your judgement should have had attention in the graduate school?" Slightly more than half of those replying to the question believed that candidates did show such weaknesses.[2]

Major shortcomings charged to the young graduates were summed up in nine findings: (1) instructors' preparation is frequently of a narrow and specialized nature; (2) instructors have the "content point of view" rather than "student point of view"; (3) they lack a suitable balance of subject matter and professional training; (4) they do not understand the junior college; (5) they fail to develop personality traits adapted to the dynamic leadership of youth; (6) they lack ability or knowledge to relate their teaching to practical everyday problems; (7) they are interested in research, not in classroom teaching; (8) they consider the junior college with an attitude of condescension; and (9) they lack appropriate work experience.[3]

The committee suggested that many of these weaknesses could be overcome by revising teacher training programs for junior college instructors. In planning this revision they strongly recommended that importance be attached to (1) training in guidance and counseling; (2) understanding of the philosophy and background of the junior college; (3) student teaching and observation in the junior college; (4) experiences in committee assignments and similar faculty services; and (5) emphasis upon the community nature of the junior college.[4]

The Committee on Junior College Teacher Preparation decided that part of its job would be to suggest practices and standards for the training of junior college teachers. In April, 1945, thanks to a gift of $2,500 by the American Council on Education, the AAJC invited representatives of the junior colleges and grad-

[2] David B. Pugh and Roy E. Morgan, "Faculty Needs and Requirements," *Junior College Journal*, XIII (May, 1943), 428.

[3] David B. Pugh and Roy E. Morgan, "Shortcomings in Preparation of Instructors," *Junior College Journal*, XIV (May, 1944), 405–15.

[4] Pugh and Morgan, "Faculty Needs and Requirements," p. 430.

uate schools of education and specialists from the U.S. Office of Education to a conference in Washington. The conference focused on the problem of the preparation of junior college teachers and made recommendations regarding the type of graduate training needed. Those attending the conference agreed that a sound graduate program would include (1) a strong liberal education, (2) adequate knowledge of subject matter fields, and (3) professional preparation to fit candidates specifically for the junior college.[5]

Growing Concern with Recruitment and Preparation

College administrators, with increasing urgency after World War II, sought teachers better prepared and more qualified than previously. Graduate schools, in their studies and reports, evidenced a growing awareness of their responsibility for recruiting talent and preparing it adequately for college teaching. In 1949 the American Council on Education and the United States Office of Education sponsored the Chicago Conference on the Preparation of College Teachers, already the subject of many conferences, research studies, and monographs.[6] However, the Chicago sessions (December 8–10, 1949) were the first nation-wide attempt to focus the thinking of educators from all sections of the country and who represented all aspects of higher education.

Harry J. Carman, dean of Columbia College, Columbia University, charged that college instruction was weak and second-rate. "The gap between educational intent and actual achievement," said Carman, "is wide and discouraging."[7] While he recognized that heavy enrollments, strained budgets, and unreasonable teaching assignments were not conducive to effective teaching, Carman thought that the principal cause for the weaknesses of instruction that characterized many liberal arts colleges lay "in the fact that our college teachers have not been selected with sufficient care and have not been prepared to teach." Carman asserted that it was a

[5] David B. Pugh, "Committee on Teacher Preparation," *Junior College Journal,* XVII (May, 1947), 388.

[6] See bibliography in Theodore C. Blegen and Russell M. Cooper (eds.), *The Preparation of College Teachers* (Washington, D.C.: American Council on Education, 1950), pp. 180–86.

[7] Harry J. Carman, "The Preparation of Liberal Arts Teachers," in Blegen and Cooper (eds.), *ibid.,* p. 15.

mistake to proceed on the assumption that knowledge of the subject and ability to do research in a chosen field of interest were
sufficient. He observed that one looked in vain for evidence of
purpose in classroom, lecture hall, and laboratory.

The only apparent purpose the observer can discover is to fill the in-
terval from bell to bell with another segment of the subject matter of
the course, which the student can and should acquire for himself. In
the wake of this purposeless procedure come habits of mind and of
work decidedly deleterious to both student and teacher. Here indeed
is human wastage.[8]

Carman concluded that every liberal arts teacher should (1) have
a broad knowledge of his own and related fields; (2) know more
about interpersonal relations in modern society and community
living; (3) have broad acquaintance with his profession; and (4)
possess an attractive personality.

Earl J. McGrath, then United States Commissioner of Education, made a distinction between the roles of graduate and professional schools. The primary responsibility of the graduate school
is to produce creative minds capable of the most original investi-
gative work; the training of men and women for professional practice, on the other hand, should be the responsibility of a professional division of a university. "The failure to recognize the
essential difference between the work of the scholar and research
worker and the work of the practitioners in the various professions," said McGrath, "and the consequent need for different educational programs for each has had particularly unfortunate conse-
quences in the case of college teachers." [9]

McGrath detailed the essential features of a program for the
education of college teachers. First, graduate schools should select
students in terms of their interest in teaching and in terms of the
qualities of mind and of character that appear to be associated
with good teaching. Second, graduate schools should broaden their
programs for future teachers. Third, graduate schools should pro-

[8] Harry J. Carman, "The Preparation of Liberal Arts Teachers," in Blegen and
Cooper (eds.), *ibid.*, pp. 16–17.

[9] Earl J. McGrath, "Graduate Work for College Teachers," in Blegen and Cooper
(eds.), *ibid.*, p. 34. McGrath was not present at the meeting but his paper was presented by Fred J. Kelly, Specialist in Higher Education, United States Office of Education.

vide professional courses in the program for the education of college teachers.[10]

At the end of the conference, the members unanimously adopted a resolution calling for the establishment of a national commission to forward projects for the improvement of the training of college teachers.[11] The following year the American Council on Education and the United States Office of Education sponsored a second conference in Chicago to consider the problems involved in improving the effectiveness of the already employed college teacher. The conference reaffirmed the resolution of the 1949 meeting and moved that the proposed national commission deal with the in-service development of college and university faculty members.[12]

Although the national commission never materialized, educators across the country were awakened to the immensity of the problem. The conferences had encouraged experimentation with various procedures for the preparation of college teachers, and had provided an opportunity to explore what the graduate schools ought to do with respect to their preparation.

Junior College Instructors

The majority of junior college instructors have been recruited from the ranks of experienced high school teachers. Suggestions have been long and loud that the junior college needed teachers with special preparation for the more distinctive responsibilities of the institution, whatever these may be. It was argued that if the junior college were a new type of institution, there should be a new type of instructor, "one that is not merely a glorified high school teacher, and one that is not a transplanted college professor." [13]

At the 1950 AAJC annual meeting William R. Wood, junior college specialist of the U.S. Office of Education, declared that the

[10] Earl J. McGrath, "Graduate Work for College Teachers," in Blegen and Cooper (eds.), *ibid.*, pp. 35–37.

[11] Appendix A in *ibid.*, p. 171.

[12] Fred J. Kelly (ed.), *Improving College Instruction* (Washington, D.C.: American Council on Education, 1951).

[13] William H. Conley, "The Junior College Instructor," *Junior College Journal,* IX (May, 1939), 507.

junior college teacher's basic concern would be people and not subject matter.

Certainly the teacher must know, or he can't teach; but knowing doesn't make him a teacher—not in the community college. His first responsibility, his point of beginning, is a study of the student. That study has no end. Let the cobwebs in our academic attic continue to multiply on the quaint and once prevalent notion that all you need to become a good teacher are enthusiasm and sufficient mastery of your subject.[14]

The junior college specialist warmed up to his task and called to account those people who were developing a feud over whether the junior college was "higher" education or "secondary" education. He called the feud as "futile and silly" as the feud between the liberal arts schools and schools of education.

A lot of hot air and hot ink will be shed before we hear the end of this one. And here come our old friends, the twin boogey men, respectability and prestige. I'm a college teacher. I'm a college administrator. I'm closer to God. I'm ashamed of myself. My job is to teach people. It is a humble task.[15]

Wood stressed that the junior college was a composite of educational services for older youths and adults. As long as the individual received the opportunity, it did not matter whether we labeled the opportunity "higher" education or "secondary" education. Wood expressed the hope that community college teachers would be too smart to get caught in the "what-level-is-it" squabble.

A 1950 work conference held at Teachers College, Columbia University, suggested differences between junior college teaching and other teaching. It charged the university with the preparation of junior college instructors who would be interested in students rather than in research, who would understand the psychology of the young adult, who would have a broad general education, "a community-mindedness, together with the ability to apply subject matter to the practical interests and concerns of the community college student." [16]

[14] William R. Wood, "Professional Personnel for Community Colleges," *Junior College Journal*, XX (May, 1950), 516.
[15] *Ibid.*, p. 519.
[16] Ralph R. Fields and Arthur H. Pike, "Community College Problems," *Teachers College Record*, LI (May, 1950), 533.

Although largely unheard by the rest of the populace, one of the noisiest disputes among university men in recent years has concerned graduate education in the United States. It will be of comfort to some and discomfort to others that the criticisms now being made of graduate education have been made, in much the same sort of language, ever since the establishment of the Association of American Universities in 1900. By 1909 the president of Harvard was deploring the "monstrous figures" attending graduate school; and in 1912 the dean of Columbia was disturbed because "proficiency rather than scholarship" seemed to be the result of graduate study. The most celebrated, and certainly the most entertaining, attack on the cult of the Ph.D. was made as early as 1903 by William James, who tangled with the many tentacles of the "Ph.D. octopus." [17]

At the 1929 convention of the AAJC, Henry Suzzallo of the Carnegie Foundation for the Advancement of Teaching anticipated the debates of the 1960's. He pointed to the need for men of broad training to teach in the junior college, and stated, in no uncertain terms, that the doctor of philosophy was not broadly trained.[18]

I object to the way in which many teachers' colleges and junior colleges are trying to borrow the 'peacock feathers' of the research man by insisting that their teaching faculties should be made respectable and half-effective for their own purpose by insisting that appointment shall wait on the acquisition of the doctorate of philosophy.[19]

Suzzallo laid down as requirements in the training of teachers for junior colleges broad undergraduate training as well as some orientation to education. He called on the AAJC to set up reasonable standards for the training of junior college teachers.

Innumerable studies of the junior college instructor and recommendations for his preparation poured from the mouths of

[17] For discussions of graduate education in the 1960's see Bernard Berelson, *Graduate Education in the United States* (New York: McGraw-Hill Book Co., 1960); Earl J. McGrath, *The Graduate School and the Decline of Liberal Education* (New York: Bureau of Publications, Teachers College, Columbia University, 1959); Oliver C. Carmichael, *Graduate Education: A Critique and a Program* (New York: Harper & Brothers, 1961).

[18] Henry Suzzallo, "The Training of Junior College Teachers," *Proceedings of Tenth Annual Meeting of AAJC*, 1929, 95-105. AAJC Archives.

[19] *Ibid.*, pp. 101–02.

speakers at AAJC conventions and from the pens of writers.[20] One junior college administrator suggested that the junior college instructor should possess certain professional characteristics. Among these should be: (1) a philosophy of education concerned primarily with general education; (2) breadth rather than narrow specialization; (3) recognition of teaching as the first duty, and of other activities as secondary and as aids to teaching; and (4) intellectual alertness which is measured by creative scholarship not necessarily in pure research. He indicated that the Ph.D. in itself did not establish the fitness of the junior college instructor. It did show, however, that the instructor was well trained, and if he were well trained and possessed the right point of view, "he can develop the distinctive background of the junior college instructor in a comparatively short period of time."[21]

In 1950 Leonard V. Koos directed a study for the AAJC Committee on Teacher Preparation, in an attempt to reach some agreement with regard to the kind of training that would prove most useful to teachers in the junior college. Koos and his associates concluded that neither the master's nor the doctoral program was well geared to the current need for teachers in junior colleges, particularly teachers of academic subjects. "The one-year program for the Master's seems too short," said Koos, "while the three-year program for the Doctor's is too long to be required of all academic teachers." [22] He thought that a two-year graduate program would be about right. He suggested the reorganization of the last two

[20] See *Proceedings of Ninth Annual Meeting of the AAJC,* 1928; George F. Zook, "The Problem of Teacher Education," *Junior College Journal,* VIII (May, 1938), 410–16; William C. Bagley, "A Unique Teaching Problem," *Junior College Journal,* VIII (May, 1938), 448–50; F. H. Dolan, "The Preparation of Junior Community College Teachers," *Junior College Journal,* XXII (February, 1952), 329–36; Harold J. Punke, "Academic Qualifications of Junior College Teachers," *Junior College Journal,* XXIII (March, 1953), 366–67, 370–79; L. L. Jarvie, "Making Teaching More Effective," in *The Public Junior College,* Fifty-fifth Yearbook of the National Society for the Study of Education, 1956, pp. 213–31; Thomas B. Merson, "Credentials for Junior College Teaching," and B. Lamar Johnson, "Six Problems in the Preparation of Junior College Teachers," in *Report of the California Statewide Conference on the Preparation, Credentialing, Recruitment and Placement of Junior College Teachers,* Calif. State Dept. of Ed., 1958, pp. 31–34, 5–11. Mimeographed.

[21] William H. Conley, "The Junior College Instructor," *Junior College Journal,* IX (May, 1939), 507–12. An address to 19th annual AAJC meeting, 1939.

[22] Leonard V. Koos, "Preparation for Community College Teaching," *Journal of Higher Education,* XXI (June, 1950), 315.

undergraduate years and one graduate year as a unified three-year span leading to the master's degree.

While it is difficult to identify valid criteria for evaluation of good teaching, there has been considerable agreement about the nature of the preparation of teachers for the junior college. This preparation should include good academic and professional education. The future junior college teacher should take courses that will help him understand and believe in the purposes of the junior college as an educational institution. He should be educated to work with adults in school and in the community and should be prepared as a teacher and not a researcher. A year's graduate work beyond the master's degree is commonly regarded as a desirable minimum.

AAJC Accomplishments

The AAJC and the junior college movement have not come very far in the area of teacher preparation since the 1930's, when Eells first raised the question of the proper training of junior college instructors. The need for well-trained junior college teachers still exists. The Commission on Instruction still discusses proper preparation of junior college teachers and effective in-service programs.[23] In order to improve instruction in the junior colleges, the AAJC has collected information on the backgrounds of junior college instructors and the practices of graduate schools and has compiled data about salaries and teaching loads. The Association has also sponsored studies to identify the competencies needed by junior college teachers and then recommended preservice and in-service programs necessary to achieve these competencies. The AAJC has disseminated such information at its meetings and through its publications.

Hope for the Future

Though the issues and recommendations have not changed much since the 1930's, two developments in the 1960's offer hope for the future. First, a grant from the Kellogg Foundation has enabled the Association to implement the work of the Commission

---

[23] Report of Meeting of the Commission on Instruction of the AAJC (March 1–5, 1960). Mimeographed. AAJC Archives.

on Instruction.[24] Second, graduate education has undergone critical self-examination in the 1960's and has responded in some measure to the demands for better prepared teachers. An example of this response was the announcement in the spring of 1962 by Teachers College, Columbia University, of the establishment of a Doctor of Education program designed to prepare undergraduate teachers. A doctoral candidate in this program specializes in his instructional field and also studies professional aspects of college teaching. "The emphasis will be on depth and breadth of scholarship rather than on the rather sharp specialization which characterizes many Ph.D. programs," said John H. Fischer, then dean of Teachers College. "While students will be well-grounded in research procedures, the new program is designed to produce scholarly teachers rather than research specialists." [25]

There has been tremendous growth in public awareness and concern for the general state of education. A shortage of college teachers exists. The time is ripe for the AAJC to take the lead and secure more and better prepared instructors for the junior colleges. The Association should constantly keep in mind that the quality of teaching is determined ultimately by the quality of the people who do the teaching.

STUDENT PERSONNEL SERVICES

Shortly after World War II, when veterans began to return to their communities fired with a desire for more education—due in part to an extensive educational system that the military services had developed, and to the availability of funds for education through government benefits—American educators suddenly realized that they were not prepared to meet these demands. Colleges and universities simply were not physically able to handle the great influx of entering students.

To many educators the situation did not appear alarming. Government benefits would run out eventually, the veterans would

---

[24] In the reorganization of the Committee system in 1959, the Commission on Instruction replaced the Committee on Teacher Preparation. The Commission planned in 1963 to establish six or eight experimental centers in universities for the preparation of junior college instructors.

[25] "College Teaching Ed.D.," *TC Topics*, vol. X, no. 3 (Spring, 1962), p. 1.

leave the colleges, and the institutions of higher education would return to a "normal" way of life. Other educators, however, were quite concerned. They realized that the war had contributed to a great social revolution in the country. Technological advancements had been rapid and created demands for highly trained, highly specialized workers. These workers required post-secondary educational programs. It was apparent, too, that people were more concerned than previously that each individual live a full, useful, and rewarding life.

A close examination of the birth rate further complicated the picture. For years it had risen steadily but slowly. Now the figures on the charts began to shoot upward at an alarming rate. Educators looked ahead twenty years and saw unprecedented numbers of young people ready to enter college.

Commission on Higher Education

On July 13, 1946, President Truman appointed a Commission on Higher Education to study and evaluate American higher education and to recommend action to meet future problems. The report of this commission, entitled *Higher Education for American Democracy,* opened with a discussion of the role of education in America.

It is a commonplace of the democratic faith that education is indispensable to the maintenance and growth of freedom of thought, faith, enterprise, and association. Thus the social role of education in a democratic society is at once to insure equal liberty and equal opportunity to differing individuals and groups, and to enable the citizens to understand, appraise, and redirect forces, men and events as these tend to strengthen or to weaken their liberties.[26]

A primary concern of the commission was the question: Who should attend college? The barriers to equal educational opportunities were another concern. After surveying the results of the Army General Classification Test, given some ten million men during World War II, the President's Commission estimated that 49 per cent of all youth of college age possess at least the minimum level of academic ability to complete the first two years of college,

[26] President's Commission on Higher Education, *Higher Education for American Democracy* (New York: Harper & Brothers, 1947), p. 5.

and that 32 per cent could successfully go on for more extended college and professional programs. Specifically, the commission recommended a doubled college and university enrollment by 1960, provision for universal free public education through the fourteenth year, federal scholarships, and elimination of inequalities resulting from racial segregation.

As might be expected, educators debated these recommendations. The Very Rev. Robert I. Gannon, then president of Fordham University, represented one point of view:

The fraud in the present campaign for educational inflation consists in spreading our national culture perilously thin and calling it "Democracy of Education." It consists in swelling the number of incompetents in American colleges and calling it equality of opportunity. . . . It has been a normal condition of American colleges for years that one-third of the so-called students were in the way, cluttering up the place and interfering with other people's intellectual progress. If we need more room to care for the boom in 1960, let us create a good part of it by clearing out the useless lumber that we have already.[27]

Chancellor William Pearson Tolley of Syracuse University represented the opposite point of view:

in every section of the report there is an earnest and sincere commitment to a democratic faith. The future of higher education is related to the struggle and growth and pattern of secondary education, to the levels and kinds of talents our young people possess, to the needs of technology for trained personnel, to the problems which beset a divided world, to the duties of citizenship, to the removal of inequalities, to the need for simple humanity, devotion, and intelligence in our relationship to persons and places, things and ideals.[28]

Growing concern about the values of higher education has paralleled the post-World War II preoccupation with numbers. The imminent influx of students in colleges and universities, and visions of the still greater crowds to come, have given impetus to searching consideration of educational values and objectives, of type of education for students who vary widely in interests, motives, dispositions, and abilities, and of the possibility of attaining a better "fit"

[27] Quoted in *Time*, LI, February 23, 1948, 52.
[28] James G. Harlow, "Five Years of Discussion," *Journal of Higher Education*, XXIV (January, 1953), 18.

between students and institutions. The oft-asked question, "Who should go to college?" has now become "Who should go where and for what?"

Claims and Accomplishments

The guidance function of the junior college is extremely important. The student in the junior college, representing the full range of characteristics of American college students, actually has less time at his disposal than the four-year student to make the proper choice of objective. Thus, the two-year student's need to determine the direction of his training is a more urgent one. The junior colleges have been more interested than the traditional colleges in providing some form of counseling for their students.

The importance of this function was recognized early. In 1927 Frank Waters Thomas designated guidance as one of the four principal functions of the junior college.[29] Educators, to the present day, have continued to stress the importance of guidance and counseling in the junior colleges. But the claims of the junior colleges have been presumptuous when compared with their accomplishments. What Thomas and other educators were identifying was more a hope than a reality.

In 1952, J. Anthony Humphreys, as spokesman for the Student Personnel Committee of the AAJC, expressed concern over some apparent deficiencies in student personnel programs. He concluded that (1) relatively few junior colleges had programs of personnel service adequate to meet the needs of their students; (2) student personnel service was not recognized in the institutions in sufficient degree as one of the major functions; (3) testing and counseling of students was not satisfactorily developed or pursued; (4) not enough professionally qualified personnel workers were available; (5) there was a lack of adequate in-service training of faculty counselors; and (6) the chief administrator or his assistant tended to carry too much responsibility in student personnel programs. Among the reasons contributing to the situation, Humph-

[29] Frank Waters Thomas, "The Functions of the Junior College," in William M. Proctor (ed.), *The Junior College* (Stanford, Calif.: Stanford University Press, 1927), pp. 11–25.

reys indicated, were the lack of acceptance of the personnel point of view, lack of money, lack of qualified personnel, lack of physical facilities, and insufficient time to implement and carry out a program.[30]

Leland Medsker included an investigation of personnel practices in his study of the two-year college which was published in 1960.[31] He summarized his conclusions in two categories: elements of strength and elements of considered weakness. As "strengths," Medsker listed: widespread acceptance of responsibility for personnel services, the establishment of "some level or type of counseling" in every junior college studied, the existence of well-developed student activity programs, and good systems of academic records in most colleges. As "weaknesses" he listed: (1) many institutions lack policy formulation, planning, and professional direction of the program; (2) the counseling program in many institutions is inadequate; (3) little research is conducted which enables the two-year college to obtain facts about their students; and (4) two-year colleges make only limited efforts to evaluate the personnel program.[32]

Despite Medsker's underlying note of pessimism, the AAJC recognized the function of student personnel services not as a frill but as a most important service, a worthy working partner of the function of instruction. Meetings hammered home to junior college administrators that classroom activities and contact with instructors outside the classrooms had to be supplemented by personnel services for complete realization of the broad education aims of the junior college.

The Committee on Student Personnel Problems

The establishment of the AAJC Committee on Student Personnel Problems in 1946 was one result of the canvass of opinion of junior college administrators concerning problems needing research. These men and women noted student personnel practices

[30] J. Anthony Humphreys, "Toward Improved Programs of Student Personnel Services," *Junior College Journal*, XXII (March, 1952), 382.

[31] Leland Medsker, *The Junior College: Progress and Prospect* (New York: McGraw-Hill Book Co., 1960), pp. 141–68.

[32] Medsker, *The Junior College*, pp. 161–64.

as one such important area. More specifically, relationships between junior colleges and high schools and procedures of placement and follow-up were found to be uppermost in the minds of
the administrators.[33]

The annual meeting held in Chicago in 1946 charged the committee with the responsibility of making a rapid survey of guidance practices for veterans in junior colleges. During 1946–47 the
committee made preliminary approaches to the investigation of
student personnel practices. It mailed a questionnaire to the administrative heads of approximately 650 junior colleges and published the results in three articles in the *Junior College Journal*.[34]

From late February, 1949, through March, 1950, the Committee on Student Personnel Problems worked toward the achievement of two goals: (1) the stimulation of a larger number of member junior colleges to develop more adequate programs of student
personnel service; and (2) the development of detailed procedures
and devices which would help junior colleges evaluate their student personnel services.[35]

In attempting to fulfill these goals the committee called for
teamwork on the part of the members of the AAJC through the
exchange of information about their several policies, practices,
and achievements. It seemed to the committee that there were
problems other than those of a research nature which merited
some consideration. Administrators, personnel workers, and others
who attended annual meetings and participated in the discussion
groups appeared anxious to know what other colleges were doing,
what they themselves could do to improve their student personnel services, and how best they could bring about improvement in
their own college. The service aspect of their duties became important to the committee. They pondered what they could do as a

[33] J. Anthony Humphreys, "Facts Concerning Student Personnel Programs,"
Junior College Journal, XIX (September, 1948), 9.

[34] J. Anthony Humphreys, "Facts Concerning Student Personnel Programs," p.
9; also William A. Black, "Student Personnel Relationships of High School and
Junior College," *Junior College Journal*, XIX (November, 1948), 145–50; and Char-
lotte Drummond Meinecke, "Placement and Follow-up in Junior Colleges," *Junior
College Journal*, XIX (October, 1948), 59–67.

[35] "AAJC Committee on Student Personnel Problems, Report to 30th Annual
Meeting of the AAJC," *Junior College Journal*, XX (May, 1950), 551.

national group to establish some kind of service for the interchange of ideas and procedures.[36]

Service Station Project

In 1953 the Service Station Project of the Student Personnel Problems Committee undertook to facilitate an interchange of ideas and information, and perhaps philosophies, concerning student personnel procedures among member colleges. The interchange was to occur by assembling, for redistribution to member colleges, packets of student personnel materials then in use in the colleges. To implement the project, regional associations cooperated by establishing committees which invited the participation of every junior college in the country. The committees collected the materials and made up packets which they sent to member colleges desiring them.

The Service Station Project, conceived with high hopes for service to the junior colleges of the country, died a rather ignoble death; by the late 1950's it had faded from the minds of the Student Personnel Committee and from the literature of the AAJC.

Student Personnel Commission

In the reorganization of the AAJC committee structure in 1960, the Committee on Student Personnel Problems became the Student Personnel Commission, and soon proved to be the most productive of the commissions. At its organizational meeting in December, 1960, in Washington, the commission proposed several projects. For short-term projects it chose to develop "How-to-do-it Bulletins" in the areas of guidance, testing, job placement, follow-up, and referral practices; to prepare a convention program on "Honesty in Colleges"; and to stimulate improved student personnel practices on junior college campuses. The commission hoped to achieve the latter by publicizing outstanding techniques in student personnel work in junior colleges.

For long-term projects it proposed the development of university centers for junior college counselor preparation and the

---

[36] F. Grant Marsh, "Service Station Project of the Student Personnel Committee," *Junior College Journal,* XXV (September, 1954), 29–30.

establishment of experimental centers in selected junior colleges to explore improved techniques of guidance, admissions, and related practices.[37]

Implementation of Short-Term Projects

To implement the project on the development of bulletins, the AAJC assigned Milton C. Mohs, dean of placement at Pasadena City College, California, to develop a bulletin on placement practices, and J. W. McDaniel, vice-president of San Bernardino Valley College, also in California, to construct one on student personnel practices. The AAJC published the two bulletins in 1962.[38] Two other publications are in preparation.

Samuel Neel, president of Manatee Junior College in Florida, directed the student honesty project. He originally conceived the project as a national survey of the practices in American junior colleges to curb cheating and to develop honesty in handling academic assignments. Pilot experiments in selected colleges were to try some of these systems and evaluate them. He also recommended the development of an annotated bibliography on the subject, as well as publication by the Student Personnel Commission of the findings of the various studies carried out in this area. He finally had to settle for a convention program devoted to the theme of student honesty; and this program was part of the forty-second annual convention held in 1962.

University Workshops

So far as the long-term projects were concerned, encouraging university centers to establish workshops for junior college counselors occupied a good deal of the time of the Student Personnel Commission. The Board of Directors of the AAJC, responding to a strong recommendation of the commission, asked eleven selected institutions to consider the establishment of workshops for junior

[37] For a complete report of the organization meeting of the Student Personnel Commission see AAJC, Student Personnel Commission, *Minutes* (December 8–10, 1960). AAJC Archives.

[38] J. W. McDaniel, *Essential Student Personnel Practices for Colleges* (Washington, D.C.: American Association of Junior Colleges, 1962); Milton C. Mohs, *Service Through Placement in the Junior College* (Washington, D.C.: American Association of Junior Colleges, 1962).

college counselors in the summer of 1961.[39] In the end, only three universities held workshops, attended by a total of twenty-eight junior college counselors. Nine attended the University of Texas, four the University of Michigan, and fifteen Michigan State University.[40]

While the AAJC recognized that each university should have the privilege of offering a program of its own design, it believed that the universities should cooperate in their plans and in the exchange of information. Junior college and university representatives conferred in April, 1961, and designated the kinds of experience that the proposed workshops would cover. While they agreed that each university should evaluate its own workshop, the commission would have the responsibility of evaluating the evaluation. "We in the Commission must become more active in defining workshop goals," said the report of the commission, "and in helping the universities understand what kind of programs are needed."[41]

And indeed, the commission did become more active in defining workshop goals for the universities, sometimes to the point of evoking a negative response by university representatives, who thought that the Association was overstepping its area of responsibility. In August, 1961, the Student Personnel Commission sent a questionnaire to junior college presidents in order to obtain recommendations to assist universities in planning workshops for 1962. They collected data on how many of their staff the presidents intended to send to a 1962 workshop; and they asked the presidents to identify the universities to which they would send their staff. They collected information on the suggested length of the workshop and what topics to discuss. They even gave themselves the responsibility of recruiting 250 junior college counselors to

[39]The eleven institutions selected were: University of California at Los Angeles and at Berkeley; San Jose State College; Los Angeles State College; Florida State University; University of Florida; Michigan State University; University of Michigan; Teachers College, Columbia University; University of Texas; and Washington State College. The AAJC invited these institutions on the basis of their having either a junior college leadership program or expressed interest in such a program, and their ability to handle such workshops effectively.

[40]AAJC, Commission on Student Personnel, *Minutes* (October 26–28, 1961). AAJC Archives.

[41]AAJC, Commission on Student Personnel, *Minutes* (October 26–28, 1961).

attend the 1962 workshops;[42] these actually enrolled 352 participants.[43]

Student Evaluation

Because junior colleges loomed large on the educational horizon of the 1960's, there was increased need for more attention to measurement of the educational effort and impact of these institutions. At the American Council of Education meeting in Chicago, October 5–6, 1960, Robert L. Ebel, vice-president of the Educational Testing Service, inquired of Edmund Gleazer whether the junior colleges had adequate testing services. Later in the month Ebel wrote to suggest a meeting with AAJC representatives to consider ways to improve tests and testing programs in junior colleges.[44]

Thomas Merson, director of the Student Personnel Commission, replied for the AAJC and expressed strong interest. He volunteered to poll selected junior college leaders in an attempt to get some idea of the merit of such cooperation, and to see if there was a need for new tests and if junior college test norms would be useful. After several preliminary meetings and discussions between representatives of the ETS and Gleazer and Merson, the AAJC Board of Directors endorsed the proposed meeting of the Washington staff with ETS representatives. But it expressed reservations, and suggested that the AAJC explore the resources of other testing agencies, and that junior colleges avoid increased reliance on tests for admission.[45]

Ebel then prepared "A Tentative Proposal for Junior College Testing Services" that the AAJC Student Personnel Commission discussed at length in October, 1961. The commission unanimously passed the motion "to encourage full exploration of the project." [46]

---

[42] AAJC, Commission on Student Personnel, *Minutes* (October 26–28, 1961). AAJC Archives.

[43] *Junior College Newsletter*, XVII (August, 1962), 2.

[44] *ETS-AAJC Conference on Junior College Testing*, November 8–9, 1961, Appendix. Mimeographed. AAJC Archives.

[45] AAJC Board of Directors, *Minutes* (July 16, 1961). AAJC Archives.

[46] AAJC, Commission on Student Personnel, *Minutes* (October 26–28, 1961). AAJC Archives. For text of proposal see *ETS-AAJC Conference on Junior College Testing*, Appendix.

Educational Testing Service and AAJC representatives met at Washington in November, 1961. A delegate from the American Council on Education and a delegate from the Department of Defense also attended. Junior college representatives from five states described tests and testing improvements needed in junior colleges. They also reported their evaluation of the desirability and feasibility of undertaking a national program directed toward improved junior college testing.

After a great deal of vigorous discussion, Ebel posed five questions for the junior college representatives to reflect upon. They were to come back the following day with their answers. The morning of November 9 proved that the junior college people had done a considerable amount of "homework." The reply of the junior college representatives to Ebel's questions indicated that a catalog of tests specifically useful in junior colleges would be helpful, but that better testing *per se* would improve junior college education. Junior colleges favored a testing program designed for the end of the sophomore year only if the tests would not become instruments for restricting admission to senior colleges or severe determiners of course content. They suggested that the next steps to take were to "identify junior colleges willing to serve as experimental centers and to compile a pool of talented junior college practitioners and test experts to develop test improvement programs without delay." [47]

The delegates at this meeting strongly believed that the impending increase in college enrollments, a rapidly changing society, and the dramatic changes in employment opportunities all imposed demanding responsibilities on the junior colleges of the nation. As the junior colleges prepared to meet these and other demands they had to use every means at their disposal to ensure every opportunity for maximum development of potential talent. The challenge of matching the diverse abilities, achievements, interests, and ambitions of the heterogeneous student body that enrolls in an open-door junior college, offering a wide spectrum of curricular opportunity, requires the use of the most precise predictors that can be assembled. The delegates felt that junior colleges required instruments of measurement designed specifically

[47] *ETS-AAJC Conference on Junior College Testing*, p. 15.

for their needs and for their students, rather than evaluation instruments designed for four-year colleges.[48]

Representatives from the ETS responded to the views of the junior college delegates by suggesting six projects considered necessary to start exploration of productive means of improving junior college instruction and guidance through better testing. These projects were:

1. To provide for the collection and dissemination of information on good measurement practices in junior colleges.
2. To develop data concerning aptitude scores useful to junior colleges.
3. To make available a testing program designed to assist in initial course placement of junior college students.
4. To explore the feasibility of a guidance testing program based on comparative prediction.
5. To relate research on new instruments to junior college interests.
6. To explore the feasibility of achievement testing programs appropriate for measuring educational development at the end of the second college year.[49]

The ETS representatives described the steps considered essential to carry out the six projects.

The junior college delegates received this report enthusiastically. Debates on project number six arose due to the known apprehension of some members of the AAJC Board of Directors regarding the possible misuse of information developed by testing sophomores. ETS stated that with or without AAJC support, it intended to move ahead on measurements of general education because so many junior colleges were asking for a substantial effort in this field.[50]

The conference finally endorsed all six projects and refused to concern itself with the politics of future action by the AAJC Board of Directors. It recommended a program that, in its opinion, would achieve the aims desired. If the AAJC Board chose to disregard its recommendations there would be time then to consider alternatives.

[48] "Proposal for Joint Action," *ETS-AAJC Conference on Junior College Testing,* Appendix.
[49] *ETS-AAJC Conference on Junior College Testing,* pp. 15–16.
[50] *Ibid.,* p. 16.

The Board of Directors of the AAJC at their January, 1962, meeting acted upon the report of the Conference on Junior College Testing. They expressed general agreement on the value and need of such a program, and indicated that the total recommended package was worthwhile to the junior colleges of the country. The board authorized the AAJC staff to proceed with projects one through six despite concern regarding project number six. They indicated that achievement testing for measuring educational development at the end of the second college year might become specific and exclusive to the junior colleges, and used as a tool that might restrict transfer to the upper division of four-year colleges and universities.[51]

At the 1962 convention the Commission on Student Personnel agreed to give top priority to project number two—to develop data concerning aptitude scores useful to junior colleges; and project number three—to make available a testing program designed to assist in initial course placement of junior college students.[52]

The AAJC generally accepts the idea that the success of junior colleges depends to a great extent on effective programs of admissions, testing, and guidance. In view of this fact the Commission on Student Personnel has attempted and continues to stimulate improved practices, and to uncover better means of serving students in the junior colleges.

[51] AAJC Board of Directors, *Minutes* (January 6, 1962). AAJC Archives.
[52] AAJC, Commission on Student Personnel Services, *Minutes* (February 26–27, 1962). AAJC Archives.

7

Professional Leadership:
Administration and Legislation

AMERICAN COLLEGES and universities perform two cardinal functions—the advancement and the diffusion of knowledge. These responsibilities have become indispensable to the security and welfare of the American people, and indeed of the world at large. Because higher education plays such a vital role in our society, and because the problems of the future are so complex, our educational institutions need better leadership and administrative direction than they have had. Administrative activity has increasingly become a universal concern of man. Administrators of social institutions as important as American colleges and universities must be dedicated to their task. They must "think, act and care deeply about individuals and society, institutions and education."[1]

GROWTH OF A PROFESSION

The American college has its roots in the great medieval universities of Europe. The earliest of these institutions—at Paris, Bologna, and Oxford—did not require administrators. They consisted of professors and students. Since the earliest colleges were places in which to reside, the administration of these institutions was merely a matter of housekeeping.

[1] Louis T. Benezet, "The Office of the President," in Gerald P. Burns (ed.), *Administrators in Higher Education: Their Functions and Coordination* (New York: Harper & Brothers, 1962), p. 108.

Historical Perspective

As recently as 1869, when Charles W. Eliot became president of Harvard University, there were only three other persons on its staff whom one might regard as administrators. They were a steward responsible for the dining hall, a regent in charge of dormitories, and a part-time registrar.[2] Until Eliot's day most college presidents had handled the presidency part time and had taught part time, but Eliot, bursting with plans to convert Harvard into a university, seems to have been the first college administrator to devote his full time to the presidency.

Neither Harvard nor any other American college until that time had had a dean, although the heads of the loosely associated professional schools held that ancient title. Determined not to be bogged down by student discipline as his predecessors had been, Eliot proposed to the Harvard governing boards that they establish the office of Dean of Harvard College. This they did in January 1870; and Eliot appointed Professor E. W. Gurney of the history department to the deanship on a part-time basis. All the present undergraduate deanships throughout the country date from Gurney's appointment. In 1890 Eliot divided the dean's responsibilities between two holders of the title, and thereby created the first office in American higher education to specialize in student personnel services.[3]

The expansion of the administrative function in higher educational institutions is well known. Harvard's administrative staff of three in 1869 had expanded by 1930 to some two hundred officers. One educator has estimated that in the 1940's there was one administrative officer for every six persons involved in instructional work in colleges and universities.[4]

The proliferation of administrative posts is a direct result of the extensive development of higher education in the last half-century. One hundred and sixty years ago no structural diversity existed in American higher education; today it teems with diver-

[2] Ronald C. Bauer, *Cases in College Administration* (New York: Bureau of Publications, Teachers College, Columbia University, 1955), p. 3.
[3] American colleges and universities had always performed these services, but until 1890 professors and presidents had handled them.
[4] Logan Wilson, *The Academic Man* (New York: Oxford University Press, 1942), p. 71.

sity. Collegiate institutions have grown not only in size but also in complexity and multiplicity of services. Enrollments have swelled and demands for increased services have brought to all campuses management problems related to physical plant, research institutes, budget and investment, business enterprises such as bookstores and cafeterias, housing, and the other extra-academic facets of a modern campus. In addition, specialization and expansion of knowledge have changed the nature of educational institutions so that participation by the administration is essential to achieving purpose and direction for colleges and universities.

Thus college administration has become a profession in itself, embracing numerous administrative specializations. "It is an inevitable development of the twentieth century, as inevitable as curriculum change, educational television, and inter-institutional cooperation." [5]

Changes in the Role of the Administrator

The growth in the size of institutions and parallel expansion of their functions have had a marked effect upon the role of the chief executive officer. Rudolph indicates that "the demands of growth, the tentacles of organization itself, the always certain uncertainty of a thousand loose ends—all this put the new university president into action on a broad front." [6]

College administration today requires not only well-trained technicians but also educational statesmen. The trend toward the decentralized administrative organization calls for an administrator who has a good working knowledge of the technical aspects of administration and who can use effectively the specialized services in finance, research, and public relations which his staff can provide.

At the same time, the administrator must be able to provide the kind of leadership that will move the faculty toward the achievement of the goals established for the institution. He must devote more time than did his predecessors to keeping his staff, the students, and the public informed about the problems confronting

[5] Bauer, *Cases in College Administration*, p. 4.
[6] Frederick Rudolph, *The American College and University* (New York: Alfred A. Knopf, 1962), p. 420.

the college and how he intends to solve them. He must be able to aid the faculty in defining issues that require study. He must keep abreast of the latest developments in both secondary education and higher education. He must be able to work with representatives of business and industry. Above all, he must be a spokesman for education.

Rutherford B. Hayes, a member of the Ohio State University Governing Board in the early 1890's, vividly described the president which university governing boards seek—even unto today.

We are looking for a man of fine appearance, of commanding presence, one who will impress the public; he must be a fine speaker at public assemblies; he must be a great scholar and a great teacher; he must be a preacher, also, as some think; he must be a man of winning manners; he must have tact so that he can get along with and govern the faculty; he must be popular with the students; he must also be a man of business training, a man of affairs; he must be a great administrator.

Hayes wisely commented to his colleagues on the Ohio State Board, "Gentlemen, there is no such man." [7]

While there may not be "such men," administrators still are more and more in positions that control the behavior and direction of individuals and of groups. The responsibility is awesome, and demands statesmen, not mechanics. They must possess both vision and principles.

The Preparation of Administrators

In the past decade administration has achieved greater recognition as a distinct professional field in education. The idea that individuals can prepare at the graduate level for administration is relatively new and still controversial. The fact remains, however, that successful administration demands executives with thorough preparation for the task of higher educational leadership today.

Algo Henderson, director of the Center of Higher Education at the University of Michigan, accepted the validity of the premise that college administration is a profession and in addition suggested that the top administrator should be an educator, organizer,

[7] James E. Pollard, *History of the Ohio State University: The Story of its First Seventy-Five Years, 1873–1948* (Columbus: Ohio State University Press, 1952), p. 136.

a keen judge of people, possess some understanding of finances, and have an understanding of public relations.[8]

Gerald Burns, executive director of the Independent College Funds of America, has stated that the ideal educational administrator of the future should have a broad undergraduate background,

preferably in the liberal arts and sciences. He should have some graduate work in an academic discipline, in pedagogy, and in administration. He should be exposed to postgraduate or in-service training in the administration of higher education, with particular reference to the specialized area in which he will work. He should serve an apprenticeship under a highly qualified senior administrator in his area. He should attend professional conferences, study, read, and write in his area.[9]

The Kellogg Foundation also was certain that administrators needed better preparation. From 1946 to 1959 it spent nearly $9,000,000 to support projects in educational administration. The foundation was positive that if the schools of the United States were to meet the challenge of the twentieth century, improvement was necessary in the effectiveness of educational leadership. "It was time for the educational administrator to leave his post as manager of technical details," said a foundation report, "and to accept the role of educational statesman." [10]

The Development of Administrative Theory

The development of a sound theory of administration is prerequisite to the professionalization of educational administration. Administrators can learn better many of the attitudes, knowledges, and skills expected of them in the perspective of sound theory. Until recently, most of the professional writings and meetings in this field dealt with an exchange of practices, observations, and personal feelings about administration. During the past decade

[8] Algo D. Henderson, *Policies and Practices in Higher Education* (New York: Harper & Brothers, 1960), pp. 219–20.

[9] Burns (ed.), *Administrators in Higher Education*, p. 228. Also see Harold W. Dodds, *The Academic President—Educator or Caretaker?* (New York: McGraw-Hill Book Co., 1962).

[10] W. K. Kellogg Foundation, *Toward Improved School Administration* (Battle Creek, Mich.: W. K. Kellogg Foundation, 1961), p. 9.

we have been moving toward the development of a body of knowledge and principles developed through systematic research.

Highly critical publications by educators such as Coladarci and Getzels[11] and Griffiths[12] have stimulated the change. So has the development of the National Conference of Professors of Educational Administration, a very active professional organization started in 1947. The timely grants of the Kellogg Foundation that resulted in the Cooperative Program in Educational Administration (CPEA) gave great impetus to the development of a new approach to the field. Finally, the formation of the University Council for Educational Administration provided a means of inter-university cooperation both in improving the preparation of school administrators and in stimulating related research.

The president of a college is usually the only person who can view its work panoramically; hence he has the best opportunity and the most insistent obligation to plan for the future. To be equal to his opportunity and obligation he must be a student of social and educational trends and apply his knowledge to the development of his college. He must be an educational statesman.

THE AAJC AND JUNIOR COLLEGE ADMINISTRATION

Committee on Administrative Problems

In 1945 the AAJC appointed a Committee on Administrative Problems. At its first meeting the committee decided to sponsor five studies. These concerned existing administrative structures in junior colleges, development of programs and standards, improvement of instruction, budget and finance, and conduct of public relations.[13]

The principle that dominated the Committee on Administrative Problems in its various studies was "that the most important function of a junior college administrator is to help the instructor

[11] Arthur J. Coladarci and Jacob W. Getzels, *The Use of Theory in Educational Administration* (Stanford, Calif.: Stanford University Press, 1955).

[12] Daniel E. Griffiths, *Administrative Theory* (New York: Appleton-Century-Crofts, 1959).

[13] John E. Gray, "Report of Committee on Administrative Problems," *Junior College Journal*, XVI (May, 1946), 423–26.

do a better job of teaching." [14] The cooperative study on administrative practices conducted by the Administrative Committee in 1946 with the Committee on Teacher Preparation, the Curriculum and Adult Education Committee, and the Research Office was an example of the application of this principle.

To the committee, the term "administration" was synonymous with management. All those service functions which supported and made possible the educational program of the institution were of concern to the Administrative Committee. The members appraised problems indicated by their colleagues in various parts of the country to determine whether they were of wide enough interest to warrant consideration by the Association. If a problem seemed to be of general significance, the next question was how to enlist help. Sometimes the assistance required was simply to furnish information. At other times discussion groups attacked a problem at the national meetings or, at the committee's request, leaders with pertinent experience wrote articles for the *Junior College Journal*. In the issue for February, 1954, Henry G. Badger of the U.S. Office of Education described current costs of operating junior colleges; the article had its origin in the questions raised by members of the committee.[15] Other projects in which the Administrative Committee had an active part were a study of alumni relationships and a study of characteristics of good junior college teachers.[16]

As the need arose the AAJC Board of Directors established special committees or subcommittees. It appointed a subcommittee on athletics for the specific purpose of formulating a statement of principles to guide junior college athletics. A second subcommittee, on public relations, was responsible for exhibition of materials at national meetings and also concerned itself with alumni relations, fund raising, and the general philosophy and approach to an effective program of public relations. Both groups functioned as subcommittees of the Administrative Committee.

[14] John E. Gray, "Report of Committee on Administrative Problems," *Junior College Journal*, XVIII (May, 1949), 530–32.

[15] Edmund J. Gleazer, Jr., "Structure and Work of the Administration Committee," *Junior College Journal*, XXV (September, 1954), 26.

[16] Edmund J. Gleazer, Jr., "Report of the Administration Committee," *Junior College Journal*, XXIV (October, 1953), 82.

The last meeting of the Administrative Committee before its reorganization as the Commission on Administration took place in 1959; it recommended that the Board of Directors sponsor studies of (1) salaries, (2) fringe benefits, (3) per-student costs, (4) preparation of junior college teachers and administrators, and (5) changes in the administrative structure of junior colleges during the past forty years.[17] The committee suggested that junior colleges needed better educational statistics and recommended that the AAJC cooperate with other professional organizations to develop standard practices in collecting and reporting data. It also recommended a study to develop a more accurate computation of junior college enrollments, and proposed that when the AAJC approved an acceptable basis it urge all junior colleges to use this method.

Several committee members at the 1959 meeting expressed concern with the growing competition among institutions of higher education in the country. Four-year institutions were planning to expand their first-year and second-year classes. State colleges were building dormitories for freshmen and sophomores. Universities were exerting increased pressure for the expansion of extension centers and the establishment of branches. The committee believed that the AAJC should state clearly and forcefully its belief in the role of the two-year junior college. It recommended the development of a statement to set forth the philosophy and advantages of the two-year junior college and its role in the orderly expansion of higher education.[18]

A recurrent AAJC concern was the need for administrators and teachers trained specifically for the junior colleges. In 1944 Homer P. Rainey, president of the University of Texas, stated that one of the real needs of junior college education in Texas "is a program of training in the University for junior college administrators and teachers. . . . A committee of the Junior College Association has discussed this problem with me and with the dean of our School of Education and has urged that the University of Texas inaugurate such a program of training as a part of our School of Education."[19] One can see the concern of the Association with well-

---

[17] Russell T. Sharpe, "Report of the Administration Committee," *Junior College Journal*, XXIX (May, 1959), 548–49.

[18] *Ibid.*, p. 550.

[19] Homer P. Rainey, "Place of Junior Colleges in Texas Education," *Junior College Journal*, XV (December, 1944), 168.

prepared personnel in the recommendation of the Administrative Committee at every one of its meetings that the AAJC Board of Directors develop a program to prepare junior college teachers and administrators.

Development of Leadership Training Programs

A special New York conference, sponsored by the AAJC and financed by the Fund for the Advancement of Education, heard Edmund J. Gleazer, Jr., in February, 1958, assert that "if there is any single factor that is most important at this particular time in junior college development, it may well be the quality of the top administrator."[20] Discussions led to the submission of a proposal by the Association to the fund for support of a program to develop administrative leaders in the junior college field. Alvin C. Eurich, vice-president of the Fund for the Advancement of Education, told the AAJC Board of Directors that the major interest of the fund was in "creative and imaginative ideas in dealing with problems of instruction."[21] Turned down by the fund, the Board of Directors of the AAJC decided to contact other foundations that might be interested in administration.

The Kellogg Foundation, involved in the field of administration since 1949, was aware of the need for administrators for the growing number of junior colleges. In statements prepared for staff hearings Maurice Seay pointed out that no programs of any significance existed for either preservice or in-service education of junior college administrators. He asserted that foundations and the federal government had neglected the junior college. The experience of the Kellogg Foundation in supporting the CPEA program had shown that the administrator "if he is well trained, may be an educational leader . . . but if he is poorly prepared, he is indeed a great handicap to progress."[22] The Division of Education recommended that the Kellogg Foundation accept the improvement of junior college administration as a major project.

In October, 1958, at Battle Creek, Michigan, Gleazer met with Emory W. Morris, president and general director of the Kellogg

[20] Edmund J. Gleazer, Jr., "Introduction to Junior College Conference," New York City, February 17, 1958. Mimeographed. AAJC Archives.

[21] AAJC Board of Directors, *Minutes* (July 21–23, 1958). AAJC Archives.

[22] Statements prepared for staff hearings of W.K. Kellogg Foundation. Kellogg Foundation Archives.

Foundation, and Seay. Both Morris and Seay expressed the Kellogg Foundation's interest in the junior college movement, and Seay invited proposals. On May 13, 1959, the AAJC held a conference in New York City to obtain suggestions and advice from individuals whose background and experience in particular areas would lend strength to the Association's request to the Kellogg Foundation. Seay indicated that university programs which recognized a certain uniqueness of the junior college would interest the foundation; because the junior college ought to have its own identity, the proposed area of instruction should not be an appendage to existing programs for the development of four-year college administrators. He also indicated that any type of program that "downgraded" professional education would not interest the foundation. Seay suggested that Gleazer bring to the meeting with the staff of the Kellogg Foundation in Battle Creek on June 10 some general idea on what kinds of university-centered programs to establish.[23]

In March, 1960, at the fortieth annual convention of the AAJC in Louisville, Kentucky, Seay announced that the Kellogg Foundation had awarded four-year grants totaling over $800,000 to five universities to establish centers for the preparation of junior college administrators at Teachers College, Columbia University, the University of Texas, the University of California at Berkeley, the University of California at Los Angeles, and Stanford University. Before the end of 1960 Kellogg grants implemented additional leadership training programs for junior college administrators in Florida State University, the University of Florida, Michigan State University, the University of Michigan, and Wayne State University in Detroit. The foundation committed a total of over $1,600,000 to finance the ten centers.

The Leadership Training Programs

The programs at these centers included efforts to identify, select, and encourage qualified young men and women to become administrators. To improve administrative performance the centers provided refresher opportunities for those already in executive

[23] Edmund J. Gleazer, Jr., "Memorandum to Board of Directors," May 22, 1959. AAJC Archives.

positions—summer institutes, workshops, periodical regional and statewide meetings, continuing seminars, and other special conferences. The AAJC Commission on Administration continues active cooperation with the ten university centers. A five-man committee of the commission serves as a liaison between the Association and the centers.

The university grants expire in 1964 but will be renewed for another three-year period. Formal evaluation of the achievements of the centers still lies in the future.

The Kellogg training programs owe their existence directly to the activities of the AAJC. To date the centers have placed all graduates of the programs in administrative posts, but the number of administrators trained by these programs has not been enough to take care of the need. Hundreds of administrators have taken advantage of the workshops and the special conferences. The centers have made vigorous efforts to recruit and select superior graduate students; they have attempted experimentation with teaching methods and curriculum organization. They have fostered internships in order to make the preparation program a meaningful part of the prospective administrator's experience.

The AAJC, the ten universities, the Kellogg Foundation, and the junior colleges of the country have joined in a team effort to raise professional standards and make each junior college administrator better equipped for his position.

LEGISLATION

Organizations coordinate human efforts to achieve recognized goals. Stresses and strains, a constant within any given organization, tend to restrict the extent to which an organization can reach its goals. One of the factors which tends either to decrease or to accentuate stress and strain is structure. While it is not the end-all in explaining the success or failure of an organization, it is certainly an important consideration in the attainment of purpose. The AAJC has attempted to improve the structure of the junior colleges of the country by suggesting to states planning or improving junior college systems legislation that accords with experience and sound principles.

Varieties of Junior Colleges

Diversity is the key word in describing the nature of American junior colleges. They differ in size from one with as few as eighteen students to another with as many as 23,000 students, both in California.[24] There are private and public junior colleges. In 1959, the 277 private junior colleges enrolled 98,213 students and employed the equivalent of 6,211 full-time faculty members. Geographically, the private junior colleges were located in each of the six accreditation regions of the United States, though the majority of them were east of the Mississippi.[25] Most private colleges were under denominational control.

In that same year 400 publicly controlled junior colleges enrolled 806,849 students; they constituted 59.1 per cent of all junior colleges listed and their enrollments were 89.1 per cent of all junior college students. A total of 17,811 full-time, or equivalent, faculty staffed the public institutions. Public junior colleges were distributed throughout the areas of the six regional accrediting agencies, but whereas private colleges were concentrated in the eastern and southern sections of the nation, public institutions were found more frequently in the central and western sections.[26]

Junior colleges also differ by unit of control. Whereas religious denominations control two thirds of the private junior colleges with about one third undenominational, several types of governmental agencies control public junior colleges.[27] States sponsor and control some directly. Others are branches of state universities or state colleges. The latter pattern is most common in Pennsylvania, Wisconsin, and Indiana. Under this system a university may organize a junior college as a separate division or as an off-campus branch.

Control may be vested in county governments, local school districts, and independent junior college districts. Florida is an

---

[24] Edmund J. Gleazer, Jr. (ed.), *The 1962 Junior College Directory* (Washington, D.C.: American Association of Junior Colleges, 1962), pp. 4–5.

[25] Edmund J. Gleazer, Jr. (ed.), *Junior College Directory, 1960* (Washington, D.C.: American Association of Junior Colleges, 1960).

[26] *Ibid.*

[27] For brief descriptions of the two-year college in the various states see Leland Medsker, *The Junior College: Progress and Prospect,* pp. 207–95.

example of a system that operates under the county unit system. Basically, the plan makes the junior colleges a part of the local public schools. The county board of public instruction is the governing board of the institution. Legislation in California permits two types of local districts to establish junior colleges. One is the unified district, which maintains and is responsible for all units of the local schools from kindergarten through the junior college; the other is the special junior college district.

Junior colleges have developed in response to local influences and are subject to the laws of the fifty states. Of the three patterns of organization—local, state, branch of a university—the locally controlled junior college is the most common and the fully state-controlled and state-supported plan has been least often adopted by those states which have recently been establishing or strengthening a junior college system.

It is important to remember that there probably is no one ideal pattern for the entire country. However, there are some principles that help provide a structure that enables a junior college system to receive adequate financial support and that establish an organizational pattern that facilitates achievement of institutional goals. The AAJC has attempted to find such principles.

The Committee on Legislation

In 1945 the AAJC established a Committee on Finance and Legislation, not to be concerned with the formulation or creation of legislative acts or bills but primarily to scrutinize and analyze legislation that might affect the interests of junior colleges as a whole. It kept abreast of proposed legislative developments and publicized their implications to the membership.[28]

Early in its history, the Committee on Finance and Legislation drew up a set of principles to guide states that were considering junior college legislation. One strong recommendation was that state laws should establish free tuition. The report of the commit-

[28] From 1946 to 1957 the *Junior College Journal* published a biennial survey and digest of state legislation pertaining to two-year colleges compiled by S. V. Martorana. In 1957 the U.S. Office of Education published a *Survey of State Legislation Relating to Higher Education*, by Ernest V. Hollis, William G. Land and S. V. Martorana. This more comprehensive survey replaced the biennial articles in the *Journal*.

tee also stressed that before enacting any legislation, a state should survey the need for junior colleges. The committee cautioned that "a junior college with an enrollment of less than two hundred students cannot be operated economically or effectively." [29]

Principles of Legislative Action

Under the reorganization of the AAJC committee structure in 1959, the Commission on Legislation replaced the 1945 committee. It then sponsored a conference on "Establishing Legal Bases for Community Colleges," held on October 20–21, 1961, in Chicago, to evaluate, test, and review some of the basic principles that they had enunciated. Another reason for calling the conference was the urgent need, demonstrated by a deluge of inquiries from many states that were studying or reviewing legislation, for a national forum to discuss legal bases for junior colleges.[30] Pennsylvania, New Jersey, Missouri, Georgia, and Rhode Island were giving serious consideration to legislation for public junior colleges. The commission stated that the conference would pool essential information and experience.

Most of the participants in the conference held positions of major responsibility and leadership in education. From the beginning the conferees realized that the meeting was concerned not so much with establishing legal bases for new junior colleges as with improving the legal bases of those already established. Forty-two states already had publicly supported two-year colleges, and thirty-four of these states had legislation whereby local jurisdiction could establish two-year colleges by following certain prescribed procedures and meeting specified conditions. In most states it was too late to establish initial legal foundations for public two-year colleges.

S. V. Martorana, chief of the State and Regional Organization, Division of Higher Education of the U.S. Office of Education, pointed out that elected officials in the state governments, not professional educators, play the primary role in legislative matters.

---

[29] Gertrude Houk Fariss, "Committee on Legislation," *Junior College Journal*, XVII (May, 1947), 387.

[30] AAJC, *Establishing Legal Bases for Community Colleges* (Washington, D.C.: American Association of Junior Colleges, 1962), p. 1.

However, the professional educator has a vital secondary role in the legislative process, for elected political officials turn to him for basic assistance and counsel. Martorana stressed the importance of cooperation between political leaders and educators; with the educator in the role of the researcher, "that is, the fact finder, analyzer and interpreter, and objective reporter." [31]

Martorana emphasized the importance of surveys. From a survey one could document the facts relative to a particular situation; and the survey would show the objectivity of the persons who were responsible for leadership in educational planning. He listed five advantages which local surveys could provide: (1) answers to such key local questions as the location of sites for the institution, the number and type of campuses feasible to operate, procedures for articulating the programs of the two-year colleges with those of the high schools from which students come and with the colleges to which graduates go; (2) assurance of the development of curricula fitted to local area needs; (3) a clear appraisal and documentation of the extent and character of local area resources available to support the establishment and operation of a two-year college; (4) an assessment of the degree of local area interest and enthusiasm for the acquisition of a two-year college; and (5) enhancement of public understanding of the role and scope of a public two-year college and its potential services to the particular area included in the survey.[32] Martorana concluded:

Ideally, there would be an overall, thorough, state-wide survey of higher education and analysis of needs for public two-year colleges before a legal basis for community colleges would be established. Then there would follow a series of continuing statewide studies, looking into specific questions more penetratingly, and many local-area studies.[33]

James L. Wattenbarger, director of the Division of Community Junior Colleges, Florida State Department of Education, described some of the characteristics of a sound plan for financing the junior colleges. The plan should provide for state and local support of the junior college. The state must establish overall procedures,

[31] *Ibid.*, p. 4.
[32] *Ibid.*, p. 7.
[33] *Ibid.*

but should provide the local college a great amount of flexibility in the administration of the budget. The plan should also (1) depend upon student tuition fees as little as possible; (2) utilize a formula which provides for all elements of necessary costs of a good junior college program; (3) contribute to stability of operation by providing a predictable income from year to year; and (4) include provision for capital outlay.[34]

The third major topic considered at the conference was patterns for the control of junior colleges. Leland Medsker, vice-chairman of the Center for the Study of Higher Education, University of California at Berkeley, enunciated several criteria for evaluating and improving the structural organization of junior colleges. Chief among these were (1) the control structure should provide for institutional integrity of junior colleges; (2) control and finance patterns are not necessarily integrally related matters in the operation of junior colleges; (3) the controlling agency of a junior college should be as directly representative of the people served as possible; and (4) the controlling agency of a junior college should be one which can have no conflict of interests between the junior college and any other institutions for which it is responsible.[35]

The legal bases of junior colleges in most states are still in the very early stages of development. Said the conference report:

Concerted and intelligent action exerted toward sound formulation, clarification, expansion, and strengthening of the laws concerning community colleges is timely and needed. The goal is to develop laws which not only make possible, but actually stimulate full and free provision of the educational services that people need and community colleges can provide.[36]

One of the latest contributions of the Commission on Legislation is an information handbook published in December, 1962.[37] The commission prepared this handbook primarily to assist and inform those persons concerned with the development of state

[34] *Ibid.*, pp. 9–13.
[35] *Ibid.*, pp. 14–18.
[36] *Ibid.*, p. 25.
[37] AAJC Commission on Legislation, *Principles of Legislative Action for Community Junior Colleges* (Washington: American Association of Junior Colleges, 1962).

legislation affecting education—members of state legislatures, survey commissions, citizen committees, municipal government officials, and local and state boards of education. The handbook incorporated the recommendations of the Chicago conference on "establishing legal bases" and set forth a group of basic principles which should govern the legal establishment of junior colleges.

The AAJC realizes full well that it will not achieve uniformity of legislation; in fact, it does not consider this as necessarily desirable. However, through the efforts of the Commission on Legislation, the Association is defining some basic principles to follow in order to secure legislation that will give maximum capability to junior colleges so that they achieve their functions effectively.

8

Progress and Prognosis

DESCRIPTION OF the American Association of Junior Colleges' activities is much easier than evaluation of its achievements and influence. The formation of an association is but one device that promotes the purposes of a professional group. Many other forces, agencies, and individuals affected the junior college movement. For example, individual institutions, state and regional associations, universities, and state departments of education all moved the junior colleges forward. But the Association was the only national organization through which the junior colleges of the country could act and speak as a unit. Few would deny, after examining the history of the AAJC, that it acted and spoke well.

REPRISE

Human nature is such that often it finds acceptance of new ideas painful. Traditions, existing institutions, laws, and definitions rally around the old concept and slow the acceptance of the innovation. Such inertia seems to apply particularly well to educational concepts.

Ever since its establishment, the AAJC has attempted to ease the pain of acceptance of the junior college idea. Through its attempts it has developed into a strong organization dedicated to the promotion of junior colleges both at home and abroad. The AAJC has become a powerful spokesman. Through meetings, publications, studies, and research this central professional organization has given direction to the movement and performed services for the membership and the entire nation.

Some of the outstanding work of the Association was done by the Commission on Junior College Terminal Education in the 1940's. The commission sponsored a nationwide study in the field of terminal education at a time when little was known, and what was known was misunderstood, about terminal education at the college level.

Another important and successful project of the Association was the development of the Associate Degree Program in Nursing. The project began through the cooperation of the AAJC, the National League for Nursing, and the Department of Nursing Education at Teachers College, Columbia University. The Associate Degree Program in Nursing began with a few pilot programs and is now offered at approximately 90 institutions, most of them junior colleges. Several foundations, including the Kellogg, made financial commitments as evidence of their interest in these programs. The two-year nursing program represents one of the best examples of sound curriculum development that can be found on any level of education.

Through its research and service commissions the AAJC made substantial efforts to improve the performance of junior colleges. The Commissions on Administration and Teacher Preparation have raised the level of competence of junior college personnel. The Association worked with the Kellogg Foundation in initiating the Junior College Leadership Training Program at university centers throughout the country. Although these programs will not necessarily produce the future presidents of junior colleges, they are graduating an increasing number of individuals who have a professional preparation for such positions, and some who eventually will attain the highest responsibilities. In support of such educational programs, it is fair to say that the average graduate leaves with greater competence than he otherwise might have had, and the more exceptional graduate leaves with better vision of the role of administrative leadership.

In the guidance field, the AAJC initiated workshops in universities, and not only coordinated the offerings at these various institutions but also recruited personnel to attend. The Association has published guidance bulletins and is working closely with the Educational Testing Service in the development of testing instruments which will be particularly applicable and useful to junior college students.

In explaining the position of the AAJC today as a leader of the two-year college movement, one cannot overlook the Association's efforts as spokesman for the junior colleges. It has always been alert to bring pressures to bear on federal legislation so that the two-year college point of view is represented. Several bills recently enacted or still in the process of consideration by the federal Congress have definite implications for junior colleges and have been vigorously supported by the Association. These include the Manpower Training Act, the Educational Television Act, the Academic Facilities Bill, and the Brademas Bill.

Stepping up its program of public relations, the Association at the close of 1961 established an office of public information. Through its monthly newsletter and the *Journal,* members are kept informed of the latest developments in junior college education. A program of professional advisory services was established in 1961 to provide more direct and specialized services to organizations concerned with junior college development. The program makes consultants available to national and international groups interested in this kind of education.

Add to these projects the legal guides the AAJC has evolved for junior college development, and it is justifiable to conclude that the AAJC has been a significant force in the junior college movement.

The AAJC as a Forum

In assessing the work of the AAJC, even more important, perhaps, than the projects are the ideas that evolved at the annual meetings. Representatives came together to exchange plans, techniques, and general information, and to renew contacts, personal and professional. Programs deliberately included a large number of university speakers. The latter delivered their messages; and the members discussed issues, considered proposals, and formulated plans. New concepts and methods were examined, criticized and evaluated. Thus, new ideas were a product of association.

AAJC meetings served as forums for the exchange of educational messages. Here junior college educators could thrash out conflicting views and attempt to reconcile differences. The meetings also served as short courses in professional stimulation and thus the AAJC performed one of its most vital services.

The AAJC as a Voluntary Professional Organization

American higher education has never conformed to one uniform pattern in organization, control, curriculum, or support. No central ministry in America has ever consolidated and centralized power. The lack of centralization has resulted in the founding of the most diverse types of institutions of higher education in the United States. In the absence of centralized authority, voluntary associations provide direction in American education. These organizations prevent the "atomization" of society into splinter groups, each pursuing its own selfish interests.

The AAJC is an example of such organizations. It voluntarily promotes the mutual interests of the junior colleges without the compulsions of governments. The AAJC established and attempted to enforce standards of practice through a code of ethics. Early it disavowed its role as an accrediting agency and stressed its role as primarily a service organization. This meant that the function of the Association was the establishment rather than the enforcement of standards.

The Association headquarters in Washington serves as a vital communication center and clearing house, both for the internal operation of the organization and for matters that require a national spokesman for junior colleges. The office, under the direction of a full-time executive director, maintains liaison with other educational and scholarly associations that have common interests and purposes. Many governmental and nongovernmental agencies have sought the cooperation and assistance of the AAJC. National and state legislatures have recognized the Association as spokesman for junior colleges. In the past three years countries such as Chile and Kenya have asked the AAJC to help found junior college systems. The Association has established itself as the appropriate agency in the United States to represent junior colleges.

Typical of the activities of voluntary professional organizations are attempts to knit together the divergent groups within the organization. In these attempts the AAJC proved no exception. Aware of regional differences, and how public and private institutions jealously guarded their interests, the Association, in its organizational structure, provided for representation of both public and private junior colleges as well as geographical representation. The AAJC, made up as it is of a variety of two-year institutions, acted as a cohesive force and served as the voice for junior colleges on a national basis.

AAJC FAILURES

Despite all the Association has done, it has failed in some very important areas. The word "image" has become a term that has been increasingly overworked in educational jargon, and one almost hesitates to use it. However, overworked and tired as it may be, a problem that still plagues the junior colleges is the establishment of a clear image of themselves which can be interpreted to the public and to educators. The American Association of Junior Colleges has not been successful in helping junior colleges define their place in the total structure of American higher education.

One of the factors accounting for the difficulty in interpreting the junior college is that there is no one image that can be set down as a party line and receive acceptance by all two-year institutions in all parts of the country. Nor should there be one image. The great variety of institutions is one of the strengths of American higher education. Yet, while diversity can be a strength, lack of a definite purpose and a philosophy can be a weakness. Lack of understanding of the place of the junior college in the total structure of American education can be confusing to the students who attend, the teachers who instruct, the public that supports, and the administrators who lead. It brings about a situation where in many parts of the country the junior college is considered part of secondary education, in other sections a part of higher education, and in a state such as Florida, a schizophrenic condition sets in where by law the junior college is defined both as secondary and higher.

The junior college is not a secondary school, nor is it a liberal arts college or a university. All these institutions have their functions to perform. The junior college must find that segment of education which it can do best, and do it. The AAJC should give immediate attention to this problem. The Association and the junior colleges have made a mistake in attempting to emphasize their uniqueness in the American educational structure rather than attempting to find their place within the pattern. The AAJC must help the two-year colleges define their purpose, taking into consideration the needs of society as well as the needs of the individual. The Association must insist that the junior college is a social invention whose assignment is the task of raising up human talent. Its work should be done with pride and competence. The AAJC must affirm clearly and persistently its basic belief in the worth of the individual, a belief in the ready accessibility of avenues of educational development appropriate for each individual, and a belief in an unstratified society.

In the decades to come the AAJC should work closely with other organizations to solve some of the basic problems that beset all higher education. One of these problems is harmonizing the disparate traditions out of which American higher education springs and of fitting them within a changing and democratic society. It is the responsibility of the AAJC—a responsibility long overdue—to make American society aware of the worth and dignity of technical education. Ours is a society which has achieved affluence through technology, and yet it has traditionally looked down upon education that is not liberally or professionally oriented. The AAJC must help those within the junior college movement and those outside of it to appreciate that in a complex society there are many respectable tasks to be performed. The educational system should be prepared to make sure that it educates its youth to perform these tasks.

The AAJC has hesitated to take firm stands on many important issues in an attempt to maintain unity. The Association must be reminded that where people refuse to decide, events will decide for them; and to allow events to decide impersonally is in itself a decision involving greater risks than affirming a point of view.

BLUEPRINT FOR THE FUTURE

One of the most important determinants of what the junior college will eventually be is its own professional organization—the AAJC. Thanks to the Kellogg grants, since 1959 the opportunities for leadership and services have greatly expanded. Nevertheless, flushed with success, the AAJC today faces its greatest test.

In their youth all organizations tend to be dynamic, outward, experimental, vital. Then they mature. The organization becomes self-satisfied and begins to feel that if it has achieved a measure of success with past performance, that performance should be perpetuated. Annual meetings seek to justify the existing nature of the institution. To the extent that the AAJC can continuously infuse life and vitality into the junior college movement by planning for the future, rather than constantly discussing what it has done and where it has been—to that extent will the Association justify its existence and the money spent on its activities.

Many forces at work within the Association and the junior college movement pose problems for the AAJC in its attempt to supply dynamic leadership. The survival and prosperity of the Association depend upon its ability to overcome internal problems and to help the junior colleges guard against conforming to outside pressures.

Internal Problems

Finance looms large in the future of the AAJC. The Kellogg grants have allowed the Association to expand its staff and services. At present the AAJC receives approximately $75,000 annually from membership dues and about $100,000 from foundations. However, a large portion of foundation grants runs out in 1967. What happens then? The leadership of the Association is optimistic that it will receive more foundation aid to subsidize its operations. If the Association becomes increasingly dependent on the largesse of foundations there is a grave danger that it would completely break down if the aid should come to an abrupt halt. The Association must make sure it has a financial program ready to take the place of foundation subsidy.

Another very important problem that the AAJC has to consider is its commission system. What are the commissions supposed to do? Are they the best arrangement to provide the services that the junior colleges need? At the present time their chief strength is the personal involvement of some one hundred members in the activities of the Association and the educational experience that this involvement supplies. Individual involvement helps keep the interest of the membership alive. Yet how long can the AAJC afford an expensive commission system whose chief function is the maintenance of an *esprit de corps?* The Association will have to define the role of the commissions and decide whether or not the achievements are worth the expenditures.

The AAJC will have to devote its attention to achieving rapport with various state and regional educational organizations. Well-laid plans conceived at the national level too often have fallen by the wayside because they were not carried through on local levels. Junior college associations, on all levels, will have to be made an integral part of the AAJC. This could be accomplished by a single membership fee and the employment of a full-time field secretary to establish liaison with the affiliated groups.

An additional concern facing the AAJC is the new generation of junior college personnel, attuned to new conditions, that is swelling the ranks of the membership. The Association must see to it that this new generation receives a hearing. It must make sure that the thinking and maxims of the 1920's do not dominate the present and, what is more important, the future. Fruitful research should be encouraged to test long-accepted educational shibboleths. For example, has two taken on the magical qualities of four? It may very well be that the present concept of a two-year college is transitory and that time periods will vary with the student and the definition of the functions of the junior college. In light of research being done it is quite possible that our traditional notions of teaching methods, subject matter to be taught, buildings, and equipment may change radically. The AAJC must be flexible enough to change as demonstrated social change occurs.

Finally, the AAJC has suffered from an inferiority complex. Often it made exaggerated claims of its influence and achievements. Its junior colleges attempted to compare themselves to senior colleges and insisted that they were their equivalent—at least in the first two years. The Association allowed itself to be influenced by the decisions of other groups. Very often it was provincial in attitude. For years the AAJC shunned the help and advice of university professors. Another kind of provincialism was excessive leaning on California for direction. There is an element of truth in the accusation made by some junior college administrators that the work of the Association was done by its executive officer and a close coterie of California junior college leaders. True or not, the Association can no longer afford to be open to such criticism. It is now a mature national organization. This maturity was recognized by the Kellogg Foundation with its timely grants. The AAJC must itself recognize its maturity and take firmer stands on issues, point out future direction, and throw off its provincialism.

External Pressures

At the present time the junior colleges stand at a crossroads. They continue to grow in numbers and in students but the direction they are traveling is taking them away from the purposes that gave them integrity and vitality. With increasing intensity educational and social pressures, within and outside the academic community, are impinging upon them, to make them become something different from what they have been traditionally. Many junior colleges are anxious to emulate the four-year liberal arts college in the mistaken notion that thereby they will achieve everlasting immortality as institutions of excellence.

Teachers with a background in academic disciplines come to the junior colleges, and are not always sympathetic to technical and continuing education. They often arrive with the idea that the two-year college will serve as a stepping stone to a position in a four-year institution. Trustees and administrators, with visions of grandeur and a lack of understanding of the institution they head, can hardly wait until their institution turns into a four-year college. Students and their parents, indoctrinated with the idea that a four-year post-high school education is the only respectable college program and that occupational education is not an appropriate concern of higher education, are willing to see their junior college ape traditional senior institutions.

Nevertheless, social and economic conditions give insistent and imperative notice that an institution like the junior college is a necessity for our times. In supplying the national leadership that will give direction to the junior colleges, the AAJC will have to make sure that the distinguishing characteristics of these colleges do not disappear.

Future Direction for Junior Colleges

The junior college developed in order to meet certain well-defined social, economic, and educational demands. It was established to provide opportunity not then available in existing institutions. It flourished because it filled an educational void and made post-high school education geographically and financially available to many who would have had this education denied them. The junior college was the democratizer of higher education.

Technological change caused a demand for the type of education youth needed to succeed in a growing industrial society. At the turn of the century, the unskilled laborer formed a significant part of the labor market. The skilled laborer was in the minority. During the first half of the twentieth century this situation has reversed itself. There has been a great proliferation not only of professions but also of subprofessions. In response to changing society, the junior colleges developed terminal technical and semi-professional programs. Basic to the growing development of technical education was a philosophy of the social equality of all useful labor. The concept of parity between the technical and the academic has a long history in American education.

Most important in the growth of the junior college is its relationship to the social philosophy out of which the American educational system developed. Equal educational opportunity has been one of the persevering concepts of our society. The American people have believed that their welfare depends upon the individual, and that the welfare of the individual and the society rise and fall together. Dedication to this belief led to the development of publicly supported elementary and secondary education. It was this belief, that every American child should have an opportunity to develop his talents to the fullest, that led to the development of numerous types of institutions designed to meet emerging social demands. The junior college, more than any other institution, has made this belief a growing reality. This institution has been responsible for flinging open the doors of higher education to increasing numbers of American youth.

The forces that influenced the junior college idea and the development of junior colleges continued to exist in our society, and will exist in the future. The American people have not lessened their commitment to equality of opportunity. A premium has been placed on higher education. It is very likely that, within the next twenty or thirty years, the expectation of college entrance will be part of the standard equipment of every student graduating from secondary school.

Technological change is increasing at a faster pace than ever. The Department of Labor predicts that in the present decade the fastest growth will occur among professional and technical occupations; there will be particular need for engineers, scientists, and technicians. The largest increases will occur in occupations requiring the most education and training. The impact of automation is being felt in production technologies. The groups which the census calls "managerial, technical, and professional" has become the largest employee group during the last decade—rapidly overtaking the semi-skilled machine operator. In addition we face a great challenge in traditional education in respect to skills. It used to be that a man who acquired a specific skill as a boy had learned what he needed for the rest of his life. Today skills may become absolete overnight—and new skills, not yet visible, may be required overnight.

It is safe to assume that in the future the nation will need an expansion of two-year junior colleges, near the homes of students, with minimum tuition fees, offering sound programs of general education, diversified technical instruction, with faculties dedicated to good undergraduate teaching, with admission standards and instruction for those of varying levels of ability, and a varied program of continuing education. In these services lies the future of the junior colleges.

Direction for the AAJC

To make sure that junior colleges supply the necessary services, the Association will have to stimulate and assist junior colleges to develop comprehensive curricula with special attention to technical education and community services. Technical training beyond the high school, interwoven with general education, is and ought to be a major concern of the two-year colleges. The need is overwhelming in this country and abroad for personnel trained at this level. National security and individual self-fulfillment require opportunities for appropriate educational development of our citizenry.

The AAJC will have to assist states to develop sound and orderly systems of junior colleges to serve a growing part of the population in each state. It will have to provide adequate information at national and state levels regarding the appropriate services of junior colleges so that legislation involving these institutions will be realistic and constructive. It is true that there are effective junior colleges operating under various patterns of organization. However, in order to continue to perform its historically acknowledged purposes, the junior college must have independence. The AAJC should use its influence to achieve state legislation that allows freedom of action to junior colleges and removes politics, as far as possible, from education.

New patterns of financial support will also have to be found. It is extremely unlikely that local property tax revenues can be looked to for a larger percentage of support. If junior colleges are to be within financial reach of prospective students, substantial support must come from state levels and, if necessary, from the federal government. The great mobility in America is a strong case for some form of national equalization of opportunity for post-high school education.

Another objective is to raise the level of competence of junior college administrators and teachers, who together further the purpose of an institution. The AAJC will have to assist in establishing strong junior college teacher preparation programs, in-service workshops, and institutes. It will have to find ways of attracting promising people to the field. The Association must utilize the talents of teachers and staff members in the junior colleges of the country. The AAJC gears its projects and national programs to junior college presidents; the presumption that approximately five hundred administrators can represent the entire junior college movement must be rectified.

There is a growing trend to establishing selective admission standards in junior colleges; the college door is closing for those who have not demonstrated academic aptitude. The AAJC will have to help junior college leaders understand that excellence and selective admission procedures are not synonymous. An excellent junior college is one which takes students of the most diverse abilities and develops their talents, whatever they may be, to the fullest. Until there exist more precise conceptions of the value of various types of human contributions to a democratic society, no institution ought to be ashamed to serve some students of modest academic ability or mediocre high school record.

Unless the American Association of Junior Colleges succeeds in these endeavors, it may very well find itself representing an institution whose name persists but whose distinguishing characteristics have long disappeared.

Appendices

Junior College Patriarchs

Thirty-four educators, the majority of them junior college administrators, met in St. Louis, Missouri, June 30 and July 1, 1920, for a "National Conference of Junior Colleges" which resulted in the organization of the American Association of Junior Colleges. Following are the names of those who attended this important conference and the positions which they then held. Walter Crosby Eells dubbed them the junior college "Patriarchs."

BAINTER, EDWARD M., Principal, Junior College of Kansas City, Missouri.

BOLCOM, W. G., Superintendent of Schools, Rochester, Minnesota.

BOWMAN, J. HALL, President, Meridian College, Meridian, Texas.

BROWN, J. STANLEY, President, Northern Illinois State Normal School, De Kalb, Illinois.

BUENGER, THEODORE, President, Concordia College, St. Paul, Minnesota.

FLEAGLE, FRED K., Dean, Marion Institute, Marion, Alabama.

HARMON, J. C., President, Cottey Junior College, Nevada, Missouri.

HAWKINS, W. J., Field Secretary, Washington University, St. Louis, Missouri.

HILL, A. ROSS, President, University of Missouri, Columbia, Misouri.

HUMPHREYS, JOHN S., President, College of Marshall, Marshall, Texas.

LEE, EDGAR D., Vice-President, Christian College, Columbia, Missouri.

LOOMIS, BURT W., President, Marvin College, Fredericktown, Missouri.

LOVE, F. S., President, Louisburg College, Louisburg, North Carolina.

McDOWELL, F. M., Dean, Graceland College, Lamoni, Iowa.

MacKENZIE, DAVID, Dean, Detroit Junior College, Detroit, Michigan.

MILLION, JOHN W., President, Hardin College, Mexico, Missouri.

MILLION, MRS. HELEN LOVELL, Dean, Hardin College, Mexico, Missouri.

NOFFSINGER, HUGH GODWIN, President, Virginia Intermont College, Bristol, Virginia.

RAYMOND, T. W., President, Mississippi Syndical College, Holly Springs, Mississippi.

RAYMOND, MRS. T. W., Principal, Mississippi Syndical College, Holly Springs, Mississippi.

REID, MARTHA MacKENZIE, Dean, William Woods College, Fulton, Missouri.

RYAN, W. CARSON, JR., educational editor, *New York Evening Post,* New York City, New York.

SERENA, JOSEPH A., President, William Woods College, Fulton, Missouri.

SHUMWAY, ROYAL R., Professor, University of Minnesota, Minneapolis, Minnesota.

SMITH, C. E., Professor and Registrar, Blackburn College, Carlinville, Illinois.

SMITH, LEWIS W., Superintendent, Joliet Junior College, Joliet, Illinois.

STEPHENS, E. W., President, Board of Curators, Stephens College, Columbia, Missouri.

STEWART, C. S., Instructor, Crane Junior College, Chicago, Illinois.

TEMPLIN, LUCINDA DE L., Dean, Lindenwood College, St. Charles, Missouri.

THOMPSON, RICHARD R., President, Crescent College, Eureka Springs, Arkansas.

WINFIELD, GEORGE F., President, Wesley College, Greenville, Texas.

WOOD, JAMES MADISON, President, Stephens College, Columbia, Missouri.

WYNN, W. T., Professor, Middle Tennessee Normal School, Murfreesboro, Tennessee.

ZOOK, GEORGE F., Specialist in Higher Education, U. S. Bureau of Education, Washington, D. C.

Annual Meetings and Officers, 1921–1963

1921 [1] February 16–17
    Chicago, Illinois
    David MacKenzie, President
    T. W. Raymond, Vice-President
    Martha M. Reid, Executive Secretary

1922 March 24–25
    Memphis, Tennessee
    George Freeman Winfield, President
    Louis E. Plummer, Vice-President
    Martha M. Reid, Executive Secretary

1923 February 27–28
    Cleveland, Ohio
    James Madison Wood, President
    Louis E. Plummer, Vice-President
    Doak S. Campbell, Executive Secretary

1924 February 26–27
    Chicago, Illinois
    James Madison Wood, President
    Louis E. Plummer, Vice-President
    Doak S. Campbell, Executive Secretary

1925 February 20–21
    Cincinnati, Ohio
    Louis E. Plummer, President
    Richard G. Cox, Vice-President
    Doak S. Campbell, Executive Secretary

1926 March 16–17
    Chicago, Illinois
    Hugh Godwin Noffsinger, President
    Lewis W. Smith, Vice-President
    Doak S. Campbell, Executive Secretary

1926 November 29–30
    Jackson, Mississippi
    Lewis W. Smith, President
    Edgar D. Lee, Vice-President
    Doak S. Campbell, Executive Secretary

[1] Indicates the year in which the annual meeting was held at which the president presided. This year was also the terminal date for the year of service in that office for other officials shown.

1928   March 12–13
        Chicago, Illinois
        Edgar D. Lee, President
        F. G. Branch, Vice-President
        Doak S. Campbell, Executive Secretary

1928   December 3–5
        Fort Worth, Texas
        J. Thomas Davis, President
        Marion Coates, Vice-President
        Doak S. Campbell, Executive Secretary

1929   November 19–20
        Atlantic City, New Jersey
        John Wayne Barton, President
        Milton R. Floyd, Vice-President
        Doak S. Campbell, Executive Secretary

1930   November 18–19
        Berkeley, California
        Jeremiah B. Lillard, President
        Warren W. Way, Vice-President
        Doak S. Campbell, Executive Secretary

1932   February 19–20
        Richmond, Virginia
        Richard Garfield Cox, President
        G. H. Vande Bogart, Vice-President
        Doak S. Campbell, Executive Secretary

1933   February 24–25
        Kansas City, Missouri
        Arthur Andrews, President
        J. W. Cammack, Vice-President
        Doak S. Campbell, Executive Secretary

1934   February 23–24
        Columbus, Ohio
        Arthur Martin Hitch, President
        J. Leonard Hancock, Vice-President
        Doak S. Campbell, Executive Secretary

1935   February 22–23
        Washington, D.C.
        Edmond Q. Brothers, President
        Guy M. Winslow, Vice-President
        Doak S. Campbell, Executive Secretary

1936 February 28–29
      Nashville, Tennessee
      Robert Johns Trevorrow, President
      H. B. Wyman, Vice-President
      Doak S. Campbell, Executive Secretary

1937 February 26–27
      Dallas, Texas
      William Wade Haggard, President
      Katherine M. Denworth, Vice-President
      Doak S. Campbell, Executive Secretary

1938 March 4–5
      Philadelphia, Pennsylvania
      Katherine M. Denworth, President
      Nicholas Ricciardi, Vice-President
      Doak S. Campbell, Executive Secretary

1939 March 2–4
      Grand Rapids, Michigan
      Nicholas Ricciardi, President
      Curtis Bishop, Vice-President
      Walter Crosby Eells, Executive Secretary

1940 February 29–March 2
      Columbia, Missouri
      Byron S. Hollingshead, President
      Clyde C. Colvert, Vice-President
      Walter Crosby Eells, Executive Secretary

1941 February 27–March 1
      Chicago, Illinois
      Clyde C. Colvert, President
      Phillip M. Ball, Vice-President
      Walter Crosby Eells, Executive Secretary

1942 January 2–3
      Baltimore, Maryland
      James C. Miller, President
      James M. Ewing, Vice-President
      Walter Crosby Eells, Executive Secretary

1943 No meeting
      John W. Harbeson, President
      Jesse P. Bogue, Vice-President
      Walter Crosby Eells, Executive Secretary

1944   January 11–13
       Cincinnati, Ohio
       Jesse P. Bogue, President
       Roy W. Goddard, Vice-President
       Walter Crosby Eells, Executive Secretary

1945   No meeting
       Roy W. Goddard, President
       Lawrence L. Bethel, Vice-President
       Walter Crosby Eells, Executive Secretary

1946   January 17–19
       Chicago, Illinois
       Lawrence L. Bethel, President
       Roscoe Ingalls, Vice-President
       Winifred R. Long, acting Executive Secretary

1947   February 20–22
       St. Louis, Missouri
       Roscoe Ingalls, President
       Eugene Farley, Vice-President
       Jesse P. Bogue, Executive Secretary

1948   February 24–27
       Kansas City, Missouri
       Eugene Shedden Farley, President
       Leland L. Medsker, Vice-President
       Jesse P. Bogue, Executive Secretary

1949   February 23–26
       San Francisco, California
       Leland L. Medsker, President
       Curtis Bishop, Vice-President
       Jesse P. Bogue, Executive Secretary

1950   March 26–27
       Roanoke, Virginia
       Curtis Bishop, President
       Eugene Chaffee, Vice-President
       Jesse P. Bogue, Executive Secretary

1951   March 6–8
       Des Moines, Iowa
       Eugene Chaffee, President
       Dorothy M. Bell, Vice-President
       Jesse P. Bogue, Executive Secretary

1952   June 25–27
       Boston, Massachusetts
       Dorothy M. Bell, President
       Charles S. Morris, Vice-President
       Jesse P. Bogue, Executive Secretary

1953   March 25–28
       Dallas, Texas
       Basil N. Peterson, President
       Fred Marston, Vice-President
       Jesse P. Bogue, Executive Secretary

1954   March 8–10
       St. Louis, Missouri
       Fred Marston, President
       Hugh G. Price, Vice-President
       Jesse P. Bogue, Executive Secretary

1955   March 3–5
       Chicago, Illinois
       Hugh G. Price, President
       Edward G. Schlaefer, Vice-President
       Jesse P. Bogue, Executive Secretary

1956   March 7–9
       New York City, New York
       Edward G. Schlaefer, President
       James M. Ewing, Vice-President
       Jesse P. Bogue, Executive Secretary

1957   March 5–9
       Salt Lake City, Utah
       James M. Ewing, President
       Edmund J. Gleazer, Jr., Vice-President
       Jesse P. Bogue, Executive Secretary

1958   March 5–7
       Grand Rapids, Michigan
       Edmund J. Gleazer, Jr., President
       Paul Gaiser, Vice-President
       Jesse P. Bogue, Executive Secretary

1959   March 10–14
       Long Beach, California
       George Kildow, President
       Marvin C. Knudson, Vice-President
       Edmund J. Gleazer, Jr., Executive Director

1960   March 2–4
        Louisville, Kentucky
        Marvin C. Knudson, President
        Henry W. Littlefield, Vice-President
        Edmund J. Gleazer, Jr., Executive Director

1961   February 28–March 3
        Washington, D. C.
        Henry W. Littlefield, President
        Oscar H. Edinger, Jr., Vice-President
        Edmund J. Gleazer, Jr., Executive Director

1962   February 27–March 2
        Denver, Colorado
        Oscar H. Edinger, Jr., President
        Charles L. Harman, Vice-President
        Edmund J. Gleazer, Jr., Executive Director

1963   February 25–28
        Seattle, Washington
        Charles L. Harman, President
        Donald E. Deyo, Vice-President
        Edmund J. Gleazer, Jr., Executive Director

APPENDIX C

AMERICAN ASSOCIATION OF JUNIOR COLLEGES
STATEMENT OF INCOME AND EXPENSES

	1930	1940	1950	1960
Income:				
Balance	$ 207.15	$ 2,158.07	$ 1,438.59	
Membership Dues	2,035.00	7,180.00	24,100.00	$ 52,610.00
Contributions and				
Grants	25.00	25,454.85[1]		53,391.29[2]
Junior College Journal		3,428.66	7,546.26	13,521.82
Newsletter			62.60	589.15
Other Publications		730.94	2,436.55	1,267.78
Other Income	125.00	481.55	2,291.72	2,039.28
TOTAL INCOME	$2,392.15	$39,434.07	$37,875.72	$123,419.32
Expenses:				
Salaries		$ 4,612.08	$13,746.00	$ 55,879.60
Retirement & Payroll				
Taxes			400.00	3,046.18
Travel			800.00	5,816.18
Office Supplies &				
Expenses		2,270.89	3,302.35	11,751.33
Depreciation				1,731.88
Board of Directors			1,343.15	4,346.95
Commissions &				
Committees			786.45	17,002.26
Annual Meeting		327.10	879.83	291.98
Junior College Journal		4,425.49	9,531.29	16,211.16
Newsletter			766.43	2,958.09
Other Publications		673.01	2,344.15	3,485.11
Miscellaneous		178.86	2,473.99	2,488.04
TOTAL EXPENSES	$2,154.32	$12,487.43[3]	$36,373.64	$125,008.76

[1] Receipts for Study of Terminal Education from General Education Board.

[2] The W.K. Kellogg Foundation contributed $43,391.29; United States Steel Corporation $10,000.00.

[3] An additional $25,454.85 was spent on the terminal education study.

1963 BUDGET

Income:

Membership Dues	$ 84,375.00
Publications	25,750.00
W. K. Kellogg Grant	114,712.86
Investment	1,500.00
Other Income	22,500.00
Miscellaneous	1,235.30
TOTAL INCOME	$250,073.16

Expenses:

Salaries and Taxes	$141,760.30
Travel	5,000.00
Rent	7,500.00
Office Expenses	14,500.00
Depreciation	2,600.00
Public Information	1,200.00
Board of Directors	5,000.00
Committees and Commissions	18,000.00
Annual Meeting	2,500.00
Publications	41,000.00
Consultants	3,000.00
Committee on the Junior College	7,600.00
Contingency	412.86
TOTAL EXPENSES	$250,073.16

Bibliography

RECORDS OF THE AAJC

Archives

Board of Directors Minutes, mimeographed, 1947–1962.

Constitutions and By-Laws.

Minutes of commissions. Since their establishment in 1960.

Official records and correspondence of the executive secretaries and, since 1958, the executive director: Doak S. Campbell, Walter Crosby Eells, Jesse P. Bogue, and Edmund J. Gleazer, Jr.

Official records and correspondence of American Association of Junior Colleges' headquarters personnel: William Shannon, Thomas Merson, Elizabeth S. Reed, and Jesse R. Barnet.

Official records and correspondence of past presidents of the American Association of Junior Colleges.

"A Proposal to the W. K. Kellogg Foundation," dated July 18, 1961.

"Sequence of Events Leading to Appeal to W. K. Kellogg Foundation," mimeographed confidential report.

Miscellaneous items.

Other Unpublished Sources

Eells, Walter Crosby. Confidential correspondence dated 1943–1946. In possession of author.

Personal interviews with Doak S. Campbell, Walter Crosby Eells, Edmund J. Gleazer, Jr., William Shannon, Thomas Merson, C. C. Colvert, Roscoe Ingalls, Henry W. Littlefield, Curtis Bishop, Leland L. Medsker, James W. Reynolds. With the exception of

209

Reynolds, who was editor of the *Junior College Journal,* these men were executive officers of the AAJC.

Publications

Zook, George F., ed. *National Conference of Junior Colleges, 1920, and First Annual Meeting of American Association. of Junior Colleges, 1921.* Bulletin No. 19, 1922. Washington, D.C.: Government Printing Office, 1922. 73 pp. First volume of AAJC Proceedings.

Proceedings, 1922–1929. Addresses and business meeting reports, published as pamphlets.

Junior College Journal. Since October, 1930. Includes proceedings and annual reports.

Junior College Newsletter. Since October, 1945. Started as *Washington Newsletter.*

Eells, Walter Crosby. *Wartime Letters,* Nos. 1–53, 1942–1945. Mimeographed.

American Association of Junior Colleges, 1920–1961. Washington, D.C.: American Association of Junior Colleges, 1961. 20 pp.

Establishing Legal Bases for Community Colleges. Washington, D.C.: American Association of Junior Colleges, 1962. 43 pp.

Proceedings, Conference on Religion in the Junior Colleges. Held at Southern Methodist University, Dallas, Texas, April 5–7, 1955. 52 pp.

A Program of Professional Advisory Services. Washington, D.C.: American Association of Junior Colleges, 1962, 4 pp.

A Report on Terminal Education in Junior Colleges with Special Emphasis on Progress Made on the Continuation Study. Second annual report. Washington, D.C.: American Association of Junior Colleges, 1942, 80 pp.

Report of the United States Technical Education Delegation to the Union of Soviet Socialist Republics, May 5–31, 1961. Washington, D.C.: American Association of Junior Colleges, 1962, 203 pp.

Gleazer, Edmund J., Jr. *Junior College Directory, 1962.* Washington, D.C.: American Association of Junior Colleges, 1962. 44 pp.

Gleazer, Edmund J., Jr., ed. *American Junior Colleges,* 5th edition. Washington, D.C.: American Council on Education, 1960. 564 pp.

OTHER EDUCATIONAL RECORDS

American Council on Education. *A Brief Statement of the History and Activities, 1918–1961*. Washington, D.C.: American Council on Education, 1944.

Biennial Survey of Education in the United States, 1952–1954. Washington, D.C.: U.S. Department of Health, Education, and Welfare, Office of Education, 1958.

Florida Community College Council. *The Community Junior College in Florida's Future: Report to the State Board of Education*. Tallahassee: State Department of Education, 1957. 71 pp.

Hollis, Ernest V., William G. Land, and S. V. Martorana. *Survey of State Legislation Relating to Higher Education, July 1, 1958, to December 31, 1959*. U.S. Office of Education Circular No. 618. Washington, D.C.: U.S. Department of Health, Education, and Welfare, Office of Education, 1960. 200 pp.

President's Committee on Education beyond the High School. *Second Report to the President*. Washington, D.C.: U.S. Department of Health, Education, and Welfare, Office of Education, 1957. 26 pp.

United States Bureau of Education. *A Handbook of Educational Associations and Foundations in the United States*. Bulletin No. 16, 1926. Washington, D.C.: Government Printing Office, 1926. 82 pp.

Zook, George F. "Speeches and Articles," January 1, 1941–June 3, 1944. George F. Zook Memorial Library, American Council on Education Building, Washington.

HISTORICAL BACKGROUND

History of Higher Education including Junior Colleges

Bogue, Jesse P. *The Community College*. New York: McGraw-Hill Book Co., 1950. 390 pp.

Brubacher, John S., and Willis Rudy. *Higher Education in Transition*. New York: Harper & Brothers, 1958. 494 pp.

Budd, Thomas. *Good Order Established in Pennsylvania and New Jersey*. Ed. Frederick J. Shepard. Cleveland: Burrows, 1902. 80 pp.

Butts, R. Freeman. *The College Charts Its Course*. New York: McGraw-Hill Book Co., 1939. 464 pp.

Butts, R. Freeman, and Lawrence A. Cremin. *A History of Education in American Culture*. New York: Henry Holt and Co., 1953. 628 pp.

Carpenter, W. W. *The Organization and Administration of the Junior College*. Columbia, Mo.: Lucas Brothers, 1939, 193 pp.

Clark, Burton R. *The Open Door College: A Case Study*. New York: McGraw-Hill Book Co., 1960. 207 pp.

Cremin, Lawrence A. *The Transformation of the School*. New York: Alfred A. Knopf, 1961. 387 pp.

Curti, Merle, and Vernon Cartensen. *The University of Wisconsin: A History, 1848–1925*. Madison: University of Wisconsin Press, 1949. Vol. I, chapter 1.

Dewey, John (ed.). *The Living Thoughts of Thomas Jefferson*. London: Cassell & Co., 1941. 170 pp.

Diekhoff, John S. *Democracy's College*. New York: Harper & Brothers, 1950. 208 pp.

Eddy, Edward Danforth, Jr. *Colleges for our Land and Time: The Land-Grant Idea in American Education*. New York: Harper & Brothers, 1956. 328 pp.

Eells, Walter Crosby. "The American Association of Junior Colleges," *School and Society*, XLIX (April, 1939), 425–27.

———. *Associate's Degree and Graduation Practices in Junior Colleges*. Washington, D.C.: American Association of Junior Colleges, 1942. 126 pp.

———. "Developments in Higher Education—Wise and Otherwise," *Journal of the American Association of Collegiate Registrars*, XVII (July, 1942), 455–92.

———. *The Junior College*. Boston: Houghton Mifflin Co., 1931. 833 pp.

Fields, Ralph R. *The Community College Movement*. New York: McGraw-Hill Book Co., 1962. 360 pp.

Folwell, William Watts. *Autobiography and Letters*. Minneapolis: University of Minnesota Press, 1933. 287 pp.

———. *University Addresses*. Minneapolis: The H. W. Wilson Co., 1909. 224 pp.

Fraser, Mowat G. *The College of the Future*. New York: Columbia University Press, 1937. 529 pp.

Fretwell, Elbert K., Jr. *Founding Public Junior Colleges: Local Initiative in Six Communities.* New York: Bureau of Publications, Teachers College, Columbia University, 1954. 148 pp.

Harper, William Rainey. *The President's Report, July, 1898–July, 1899.* Chicago: University of Chicago Press, 1900. 224 pp.

––––––. *The Prospects of the Small College.* Chicago: University of Chicago Press, 1900. 46 pp.

––––––. *The Trend in Higher Education.* Chicago: University of Chicago Press, 1905. 390 pp.

Henderson, Algo D. *Policies and Practices in Higher Education.* New York: Harper & Brothers, 1960. 338 pp.

Henninger, G. Ross. *The Technical Institute in America.* New York: McGraw-Hill Book Co., 1959. 276 pp.

Hillway, Tyrus. *The American Two-Year College.* New York: Harper & Brothers, 1958. 276 pp.

Hinsdale, B. A. *History of the University of Michigan.* Ann Arbor: University of Michigan Press, 1906. 376 pp.

Hofstadter, Richard, and C. DeWitt Hardy. *The Development and Scope of Higher Education in the United States.* New York: Columbia University Press, 1952. 254 pp.

Horn, Jefferson Lee. "William Rainey Harper and Alexis Frederick Lange, Productive Pioneers in the Junior College Movement." Unpublished Ph.D. dissertation, University of Texas, 1952.

Houghton, Alcina B. "A Survey of the History of the Junior College." Unpublished Master's thesis, New York University, 1933.

Hutchins, Robert M. *Conflict in Education in a Democratic Society.* New York: Harper & Brothers, 1953. 112 pp.

Janney, Samuel M. (ed.). *The Life of William Penn.* Philadelphia: Friends' Book Association, 1882. 591 pp.

Jordan, David Starr. "The College and the University," *Science,* XXVII (April 3, 1908), 531–32.

Kabat, George J. "The People's College," *Journal of Higher Education,* XI (February, 1940), 85–89.

Koch, Adrienne, and William Pedan, eds. *The Life and Selected Writings of Thomas Jefferson.* New York: Random House, 1944. 730 pp.

Koos, Leonard V. *Integrating High School and College: The Six-Four-Four Plan at Work.* New York: Harper & Brothers, 1946. 208 pp.

———— *The Junior College Movement.* Boston: Ginn & Co., 1925. 436 pp.

————. "A Quarter Century with the Junior College," *Journal of Higher Education,* IX (January, 1938), 1–6.

————. "Rise of the People's College," *School Review,* LV (March, 1947), pp. 138–49.

McDowell, F. M. *The Junior College.* U. S. Bureau of Education Bulletin No. 35. Washington, D.C.: Government Printing Office, 1919. 139 pp.

McLain, Charles W. "The Present Status of the Junior College in the United States." Unpublished Doctor of Education project, Colorado State University, 1953.

Medsker, Leland L. *The Junior College: Progress and Prospect.* New York: McGraw-Hill Book Co., 1960. 367 pp.

Mumford, Frederick B. *The Land Grant College Movement.* Columbia, Mo.: University of Missouri, 1940. 140 pp.

National Society for the Study of Education. *The Public Junior College.* Fifty-fifth Yearbook, Part I. Chicago: National Society for the Study of Education, 1956. 347 pp.

Padover, Saul K. (ed.) *Thomas Jefferson on Democracy.* New York: D. Appleton Century Co., 1939. 291 pp.

Phenix, Philip H. (ed.) *Philosophies of Education.* New York: John Wiley & Sons, 1961. 137 pp.

President's Commission on Higher Education. *Higher Education for American Democracy.* New York: Harper & Brothers, 1947. Six volumes.

Proctor, William Martin. *The Six-Four-Four Plan of School Organization in Pasadena, California.* Pasadena: Board of Education, 1933. 201 pp.

Proctor, William Martin, ed. *The Junior College: Its Organization and Administration.* Stanford, Calif.: Stanford University Press, 1927. 226 pp.

Ricciardi, Nicholas. "Reorganization of the American Association of Junior Colleges," *School and Society,* XLVIII (August, 1938), 200–201.

Rockefeller Brothers Fund. *The Pursuit of Excellence: Education and the Future of America.* Garden City: Doubleday & Co., 1958. 48 pp.

Roemer, Joseph. "The Junior College—the People's College," *Proceedings of the Northwest Association of Secondary and Higher Schools.* Spokane, Wash.: The Association, 1938, pp. 26–28.

Rudolph, Frederick. *The American College and University.* New York: Alfred A. Knopf, 1962. 516 pp.

Rutledge, Lawrence Adrian. "A History of the American Association of Junior Colleges, 1920–1950." Unpublished Doctor of Education project, University of Texas, 1951.

Scott, Paul T. "The 6-4-4 Plan at Work," *Journal of the National Education Association,* XXVIII (December, 1939), 272.

Seashore, Carl E. *The Junior College Movement.* New York: Henry Holt & Co., 1940. 160 pp.

Sexson, John A., and John W. Harbeson. *The New American College: The Four-Year Junior College.* New York: Harper & Brothers, 1946. 312 pp.

Smith, Leo F., and Laurence Lipsett. *The Technical Institute.* New York: McGraw-Hill Book Co., 1956. 319 pp.

Starrak, Jaames A., and Raymond M. Hughes. *The Community College in the United States.* Ames, Iowa: Iowa State College Press, 1954. 114 pp.

Tappan, Henry P. *University Education.* New York: George P. Putnam, 1851. 120 pp.

Thornton, James W., Jr. *The Community Junior College.* New York: John Wiley & Sons, 1960. 300 pp.

Vanaria, Louis Michael. "The National Council for the Social Studies: A Voluntary Organization for Professional Service." Unpublished Ph.D. dissertation, Teachers College, Columbia University, 1958.

Wesley, Edgar B. *NEA: The First Hundred Years.* New York: Harper & Brothers, 1957. 419 pp.

White, Robert, Jr. "Feasibility of a 6-4-4 Reorganization in School Systems with Junior Colleges," *School Review,* LIV (March, 1946), 140–47; LIV (April, 1946), 222–30; LIV (June, 1946), 351–59.

Whitney, Frederick Lamson. *The Junior College in America.* Colorado Teachers College Education Series No. 5. Greeley: Colorado State Teachers College, 1928. 258 pp.

Willey, Malcolm M. *Depression, Recovery and Higher Education.* New York: McGraw-Hill Book Co., 1937. 543 pp.

Winfield, George F. "The Junior College." Unpublished Master's thesis, Southern Methodist University, 1916.

Woody, Thomas (ed.). *Educational Views of Benjamin Franklin.* New York: McGraw-Hill Book Co., 1931. 270 pp.

Purposes and Functions of the Junior College

Anderson, Albert T. "An Appraisal of the Junior College Journal, 1946–1953." Unpublished Doctor of Education project, Teachers College, Columbia University, 1954.

Brumbaugh, Aaron J. "The Junior College of the Future," *Bulletin of the Department of Secondary School Principals,* XXIII (January, 1939), 7–11.

Buck, J. P. "Public Junior Colleges as a New Unit in Our Educational Program," *Texas Outlook,* XII (July, 1928), 60–61.

Campbell, Doak S. *A Critical Study of the Stated Purposes of the Junior College.* Contribution to Education No. 70. Nashville: George Peabody School for Teachers, 1930. 126 pp.

———. "The Purposes of the Junior College," *Journal of the National Education Association,* XXI (October, 1932), 221–22.

Charters, W. W. "The ABC Degree," *Journal of Higher Education,* XIII (May, 1942), 281–82, 286.

Eells, Walter Crosby. "The Community's College," *Adult Education Journal,* IV (January, 1945), 13–17.

———. "The Junior College—Its Character and Prospects," *Journal of the National Education Association,* XXII (May, 1933), 157–58.

Esterly, Virginia Judy. "The Junior College: A Solution," *Proceedings of the 69th Annual Meeting of the National Education Association,* LXIX (1931), 395–401.

Gleazer, Edmund J., Jr. "Facing Up to Basic Issues in the Junior College Field" (paper delivered at the third annual Summer Work Conference, for Community and Junior College Administrators, Teachers College, Columbia University, New York, June 18, 1962).

Goddard, Roy W. "Basic Issues for Junior Colleges in the Postwar Period," *North Central Association Quarterly,* XIX (October, 1944), 184–89.

Gummere, Richard M. "The Bisected A.B.," *Southern Association Quarterly,* VI (August, 1942), 339–45.

Harbeson, John W. "Advantages of the Four-Year Junior College," *School Executive,* LIX (March, 1940), 17.

————. "The Rechristening of the Junior Colleges," *California Journal of Secondary Education,* XIX (April, 1944), 204–07.

Johnson, B. Lamar. "The Implications of Democracy for the Junior College," *Bulletin of the National Association of Secondary School Principals,* XXIV (February, 1940), 134–39.

Kefauver, Grayson N., and Catherine Bullard. "The Organization of the Junior College as an Agency of Democracy," *Proceedings of the 69th Annual Meeting of the National Education Association,* LXIX (1931), 604–07.

Kelly, Frederick J. "The Line Between Secondary and Higher Education," *School Life,* XXIII (November, 1937), 65–66, 72.

Koos, Leonard V. "The Bachelor's Degree to College Sophomores: Considerations Pro and Con," *School Review,* L (September, 1942), 494–503.

————. "Then and Now on the Place of the Junior College," *School Review,* XLVI (October, 1938), 571–73.

Lange, Alexis F. "The Junior College—What Manner of Child Shall This Be?" *School and Society,* VII (February, 1918), 211–16.

Loder, Eugenia Cruzen. "The Community College: A Program of Community Participation in Education." Unpublished Doctor of Education project, Stanford University, 1945.

McGrath, Earl J. "Does the Community College Have a Future?" *The Educational Forum,* XXVII (November, 1962), 5–13.

EDUCATIONAL ISSUES

Curriculum

American Council on Education. *A Design for General Education for Members of the Armed Forces.* Studies series 1. Reports of Committees and Conferences no. 18. Washington, D.C.: American Council on Education, 1944. 186 pp.

Beard, Charles A. *A Charter for the Social Sciences in the Schools.* Part I, Report of the Commission on the Social Studies of the American Historical Association. New York: Charles Scribner's Sons, 1932. 122 pp.

Bird, Grace V. "General Education in Junior Colleges," *California Journal of Secondary Education,* XXII (March, 1947), 158–61.

Brown, Esther Lucile. *Nursing for the Future.* New York: Russell Sage Foundation, 1948. 198 pp.

Bryson, Lyman. *Adult Education.* New York: American Book Co., 1936. 208 pp.

Buechel, J. F. Marvin. *Principles of Administration in Junior and Community College Education for Nursing.* New York: G. P. Putnam's Sons, 1956. 255 pp.

California State Department of Education. *Technical Education in California Junior Colleges: A Study of Problems and Procedures.* Sacramento: California State Department of Education, January, 1953.

———. *Vocational Education in the Junior College.* Sacramento: California State Department of Education, 1949.

Carnegie Foundation for the Advancement of Teaching. *State Higher Education in California.* Sacramento: California State Printing Office, 1932. 82 pp.

Colvert, C. C. *The Public Junior College Curriculum.* Baton Rouge: Louisiana State University Press, 1939. 177 pp.

Committee for the Study of Nursing Education. *Nursing and Nursing Education in the United States.* New York: The Macmillan Co., 1923. 585 pp.

Committee on the Grading of Nursing Schools. *Nursing Schools Today and Tomorrow.* New York: Committee on the Grading of Nursing Schools, 1934. 269 pp.

Dixon, Henry Aldous, *et al. The Organization and Development of Terminal Occupational Curricula in Selected Junior Colleges.* Ogden, Utah: Weber College, 1944. 181 pp.

Eells, Walter Crosby. *Present Status of Junior College Terminal Education.* Washington, D.C.: American Association of Junior Colleges, 1941. 340 pp.

———. *Why Junior College Terminal Education?* Washington, D.C.: American Association of Junior Colleges, 1941. 365 pp.

Emerson, Lynn A. *Vocational-Technical Education for American Industry.* U.S. Office of Education Circular No. 530. Washington, D.C.: U.S. Department of Health, Education and Welfare, Office of Education, 1958. 25 pp.

Engleman, Lois E., and Walter Crosby Eells. *The Literature of Junior College Terminal Education.* Washington, D.C.: American Association of Junior Colleges, 1941. 322 pp.

Harris, Norman C. "The Community Junior College—A Solution to the Skilled Manpower Problem" (paper read at the 17th National Conference on Higher Education sponsored by the Association for Higher Education, Chicago, March 5, 1962). Mimeographed.

Harvard University. Committee on the Objectives of a General Education in a Free Society. *General Education in a Free Society.* Cambridge, Mass.: Harvard University Press, 1945. 267 pp.

Houle, Cyril O. "What Lies Ahead in Adult Education," *Sierra Educational News,* XLII (October, 1946), 25–27.

Jensen, George C. "An Analysis of the Report of the Carnegie Foundation Survey and Recommendations," *California Quarterly of Secondary Education,* VIII (October, 1932), 58–67.

Johnson, B. Lamar. *General Education in Action: A Report of the California Study of General Education in the Junior College.* Washington, D.C.: American Council on Education, 1952. 409 pp.

McGrath, Earl J. "The Future of General Education," *Journal of Higher Education,* XXIV (March, 1953), 121–26.

McGrath, Earl J., *et al. Toward General Education.* New York: The Macmillan Co., 1948. 224 pp.

Mohr, J. Paul. "Junior College Terminal Education and the War," *Journal of the American Association of Collegiate Registrars,* XVIII (July, 1943), 416–21.

Montag, Mildred L. *Community College Education for Nursing.* New York: McGraw-Hill Book Co., 1959. 457 pp.

———. *The Education of Nursing Technicians.* New York: G. P. Putnam's Sons, 1951. 146 pp.

National Committee for the Improvement of Nursing Service. *Nursing Schools at the Mid-Century.* New York: National Committee for the Improvement of Nursing Services, 1950. 88 pp.

National League for Nursing. *Report on Associate Degree Programs in Nursing.* New York: National League for Nursing, 1961. 44 pp.

National Society for the Study of Education. *General Education in the American College.* Thirty-eighth Yearbook, Part II. Bloomington, Ind.: Public School Publishing Co., 1939. 382 pp.

Russell, John Dale (ed.). *Terminal Education in Higher Institutions.* Chicago: University of Chicago Press, 1942. 198 pp.

Sindlinger, Walter Eugene. "Experimentation in Education for Nursing at Orange County Community College." Unpublished Doctor of Education project, Teachers College, Columbia University, 1954.

Snedden, David. "A Vision of the Future in Vocational Education," *School and Society,* XXXII (December, 1930), 819–31.

Thomas, Russell. *The Search for a Common Learning: General Education, 1800–1960.* New York: McGraw-Hill Book Co., 1962. 324 pp.

Ward, Phebe. *Terminal Education in the Junior College.* New York: Harper & Brothers, 1947. 282 pp.

Teachers and Students

American Council on Education. *Wanted: 30,000 Instructors for Community Colleges.* Washington, D.C.: American Council on Education, 1949. 52 pp.

Berelson, Bernard. *Graduate Education in the United States.* New York: McGraw-Hill Book Co., 1960. 346 pp.

Blegen, Theodore C., and Russel M. Cooper (eds.). *The Preparation of College Teachers.* Series I—Reports of Committees and Conferences, vol. XIV, No. 42. Washington, D.C.: American Council on Education, 1950. 186 pp.

California State Department of Education. *Report of the California Statewide Conference on the Preparation, Credentials, Recruitment and Placement of Junior College Teachers.* Sacramento: California State Department of Education, 1958.

Carmichael, Oliver C. *Graduate Education: A Critique and a Program.* New York: Harper & Brothers, 1961. 213 pp.

"College Teaching Ed.D.," *TC Topics,* X (Spring, 1962), I.

Fields, Ralph R., and Arthur H. Pike. "Community College Problems," *Teachers College Record,* LI (May, 1950), 528–36.

French, Sidney James (ed.). *Accent on Teaching: Experiments in General Education.* New York: Harper & Brothers, 1954. 334 pp.

Harlow, James G. "Five Years of Discussion," *Journal of Higher Education,* XXIV (January, 1953), 17–24.

Kelly, Fred J., ed. *Improving College Instruction.* Series I—Reports of Committees and Conferences, No. 48, vol. XV. Washington, D.C.: American Council on Education, 1951. 195 pp.

Koos, Leonard V. "Preparation for Community College Teaching," *Journal of Higher Education*, XXI (June, 1950), 309–17.

McDaniel, J. W. *Essential Student Personnel Practices for Junior Colleges*. Washington, D.C.: American Association of Junior Colleges, 1962. 54 pp.

McGrath, Earl J. *The Graduate School and the Decline of Liberal Education*. New York: Bureau of Publications, Teachers College, Columbia University, 1959. 65 pp.

Mohs, Milton C. *Service Through Placement in the Junior College: The Organization and Operation of a Junior College Placement Bureau*. Washington, D.C.: American Association of Junior Colleges, 1962. 102 pp.

Mueller, Kate Hevner. *Student Personnel Work in Higher Education*. Boston: Houghton Mifflin Co., 1961. 570 pp.

National Education Association of the United States, Educational Policies Commission. *Education for all American Youth*. Washington, D.C.: Educational Policies Commission, National Education Association, 1944. 321 pp.

Warner, W. Lloyd, Robert J. Havighurst, and Martin B. Loeb. *Who Shall Be Educated?* New York: Harper & Brothers, 1944. 190 pp.

Wise, W. Max. *They Come for the Best of Reasons: College Students Today*. Washington, D. C.: American Council on Education, 1960. 65 pp.

Administration and Legislation

Bauer, Ronald C. *Cases in College Administration*. New York: Bureau of Publications, Teachers College, Columbia University, 1955. 213 pp.

Burns, Gerald P., ed. *Administrators in Higher Education: Their Functions and Coordination*. New York: Harper & Brothers, 1962. 236 pp.

Coladarci, Arthur P., and Getzels, Jacob W. *The Use of Theory in Educational Administration*. Stanford, Calif.: Stanford University Press, 1955. 28 pp.

Corson, John J. *Governance of Colleges and Universities*. New York: McGraw-Hill Book Co., 1960. 209 pp.

Dodds, Harold W. *The Academic President—Educator or Caretaker?* New York: McGraw-Hill Book Co., 1962. 294 pp.

Griffiths, Daniel E. *Administrative Theory*. New York: Appleton-Century-Crofts, 1959. 123 pp.

W. K. Kellogg Foundation. *Toward Improved School Administration*. Battle Creek, Mich.: W. K. Kellogg Foundation, 1961. 68 pp.

McGrath, Earl J. "The Evolution of Administrative Offices in Institutions of Higher Education in the U. S. from 1860–1933." Unpublished Ph.D. dissertation, University of Chicago, 1936.

Stoke, Harold W. *The American College President*. New York: Harper & Brothers, 1959. 180 pp.